THE CONDUCTOR'S GESTURE
A Practical Application of Rudolf von Laban's Movement Language

THE COMPANION DVD

The Conductor's Gesture

JAMES JORDAN

with

MEADE ANDREWS

THE CONDUCTOR'S GESTURE
A Practical Application of Rudolf von Laban's Movement Language

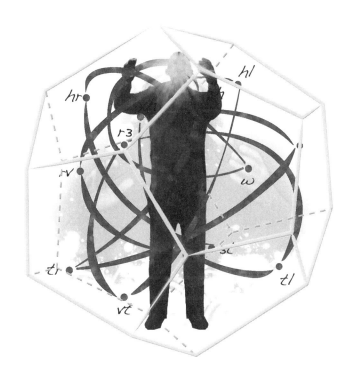

JAMES JORDAN
with Giselle Wyers and Meade Andrews

GIA PUBLICATIONS, INC.
CHICAGO

G-8096

GIA Publications, Inc.
7404 S. Mason Ave.
Chicago, IL 60638
www.giamusic.com

Copyright © 2011 GIA Publications, Inc.
All rights reserved.
Printed in the United States of America.

Cover Design and Layout by Martha Chlipala

ISBN: 978-1-57999-858-5

To

Gail B. Poch
master teacher, mentor, inspirational conductor, and friend

Sarah Alberti Chapman
my Laban guide and Laban mentor in my doctoral study

David Milne
my mentor and teacher in psychology at Bucknell University

This book and the ideas presented within would not have been possible without their inspired teaching, patience, insights, and guidance.

The research for this book was funded by a generous Doctoral fellowship from Temple University.

Other Publications by James Jordan
Relating to the Content of This Book

Evoking Sound
Second Edition with DVD
(G-7359)

Music for Conducting Study
with Giselle Wyers
(G-7359A)

The Musician's Breath
(G-7955)

The Anatomy of Conducting
Architecture & Essentials: Choral and Instrumental
with Eugene Migliaro Corporon
DVD (DVD-745)
Workbook (G-7358)

The Choral Rehearsal
Vol. 1: Techniques and Procedures (G-7128)
Vol. 2: Inward Bound—Philosophy and Score Preparation (G-7129)
DVD (DVD-720)

Table of Contents

Foreword by Eugene Migliaro Corporon xv
Philosophical Foreword by Gerald Custer xxi
Preface xxv

PART 1
The Theories and Work of Rudolf von Laban:
An Examination of the Perception of Movement. 1

CHAPTER 1
Introduction 5

Laban as a Gestural Morphology 10
The Pitfalls of Pedagogical Impatience 11

CHAPTER 2
The Beginnings 15

Conducting: Movement Analogues through Effort/Shape 16

CHAPTER 3
The Consequences of Gesture 21

Developing Observation Skills and Awareness of Movement 24
The Real Issue 24
A New Pedagogy and Theory for Conducting 25

CHAPTER 4
An Overview of the Psychological Research:
Kinesthesia, Body Mapping, and the Influence of Mirror Neurons 29

Introduction to the Research 30
A History of the Development of the Theories of Kinesthetic Sensation
    for Movement Perception 31
Perception as Examined by the Empiricist Philosophers
    and the Associationist Psychologists 31
Early Phenomenology 33
Modern Psychological Phenomenology 34
The Associationists 35
William McDougall: Hormic Psychology and the Nature of Instincts 36
Edward Bradford Titchener: Context Theory and Structural Psychology . . 37
William James: Muscular Theory—Eccentric Projection of the Feeling . . . 38
Gestalt Psychology 39

The Differentiation Theory of Werner 41
Twentieth-Century Developmental Psychology 41
Studies Concerning the Origin and Development
  of Movement Patterns in Young Children 44
James J. Gibson; Gunnar Johansson 46
Behaviorism 47
Music Education 49
Modern Educational Dance 51
Rudolf von Laban 52
  Philosophical Basis of the Work of Laban 53
  Effort 55
  The Effort Elements 57
  The Effort Elements in Combination 58
  The Projective Geometry of Laban 61
  The Rhythm of Movement and Phrasing in the Theories of Laban 61
  Summary 63
The Importance of the Body Map and the Theories of Antonio Damasio:
  Connections with William James and "Feelings of Knowing" 64
The Pedagogical Mandate of This Book 65
How Movement and Conducting Affects Ensembles:
  Understanding the Power of Body Mapping and Mirror Neurons 65

CHAPTER 5
A Morphology of Conducting: Outlining the Laban Path through
Spatial Imagination and Projective Geometry 69

The Morphology: A Movement Learning Theory 71
An Explanation of the Morphology 73
Specifics of the Morphology 74

CHAPTER 6
Toward an Understanding of Effort 77

CHAPTER 7
An Overview of the Importance of Breath
and Its Relationship to Movement 81

CHAPTER 8
The Dimensional Architectures of Movement .87

Rhythm Impulse and Conducting Are Inseparable 89
Kinesthetic Oral/Aural 90

Teaching the Architecture of Sound 91
Always Moving in Cross Dimensions: Space Orientation. 92

CHAPTER 9
The Theory Underlying the Perceptions of Personal Space. 95

The Line of Embrace 97
The Sound Membrane or Door Plane. .98
Simultaneous Conducting Planes: The Three Dimensional Planes. 98
Connecting Core to the Distal Relationships of the Body 102
The Starfish Connection. 102

CHAPTER 10
Laban's Conceptions of Spatial Architecture Applied to Conducting. 105

Rudolf von Laban 108
    Philosophical Basis of the Work of Laban 109
    Using the Architecture of the Body to Conducting Advantage. 110
    Simultaneous Conducting Planes: The Three Dimensional Planes 111
    The Laban Effort Elements: Flow, Weight, Time, and Space. 113
    Experiencing the Efforts in Combination. 114
    Connecting Sounds to Gesture: Sounding Musical Line 125
    Summary. 127
Other Laban Organizations 127
Laban-Related Organizations 128
Laban-Related Programs and Projects 128
Lims' Partner Organizations 129

PART 2
The Impulse to Move:
Harmonic Rhythm 131

CHAPTER 11
Harmonic Progression: The Genesis for Movement. 133

The Importance of Harmonic Rhythm. 134
Hierarchy of Chord Progressions (as suggested by Arnold Schoenberg) . . . 136
The Intentionality and Imperatives of Harmonic Progression 139
Explanation of Exercises in Skill Set Eight. 140

PART 3
States and Drives 141

CHAPTER 12
Portal to Expressivity: Laban's States and Drives for Conductors 143
Giselle Wyers

A Preface to This Chapter *Geoffrey Boers* 144
Review of Single Effort Elements 146
Effort States 147
Effort Drives 148
Full Effort Action 148
Reviewing Single Effort Elements: Suggested Exercises 148
Experiencing Weight: Strong and Light 149
    Strong Weight 149
    Light Weight 150
Experiencing Flow: Bound and Free 151
    Bound Flow 152
    Free Flow 153
    Combinations of Bound and Free Movements 153
Experiencing Space: Direct and Indirect 154
    "Out of Space" 155
Experiencing Time: Quick and Sustained 156
Efforts in Combination: States 157
    Dream State 158
    Awake State 159
    Mobile State 160
    Stable State 160
    Remote State 161
    Rhythm State 161
Efforts in Combination: Drives 162
    Action Drive (Space, Time, Weight) 162
    Passion Drive (Weight, Time, Flow) 163
    Vision Drive (Space, Flow, Time) 163
    Spell Drive (Space, Weight, Flow, Lacks Time) 163
Experiencing the States 164
Experiencing the States in Rehearsal 164
Beyond the Action Drive 165
Movement Signatures 166
Expressivity in Conducting 167
Listening with Laban: Creating a Kinesthetic Analysis of the Score . . . 172
Musical Elements 172
Exploring Choral Works in Detail 175

Morten Lauridsen's *Dirait-On* 175
Michael McGlynn's *Dulaman* 176
Samuel Barber's *Agnus Dei* 176
Claude Debussy's *Dieu! Qu'il la fait bon regarder* 177
A Brief Discussion of Laban's "Shape" System 178
Shape Qualities (Affinities) 178
Modes of Shape Change 179
Conclusion 179

PART 4
Bodying Forth:
Developing a Kinesthetic Vocabulary and Movement Language 181

CHAPTER 13
The Laban Connection to Mirror Neurons:
The Importance of Learning and Re-Learning Movement 183

Understanding Mirror Neurons 185
Laban, Mirror Neurons, and Breath 187

SKILL SETS
Acquiring Conducting Technique Using the Principles of Laban 189

SKILL SET ONE
Developing Movement Observation and Self-Perception Skills 191

Body Kinesthetic Exercise 1: Weight at Center 192
Feeling Weight at Your Center 192
Body Kinesthetic Exercise 2: Learning the Kinesthetic
of Withholding Weight 195
Body Kinesthetic Exercise 3: Learning the Kinesthetic of the Body
Interacting with the Effort of Weight in Relative Isolation 197
Experiencing Dimensions of Time 197
Experiencing Various Interactions of Time, Weight,
and Space Using the Body 198

SKILL SET TWO
Unlocking the Conductor's Architecture 201

The Unlocking Joint: The Point of Gestural Release 202

SKILL SET THREE
Accurately Perceiving Your Architecture ... 205

The Crystals ... 207
The Body: A System of Levers ... 208
The Study of the Body Architecture
    and Its Hierarchy of Resultant Gravity Pulls ... 210
    Geometric Divisions of the Body for Study and Self-Perception ... 210
    Perceiving Your Kinesphere and Interactive Gravity Pulls ... 211
    Spatial Distinctions and Zones for Movement ... 213
Sequential Exploration of the Organization of the Body
    with Corresponding Gravity Pulls ... 214
    The Defense Scale: The Foundation of Kinesthetic Experience
        for Conductors ... 214
Experiencing Two-Dimensional Movement Around the Axis:
    Movement in the Octahedron ... 216
The Door, Wheel, and Table Planes: Two-Dimensional Movement ... 217
Movement within the Cube: The Experience of Three
    Interactive Gravity Pulls ... 220
Moving from Full Body Movement to Focusing
    the Movement World on the Upper Body ... 224
Modified Diagonals and the Dynamic of Movement
    Among and Between Diagonals Create the Icosahedron ... 226

SKILL SET FOUR
Developing a Kinesthetic Vocabulary of Effort Combinations
through Awakening Movement Imagination ... 229

Experiencing the Efforts in Combination ... 231

SKILL SET FIVE
The Movement Imagery Exercises ... 243

SKILL SET SIX
The Sixteen Movement Themes ... 247

Basic Themes ... 248
Advanced Themes ... 249
Laban Movement Experience DVD: Experiencing the Movement Themes ... 250

SKILL SET SEVEN
Predicting and Imaging Movement to Evoke the Music:
Laban Movement Score Analysis (LMSA) ... 251

Choosing Appropriate Efforts in Combination ... 259

SKILL SET EIGHT
Music Exercises for Practice. 265

Dab and Glide 267
Glide, Press, Float, Dab, and Punch .268
Float, Dab, Wring, Glide, and Press 270
Press and Wring 271
Dab and Glide over Float and Glide .272
The Zoo 273
Mixolydian Conducting Round 274

SKILL SET NINE
The Movement Experience DVD 275

The Discipline of Etudes for the Development of Conducting Technique 277
F. M. Alexander and Rudolf Laban:
    A Symbiotic Relationship   Meade Andrews 278
How to Use the DVD for Practice and Study 279

Self-Study Outline:
The Conductor's Gesture DVD

Introduction   James Jordan 280
Chapter 2: The Laban Masterclasses   Meade Andrews 281
    The Architectural Design of the Body: The Interaction and
        Mutual Dependence of Laban and Alexander Technique 281
    Defining and Delineating Your Personal Space:
        Exploring the Dimensions of Movement 281
    Exploring the Planes of Movement:
        The Door Plane, Wheel Plane, and Table Plane 282
    Experiencing the Diagonals of the Cube 284
    The Defense Scale: Definition and Application Using
        Time, Weight, and Space 285
    Exploring the Isolated Efforts through Movement:
        The Building Blocks of Expressive Conducting Gesture 285
    Experiencing the Efforts in Isolation through Life
        Movement Situations 286
    Experiencing the Efforts in Combination through
        Movement Experiences 286
    Acquiring a Movement Vocabulary through Effort in
        Combination Experiences 286
    Experiencing Efforts and Efforts Juxtaposed 286

Chapter 3: Applying the Efforts in Combination to Patterns:
Drill and Practice Examples   *James Jordan* .287
Chapter 4: Choral Conducting Masterclass—Practical
Application   *James Jordan and Meade Andrews* 287
Chapter 5: Instrumental Conducting Masterclass—Practical
Application   *James Jordan* 288

SKILL SET TEN
Preparatory Audiation and Laban Efforts
CD/mp3 Download for Conducting Technique Development 291

The Acquisition of Conducting Analogues 292
Using Movement Imagery for Conducting Study 292
Pedagogical Concept Behind the CD/MP3: Movement Imaging 293

SUMMARY

A Retrospective on a Conducting Method Based Upon
    the Theories of Rudolf von Laban 295

A Compendium of Thoughts for Re-Study 296

Bibliography 307
Rhythm Bibliography 317
About the Authors 327

Foreword

Eugene Migliaro Corporon

Without a doubt, conducting is the embodiment of non-verbal communication. It is so very true that music begins where words fail. This makes it imperative for conductors to develop a gestural vocabulary that has the power to express emotions and elucidate ideas. Artistic conducting relies on the ability to develop syntax when using that vocabulary. Igniting the musical moment requires conducting that is spontaneously combustible. This kind of conducting is by its very nature improvisational and cannot be choreographed. First and foremost, it must be instigative.

Conductors embody the skills of an illusionist because in Frank Zappa's words: "They create designs in the nowhere that are interpreted as signals…" that impact and influence invisible sound. They are also able to convert thoughts and feelings into movement that is presented in the space that surrounds them. Through a process of "space-forming" or "space-sculpting," ideas and emotions that are encoded in the score and imbedded in the musicians are converted into shaped vibrations that transmit messages through the air to others. Even though the music cannot be seen, the consequential sensations can be heard and felt. Therefore, conducting remains a tactile and mystical act that triggers human interaction and reaction.

To reach our full potential as conductors, we have to become comfortable with our ability to elegantly and naturally portray sound in time through movement. Comfort, however, can be deceiving. Ones comfort level may not be the best indicator of gestural effectiveness, especially if you are working to re-map your body in space. Becoming too comfortable with the known can restrict creativity and limit growth. As you incorporate new concepts of movement into your kinesthetic presentation, the best gauge of success is the resultant sound. Evolution is paramount even though it can sometimes be uncomfortable.

Eventually, the comfort level will return as new and more effective gestures are blended into muscle memory. This book concentrates on advancing conductors to new levels of effective and affective interaction between movement, sound, and the people who make and receive it.

While there are some differences in tactics, the basic pedagogy of conducting is taught worldwide in a very similar manner. Philosophies and fundamentals are well presented in a multitude of outstanding texts. Because of limited contact hours, basic conducting classes are often more choreographic than creative. Unfortunately, too little time, usually only two semesters, is devoted to conducting in undergraduate curriculums. This makes it nearly impossible to reach beyond the basics to true artistry. As a result, finding a way to develop genuine gestures that elicit the most applicable musical sound at just the right moment is too often left to chance.

For years James Jordan has explored the world of movement through the work of Rudolf Laban and searched for ways to elevate the teaching of conducting from basics to brilliance. Any conductor who spends time with this book will surely profit from his tireless mission. What is contained between its covers is the result of decades of observation and thought put into action. It offers a way forward for conductors who seek to cultivate their expressiveness while increasing their effectiveness. The concepts are well defined and take much of the vagueness and confusion out of the perplexing world of movement. Jordan takes a fresh approach to existing Laban models that help increase comfort and competence when it comes to developing effortless, flowing, and appropriate movement that engenders the best possible sound.

As an avid reader of Jordan's work, I marvel at his ability to unite and codify information from a diverse range of sources. He truly has a gift that is enhanced by a great deal of experience, research, hard work, and consummate amounts of Starbucks coffee. His distillation process allows him to gather a variety of viewpoints, evaluate their significance, extract the salient information, and artfully present a thoughtfully blended conclusion. Having soaked up the essence of the material, he is able to make connections and correlations that lead others to comprehension and growth.

Jordan's application of the Laban philosophy is well thought out. More importantly, it has been field-tested. Jordan is a person who keeps a careful and inquisitive eye along with a discerning and critical ear on the teaching process. He is willing to investigate why something did not work and makes it a point to learn as much from his disappointments as he does from his successes.

His approach to elevating the conductor's ability to affect and expand the musicing is prophetic.

It is ironic that two of the most fundamental elements of conducting, pulse and pattern, are at once indispensible and constricting. Pulse and pattern, which are primarily informational, give the conductor something to do. However, they are not always the right things to be doing. Rudimentarily keeping time and organizing the meter are a minimal part of what ought to be coming from the podium. Once mastered, these vital constructs can work against heightening artistry, sometimes putting the conductor in a straight jacket that can restrict motion and impair expression for life.

The key is to develop freedom and clarity within a gestural range that affords one the ability to choose exactly the right movement to portray the desired sound generated by the imagined ideal. There are limitless possibilities when it comes to the interaction of movement and sound. The ability to show what sound looks like is central to experiencing success as an ingenious and imaginative conductor who has a convincing inner vision along with the technique to share it with others.

Instigating sound…monitoring sound…adjusting sound…resonating sound… sculpting sound…finishing sound…impacting silence—these are all part of the process. It is important to note that stillness is to motion what silence is to sound. Stillness draws attention to the motion that follows. Knowing when not to move is just as important as being in motion. Like everything artful, a balance must be achieved. Finding center and breathing into the sound are two of the fundamental tenants of this methodology.

The system of advanced gestural development that Jordan offers takes all of these relationships into account. Gestures that have the greatest meaning are formed in the inhalation of the breath. They come from stillness and return to stillness in much the same way that music of significance comes from silence and returns to silence. Moving conductors beyond fundamentals to a deeper awareness of these principles is one of the goals of this book.

According to Laban, Space, Weight, and Time are our allies in this pursuit. Energy, Direction, Distance, Resistance, and Speed also play a principal role. The interactions of these efforts combine to yield an inexhaustible thesaurus of gestures that can contain subtle and significant meaning.

Until now it has been difficult to find an efficient and cogent way to introduce advanced concepts of movement into the conducting curriculum. Jordan has opened the door to a pedagogical system that streamlines the process and offers a detailed plan that allows conductors to cultivate the sound-scape and reap a viable and uncomplicated harvest of refined artistry and expanded creativity. His blueprint supports and reinforces the premise that body, mind, and spirit have to be unified and passionately engaged to make meaningful progress.

Conducting gestures must portray the imagined-ideal, along with the innermost concept of the sounds and their implication. This book provides a readable and usable treasure map to the hidden places that you want your musicing to go. It enhances the awareness of not only what you see and hear, but also how to reveal implied meaning through instinctive and purposeful movement. Developing awareness is critical to finding a decipherable and reliable gesture that causes the exact sound image to emerge. Conducting has to lead the cause-effect relationship in order to be beneficial. In other words, conducting is first and foremost concerned with predicting the future, followed by monitoring and adjusting the subsequent sound that has materialized so it mirrors the sound image.

The essential focus of conducting should be on connecting and communicating with people. Over and above our own feelings, concepts, and energy, the space we work in (the kinesphere) contains the spirit of the musicians who offer the sounds as well as the soul of the composer who envisioned the piece. We all meet out there in Zappa's "nowhere" to collaborate and conjoin for one important reason: to make the best possible music. The result of this synergetic relationship can be life changing if and only if the movement embodied by the conductor liberates and protects the human energy in the space.

The honesty and integrity of the gesture will bring forth the most appropriate sound for each and every moment. Static and regulated actions will elicit music that is the same. Jordan reminds us that every movement is engendered by the desired sound. He offers natural and fluid solutions to common conducting problems. The ability to instigate events originates from a well-conceived sound. The conductor needs to be a visionary with an active and rich imagination that is proficient at developing a sub-text or back-story that can inform and augment the character and style of the music. A vivid imagination capable of creative visualization and actionable audiation is required to design gestures that expose just the right sound at just the right moment.

Conducting technique should demonstrate a balance of craft: the objective work of dispensing information and artistry, the subjective exploration of inspirational possibilities. Artists are responsible for developing their own imagined-ideal or aural model of a composition. Jordan cautions us that copying or mimicking someone else completely negates or defeats the creative process. When conducting technique is real, truthful, and in the moment, it generates from the inside out. To accomplish this, you need to broaden the movement potential within your body and eliminate whatever interferes with the musical goals.

The most any conducting pedagogical system can hope to accomplish is to enhance gestural vocabulary, facilitate movement, illuminate ideas, and deepen feeling while developing a multitude of options that can intensify creativity and improve sound. This book has the power to do all of that in addition to developing authenticity, inner strength, and individuality in those who have the responsibility of leading the musicing of others.

I encourage you to read every word, immerse yourself in the exercises, and work to make these ideas your own. It has been said that you have not really learned something until you have forgotten that you know it. Consequently, you must become so familiar with the theories offered in this text that they become an intuitive component of your subconscious toolbox that can be applied in an instant.

The personal investment of time, energy, and attention will be transformative and allow you to share the most intimate details of your objective artistic discoveries and subjective visualizations of the music. An Andrew Carnegie quote seems most applicable here: "If you do what you have always done, you will get what you have always gotten."

Throughout this incomparable endeavor, James Jordan has once again delivered a significant resource that provides an opportunity for all of us to break away from what we have always done and introduce something new into our work. He has furnished not only the motivation but also the materials and tools to help redesign the way we use space and move through time to innately sculpt sound in the "nowhere." With his guidance, we can get results that we have never gotten before and break down the barriers that block access to informed, effortless musical movement that enriches, magnifies, and amplifies the way sounds are generated, received, and perceived.

Philosophical Foreword

Why Gestural Pedagogy Matters

Gerald Custer

The book you are about to read is unlike any conducting text you've ever seen. It marks a radical break with the past in two important ways: It offers a cohesive, integrated course of study about an aspect of conducting that is seldom properly understood—gesture. And it presents this material in a unique way—pedagogically.

What's so important about gesture? Why does pedagogy matter?

Like singers and instrumentalists, conductors must learn and refine a technique that enables them to accomplish what other musicians do routinely: understand the musical content of the score and communicate its meaning to others with artistry and expression. For conductors, gesture is the essential visible point of contact between the music and the musicians they direct. Acquiring and mastering a robust gestural vocabulary is critical to successful conducting technique.

Yet gesture is greatly misunderstood. Far too often, it is defined narrowly and mechanically. Many well-known conducting texts (Max Rudolf's *The Grammar of Conducting* and Elizabeth Green's *The Modern Conductor,* for example) erroneously equate time beating and beat patterns—the so-called "manual technique"—with gesture. Beginning conductors, who frequently confuse conducting with "taking charge" or "being in control," routinely make this same mistake as well. This should hardly be surprising. The instruction they get rests on the same flawed set of assumptions, and those giving that instruction were very likely trained the same way themselves.

As a result, newly minted conductors typically approach their first professional engagements as little more than living metronomes, fueled by ego and operating under the magical illusion that somehow they "make the music happen" simply by beating time patterns clearly. This sorry state of affairs (a vicious cycle, really) gets perpetuated because as conductors we do not fundamentally understand what gesture truly comprises or what a pedagogy of conducting should look like.

Gesture is far more than patterns of manual technique or time beating. It is what allows us to "look like the music" we conduct. Although it has a metric dimension, gesture communicates a host of information besides meter. It expresses tempo and dynamics, articulation and weight, the degree of decay or sostenuto in the line, character and timing of breath, overall phrase shape and direction, and choral texture and balance.

More than this, gesture is an integrated set of simultaneous mind-to-body coordinations that encompass the whole of our physical being: alignment, mechanisms of breath and phonation, eyes and face, torso, arms, hands, and fingers. Finally, gesture flows from a deep understanding of the score's contents, demands, and challenges, and from a thorough appreciation of how the voice works and what the specific needs (and limitations) of the singers at hand may be.

Defining gesture in a multi-dimensional way has significant implications for the study and teaching of conducting. It means that developing an accurate anatomical picture is crucial and that correcting our body maps and understanding body structures and mechanics are necessary prerequisites to accessing gesture with freedom and using it fluently.

It also means that understanding and using a wide range of analytical tools—harmonic analysis, structural analysis, historical/critical analysis, textual analysis, and others—is essential in forming a robust gestural vocabulary, since these approaches identify and unlock the data that flows into a conductor's gestures. And it means that familiarity with the singing voice and the principles of group vocal technique will play an important role in the gestures a conductor ultimately selects and employs.

It may be easier to grasp this enhanced definition of gesture by graphically illustrating it as multiple knowledge sets that intersect:

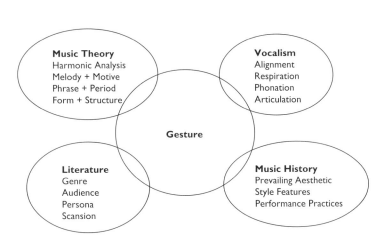

Audiation, rehearsal planning and management, sectional voicing, and error detection and correction (among other skills) are vital. But gesture remains the central expression of our technique as conductors. It is the most important avenue available to us to effect the revelatory transference that lies at the heart of choral rehearsing and choral performance: interiorization of the score and its contents, transfer of ownership to the ensemble, and ultimately forging an experience of life-changing *communio* with the listeners.

That's why how we *teach* gesture matters just as much as how we *define* it. And here we encounter a problem.

Violinists study string pedagogy, singers learn vocal pedagogy, and theorists and composers are able to study theory and composition pedagogy. But conducting is still largely taught through mentorship and imitative initiation at a personal level. The professional training of conductors resembles the guild approach of the Middle Ages more than anything else. The guild model is still how carpenters and electricians are trained today: through a sequential combination of hands-on experience, one-on-one coaching, modeling, and the transmission of lore anecdotally.

As a result, many conductors conduct in a style that resembles the approach of those with whom they studied and—for better or worse—teach conducting to others as they were taught it initially. Perhaps more troubling is that most conducting DMAs are expected to teach undergraduate courses for which they have received no formal instruction in teaching. We need a pedagogy of our own.

Pedagogy is a comprehensive, coordinated, and systematic approach that enables teachers to reliably communicate knowledge (both content data and specific skills) in a replicable manner about a given subject area to those who are learning it. It encompasses both minimum levels of competencies—what must be known and what must be done—and how best to teach that content and those skills.

A robust pedagogy includes a body of knowledge, core content whose inclusion is the result of consensus by content experts and master practitioners; an understanding of the various avenues through which students acquire and master that body of knowledge, including awareness of different learning styles and multiple modalities of effective teaching; and optimized sequencing of content within the body of knowledge (skills, topics, knowledge areas) that appropriately matches student learning styles and expected levels of content mastery across the educational spectrum.

In addition, a pedagogy worthy of the name incorporates reliable methods to measure and validate student mastery of core content and skills. It is driven by discrete, explicitly stated educational outcomes where achievement can be tested and measured in pragmatically meaningful and statistically reliable fashion. It should include an intentional program of study that enables future teachers to understand, practice, and improve their own skillfulness in teaching and in evaluating acquisition of content by their students. And it should feature ongoing research to continually improve the sequencing, presentation, and testing of this body of knowledge.

Creating and refining a pedagogy for choral conducting is no small task. Yet the benefits of doing so hold great promise: better conducting teachers will make for better conductors; better conductors will make for better choirs; better choirs will attract more potential singers to join them and touch a world hungry for the beauty only music can provide. It is a challenge worth addressing. And this book marks an important step toward doing just that.

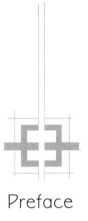

Preface

Acquiring Our Sixth Sense

James Jordan

Kinesthesis (the "muscle sense" or "sixth sense") is defined as the sensual discrimination of the positions and movement of body parts based on information other than visual, auditory, or verbal. Kinesthetic perception involves judging changes in muscle tension, body position, and the relative placement of body parts…. Without any difficulty we know where the body is, and where it is going, at any moment, with eyes shut. (p. 48)

—*Carol-Lynne Moore*
in *Beyond Words*

Where does the impulse of motion lead? —into space. Therefore, the mastery of the surrounding space is necessary. The training has thus, as one of its aims, to reach every point of the space surrounding the body. People can be made aware of the main zones of space which can be reached according to the anatomic structure of the various parts and limbs of the body in the best way. This awareness must be acquired through practical movement experience. (p. 27)

—*Rudolf Laban*
in *Modern Educational Dance*

> The person who has learnt to relate himself to Space, and has physical mastery of this, has attention. The person who has mastery of his relation to the Weight factor of effort has Intention and he has Decision when he is adjusted to time. Attention, intention and decision are the stages of inner preparation of an outer bodily action. This comes about when through the Flow of movement, effort finds concrete expression in the body. (p. 251)
>
> —*Rudolf von Laban*
> in *Laban for All*
> Jean Newlove and John Dalby

To interpret the work of one of the great movement geniuses of the twentieth century is a daunting task to be sure. It is almost thirty years since I first heard of Laban. From my very first exposure to his work, I sensed its gravitas for the career I was to embark upon—conducting. His work has found its way into my way of thinking about the conducting art, how I teach, and how my students learn to conduct. Laban's gift for describing movement and visualizing movement space is a gift I believe all musicians should embrace. Since movement is vital to our work, and because we as musicians come to movement almost "through the back door," Laban has much to offer as a communicative language and as a way to deepen our "sixth sense" (our kinesthesia, or feeling about what it is to move).

Laban understood the sacred "dance" between sound and movement, and how the alchemy of those two things could move the human spirit in the most powerful of ways. From the beginning of my work with these ideas, the application (or rather transfer) of Laban's ideas seemed a comfortable, if not natural, fit to the art of conducting—at least to me! While it was somewhat clear even in the early days of my work with Laban just how the material could be applied to both conducting and rhythm pedagogy, the specific method has taken much longer to sort out.

My pedagogical way of thinking was deeply influenced by my music psychology teacher and mentor, Edwin Gordon. Dr. Gordon not only taught me a deep and abiding respect for pedagogy, but he also impressed upon me the importance of refining and defining pedagogy in such a way so music could have the voice it deserves to touch people. Pedagogy, or rather method, is a painstaking process of becoming more efficient, and therein lay the challenge. Dr. Gordon also taught me how to craft the written word to accurately describe the pedagogical ideas, including how that pedagogy is both taught and learned. It is a privilege to call him my teacher, and none of this would have been possible without his teaching in those early years.

While many of the specific applications have come about through both thought and teaching, the inspiration for all of this lay with one of my conducting teachers and mentors, Gail B. Poch. For those who know Gail, I am sure all would agree he was a teacher among great teachers who prided himself on not only good teaching, but also compassionate teaching. Mr. Poch introduced me to the world of Laban. He and I attended the Laban Institute for Movement Studies to try to further "decipher" and experience firsthand the message of Laban. He was both my inspiration and my sounding board. This book is a tribute to his teaching genius and a small repayment for all the care and love he showed me as a young conductor. Without his germinating idea and insights, none of this would have come to pass. Mr. Poch drafted an initial interpretation of the application of Laban to conducting. I had hoped to incorporate that manuscript into this book, but through a series of unfortunate situations, that was not possible.

Professor David Milne was my major professor at Bucknell University, where I did much of my graduate study in psychology related to my doctoral program. He guided me through the history of psychology as I dug for related research questions regarding Laban. Much of the work of Chapter 4 was done under his guidance. He helped me formulate research problems and, in so doing, strongly influenced how I interpreted Laban's work as a musician/psychologist. It was Dr. Milne who made me understand that there is a difference between the perception of someone else moving and one perceiving one's own movement. Laban's genius rests in the fact that he knew that both must be understood and studied if one was to truly understand movement as an expressive language. Without Dr. Milne's guidance, I am not sure any of my ideas, much less a methodology, would have evolved to their present form.

The material by Giselle Wyers in this book not only shows profound insights into Laban and its applications but also provides compelling examples of practical application to our conducting and rehearsal art. Dr. Wyers is a gifted musician, teacher, and conductor in her own right. But she has taken Laban's intent and transformed it into a living and vibrant pedagogy. She is able to bridge theory to practice. Readers of this text would do well to spend much time with her material. Her chapter deepens the applications of Laban for the broader context of evoking and influencing sound. I am honored to have her help in this collaboration. Her work is profoundly innovative and provides the vehicle for direct application of Laban's principles to conducting using specific examples from the choral literature.

And then there is Meade Andrews. I often hesitated to complete this book because I could not find the final piece: the practical application. For me, it was moving through space and then experiencing the Efforts in Combination through actual life experiences that ignited the ideas in this book. While I have written about Laban in several different resources, many questions remained unanswered because it is so difficult to write about moving—one must move and experience!

While I knew I could probably cobble together a "re-enactment" of my training at the Laban Institute, I searched for someone for whom movement was a significant part of their artistic life. Dr. Andrews arrived at Rider University as an artist-in-residence. To my surprise, I found out that she and I had studied at the same Laban Institutes and with many of the same teachers! A dancer, recognized Alexander Technique specialist, and theater professor, she was able to add another dimension to the application of Laban's work to conducting (as can be seen on the DVD that is contained with this book). Her innate ability as a dancer to guide us into the movement world completed what I believed necessary for a book of this scope. Study the DVD and move with Dr. Andrews as she teaches my students. Moving is the only "way in" to this Laban world, and Dr. Andrews is the best explorer I have seen of Laban's world. She reminds us that an expressive body is an aligned body through her deep and intuitive understanding of Alexander Technique. Her teaching and expertise provides additional depth and movement experience to us all.

Eugene Migliaro Corporon and I share a passion for teaching conducting and for the miracles that become what conducting "does." We believe in many of the same human things that make for great musicing, and we have an additional abiding passion for conducting pedagogy. His career has been marked by a pedagogical curiosity that asks us to examine and re-examine what we do and how we do it. Collaborations in the past have yielded such projects as *The Anatomy of Conducting*. His generous offer to use the Wind Symphony of The University of North Texas on the DVD companion to this book enriches this project immeasurably. His friendship and support mean more to me than words can express.

What is presented in the pages that follow is a way that Laban can be applied to conducting and, hopefully, how we teach conducting. It is a method for the sequential acquisition of conducting technique. This application is through my eyes, but I have at all times tried to remain true to Laban's original language and his intent. Sara Alberti Chapman, who was an advisor on my Ph.D. dissertation, is a leading authority on Laban *Effort Shape* and *Modern Educational Dance*. It was her continued admonitions throughout my study with her to remain true to all of the original Laban sources.

Great geniuses are those people who can see things that others cannot. In fact, they see things so simply and clearly that they seem obvious once pointed out. Part of the genius of Laban is that he was able to take what is a complex language-movement and place it in the most simple and direct language so that movement not only can be felt but also can be communicated to others and recalled from other parts of our movement life. As human beings, Laban believed that we come with a full movement "vocabulary" at birth. That vocabulary falls into disuse because of environmental and other influences. Laban's language of the Effort Elements allows us to rekindle the movement world that is in each one of us so we can rediscover our "sixth sense." If you approach the art of conducting as acquiring the skills for a new "sixth sense," then the importance of Laban's work will take root in your expressive and teaching life as a conductor. As time goes on, I hope others will have insights beyond those in these pages. But for now what I do know is that through Laban, my students have grown immeasurably and have gained insights into the symbiotic relationship of gesture and sound. And through Laban, my own conducting has developed an expressive language that allows for the spontaneity of the music making experience that I believe is at the very core of what we do.

This book has been a long time in the making and is the culmination of a very long and exciting pedagogical journey. I am glad to be able to share this with all of you. May you find the material as life-changing and empowering as I have.

—James Jordan
Yardley, Pennsylvania

PART 1

The Theories and Work of Rudolf von Laban:
An Examination of the Perception of Movement

In rhythmic waves regularly spreading, the ether trembles, the small, most minute particles of matter tremble. If there were no movement at all, all things would be lying dead in absolute rigidity and complete apathy. No ray of light, no sound would bring messages from one thing to another.

Movement not only speaks through an object; a living organism owes its final form to it; movement leads to growth and structure.... (p. 1)

> —Rudolf von Laban
> in Irmgard Bartenieff,
> *Body Movement*

CHAPTER 1
Introduction

Few people will realize that a page of musical notes is to a great extent a description or prescription of bodily motivations or of the way how to move your muscles, limbs, breathing organs…in order to produce certain effects. (p. 39)

—Rudolf Laban
in Karen K. Bradley,
Rudolf Laban

We body forth our ideals in personal acts, either alone or with others in society. We body forth felt experience in a poem's image and sound. We body forth our inner residence in the architecture of our homes and common buildings. We body firth our struggles and our revelations in the space of theatre. That is what form is: the bodying forth. (p. 39)

The artist is a birther of form and form means "bodying forth." All art is a "bodying forth." (pp. xv–xvi)

—M. C. Richards
in *Centering*

Man moves in order to satisfy a need. He aims by his movement at something of value to him. It is easy to perceive of the aim of a person's movement if it is directed to some tangible object. Yet there also exist intangible values that inspire movement. (p. 1)

—Rudolf Laban
in *The Mastery of Movement*

Looking at the whole range of innate and acquired impulses of man, one is tempted to search for a common denominator…this denominator…is movement with all its spiritual implications. (p. 17)

>—Rudolf Laban
>in Hodgson and Dunlop,
>*Rudolf Laban*

Movement must be approached at multiple levels if it is to be properly understood. (p. 186)

>—Carol-Lynne Moore
>in *Beyond Words*

Movement can be studied like any other reality of existence. One can see its mechanical implications, coming from the instrumental character of our body. The parts of our skeleton are levered by our muscles in a way not dissimilar from the function of a mobile crane with which we lift and transport merchandise. But in the crane sits a mastermind, the crane driver, who organizes the motions of the crane, enabling this contraption to serve a definite job. We can all know about every single screw and pulley of the crane without being able to drive it by our thinking only. For the driving we need movement.

The body is the crane and crane-driver in one assembled unit, and this unit follows—knowingly or unknowingly—the invariable rules of the bodily and mental motion. (p. 5)

>—Rudolf von Laban
>in *The Laban Art of Movement
>Guild Magazine*, No. 19 (November 1957)

I have seen all too many dancers who throw themselves into the air without any sign of inner participation. On the contrary, such large movements are frequently very externalized, comparable to hollow shells in which not the slightest indication of real life or an integration of body and mind could be discovered. (p. 7)

>—Rudolf von Laban
>in an unfinished article entitled
>"The Educational and Therapeutic Value of Dance"
>*The Laban Art of Movement
>Guild Magazine*, No. 22 (May 1959)

INTRODUCTION

Chapter 1

Rhythm is the result of interaction of natural forces.

> —Alice Parker
> Westminster Choir College Seminar
> (July 2009)

Many of us have experienced frustration in teaching conducting. How does one guide a student to comprehend the relationship of gesture (movement) to music, and at the same time remain within the confines of traditional orientation and clarity? Texts on conducting deal only with the spatial reproduction of patterns, minimal introduction to cueing, dynamics, phrasing, etc. Some recognize the difference in style of beat, but none provide tangible methods for developing those differences. The problem: Conducting is initially an imitative form of communication dictated by conventional patterns of movement which have evolved into a series of universally understandable gestures. It is possible for a student to learn to articulate these gestures through imitation, yet the movement patterns fail to successfully convey the basic demands of a score. The communication of stylistic qualities or musical sensitivity is beyond the realm of possibility when a conductor is only imitating the gesture.

> —Gail B. Poch
> in *The Choral Journal* (January 1982)

The value of characterization through dance-like mime movements lies in the avoidance of the simple imitation of external movement peculiarities. Such imitation does not penetrate to the hidden recesses of man's inner Effort. We need an authentic symbol of the inner vision to effect contact with the audience, and this contact can be achieved only if we have learned to think in terms of movement. (p. 20)

> —Rudolf Laban
> in *The Mastery of Movement*

Thus Laban shares his perspectives on the role of theater performance in the lives of human beings, and thus he prescribes the ways in which performers can master the art of being fully human. With stories of the heart at every performance, the goal was to help people find their way to the essence and truth of those stories we tell ourselves over and over, hoping to learn anew. (p. 46)

> —Karen K. Bradley
> in *Rudolf Laban*

Everything about the art of conducting is about being in a constant state of awareness. In fact, teaching one to be aware may be the most difficult task facing any conducting teacher or student. Being aware of one's own body and sound in the same instant poses pedagogical challenges. Music is also about forward motion. Awareness of sound, awareness of how music moves forward, and awareness of breath, among other things, form the basis of how we not only teach music to ensembles but also conduct them and connect to them in the most profoundly human way. If we believe that conducting is enabling sound to move forward, then conductors must be aware movers at their very core. The perplexing dilemma is that conductors (and musicians in general) are not movers by nature. The pedagogy of teaching conducting has not begun with some paradigm to help us understand movement in its most organic sense and what it is to move while we are hearing sound. How is it that we acquire the knowledge of *how* to move and influence sound? So much of a conductor's movement seems to be an awareness *after* the sound is heard. In reality, conductors should be equipped with the kinesthetic tools to imagine and feel movement and sound as one interrelated and interdependent experience.

The more basic problem conductors face was stated very beautifully by my conducting teacher, Gail Poch, in a November 1982 article in *The Choral Journal*, which was the first such pedagogical claim to the use of Laban for conducting pedagogy. (The article appears in original form in a chapter that follows.)

> Many conductors achieve a well-defined presentation as the result of skillfully developed rehearsal procedures. However, the performance can never exceed the rehearsed level because of the conductor's inability to spontaneously create that unique atmosphere which elevates a performance to a special quality of musical excellence. This does not imply that the conductor does not desire a response of great artistic accomplishment. In many instances, he simply does not understand, or have the ability to transmit those subtleties, which accompany tempo, dynamics, and phrasing in order to communicate the full essence or excitement of a score. (*The Choral Journal*, November 1982)

INTRODUCTION

For me, the work of Laban provides the perceptual vehicle and framework by which conductors can develop and manifest their audiational kinesthesia and translate that complex perception of how music moves immediately into a gestural language that has immediate, intimate, and tangible meaning to all who perceive it. For over thirty years since this material was introduced to me by Gail Poch, and clarified in my doctoral study with Sarah Chapman at Temple University, I have wrestled with its profound pedagogical implications for conductors.

Because Laban's work was primarily developed for dance education and dance notation, applications of his work to conducting have occurred through various interpretations of his writings, by both inference and teaching experience. The focus of this book is to consider *how* the work of Laban can and should be applied to assist conductors in their musical journey. This is an inside out journey, where we learn to access the world of movement that is contained within us. The views contained in this book grow out of primary sources written by Laban, especially *Modern Educational Dance* and all the articles he wrote for *The Art of Movement Guild Magazine*, my study at the Laban Institute for Movement Studies, and my work with Sarah Chapman for my Ph.D. dissertation. For me, this has been an academic pilgrimage, walking hand in hand with my growth as a conductor for over thirty years.

So why am I only writing this book now? The answer is fairly straightforward. On the surface, this material seems immediately applicable to conducting. However, applied in a haphazard way, Laban could become a choreographic method that allows conductors to move "to the music." There may be some worth to such an approach. There are several approaches that utilize Laban in this role as movement "facilitator." In my first blush with this material in the early 1980s, that seemed to be the role I had assigned to it in my own mind. However, as I grew to understand my own movement and the true expressive power that inside-out movement embodies through my work at The School for the Hartford Ballet in the late 1980s, I began to take a journey with myself and with my conducting students through the music we were making that changed my views on the application of Laban's ideas.

Any pedagogy is like a kaleidoscope. An incredible kaleidoscope sits on my piano at home as a reminder of my role in applying Laban to our art. I feel like I have turned not only the Laban kaleidoscope, but also the movement perception kaleidoscope, in many ways throughout my thirty plus years of teaching and conducting, and I now can see an image of the application of this material clearly enough to write about it and make direct applications, albeit my applications, to conducting.

I have approached some of these applications in my writings over the years. In the first edition of *Evoking Sound* (1996), I included a chapter to break ground with conductors; the response to that material was overwhelming and gratifying. I then made some connections to rhythm pedagogy in *The Choral Rehearsal*, Vol. 1 (2007). I presented an application of Laban to score analysis in *The Choral Rehearsal*, Vol. 2 (2007). I then revised and clarified my Laban thought further in the Second Edition of *Evoking Sound* (2009). Now, this text brings all of those sources together in one location and offers the "connective tissue" to complete what I believe is a strong pedagogical method for enabling conductors to make an intimate and organic connection to the sounds they hear and their body.

Laban as a Gestural Morphology

Instead of using the word "method," I would like to propose that this text is a morphology of conducting gesture. Any morphology, by its very definition, examines in the most profound way the beginning, middle, and end of a life of something. If conducting gesture is to have any honesty and any ability to express anything, then conductors must understand how sound is bound, like blood to bone, with movement. Laban provides such a morphological viewpoint. It provides the perfect model by which we can bind the sound inside us to a meaningful gesture that is both honest and expressive, and never contrived. In *The Musician's Breath* (2010), I made the case to conductors that breath is the carrier of all things musical. I set out to complete the journey in this book by providing conductors with a way to manifest what is embodied in the breath in their every movement.

Gail Poch alluded to such a morphology when he wrote about conducting as movement analogues:

> Music has movement analogues—music originates from movement: the flow of a line, the weight of maestoso, the quickness of staccato, the relaxation of a cadence, the irregularity of recitative, or the ease of jazz. What a conductor must accomplish through his gesture is the recovery of these movement analogues in order to represent the expressive origins of the music. This quality of the gesture must convey the inherent movement in the music. (*The Choral Journal*, November 1982)

INTRODUCTION

All of this is nothing short of a miracle. Conducting can be a miracle of human communication and human connection if the conductor understands the morphology of that miracle. Gesture grows out of sound, and that gesture is re-ignited through a kind of movement memory that recalls movement we have already experienced as part of life. It is my hope (and dream) that this book will provide for conductors a deeper understanding of their innermost impulse to move and have a relationship with sound—that their conducting life will gain clairvoyance with this material. I know that it has provided me with a clear path of cognitive and perceptive tools, which has allowed me to marry what is both spiritual and physical in conducting. I hope that all of you reading this will make this material your own and that your movement/movement imaginations become both more fertile and more alive. I am excited to finally share my discoveries and ideas with you. Begin your morphological conducting journey on the firm foundation of Rudolf von Laban, one of the great creative minds of the twentieth century.

One final note about this text: You will find that similar material is presented at several different places in the book. For example, the concept of Effort and Efforts in Combination is introduced in an early chapter and then repeated in the skill set chapters. The repetition is deliberate. I have found if effective to keep this material fresh by revisiting it.

The Pitfalls of Pedagogical Impatience

> And this was the best of all, and perhaps the greatest of all pedagogical achievements; to be given not only one's artistic independence, but to be forced into an absolute self-responsibility. (p. 161)
>
> Did I comprehend at all at that time what Laban had in mind? I was young and impatient, I wanted to dance, I wanted to create and communicate something that concerned other people too. What was a theory to me? I believe that the foundations of my career as a dancer as well as a dance pedagogue were laid in those few weeks. Objectivity and responsibility, patience, endurance and self-discipline! (p. 134)
>
> —Mary Wigman
> in Mary Anne Santos Newhall,
> *Mary Wigman*

All of us have been "here" for some reason—that place where we plunge into conducting study with an urgent want and impatient urge to conduct. We want to learn what we have to learn as quickly as possible to "get on with things." Impatience with our artistic craft seems to be not only the calling card for artists, but in many ways either the downfall or stumbling block. A common tendency in people is to bypass anything that might slow them down in achieving a goal. In conducting, any pedagogy seems to tax one's patience and ability to focus.

I have conducted many workshops where I would have liked to speak of interpretative ideas or sound ideas but soon discovered that the students do not have the technical tools to bring interpretive ideas that are in their audiation to life. A "return to basics" has always yielded incredible results. When that return to basics is structured along a method, then progress seems to occur much more rapidly. Realizations become more apparent, and progress is made at a much faster pace.

The quote above by Mary Wigman, one of Laban's finest students, supports this point of view (and the trap that so many of us fall into). So many of us who are experienced conductors learned our craft devoid of any pedagogy, let alone a patient, structured approach to acquiring our technique. We acquired technique (both good and bad) through a kind of mimicry. It is only when we were forced to stop and closely examine the intimate relationship between gesture and sound that both our understanding and expressivity grew.

I ask you to trust in the material presented in these pages. Laban's visions of how we move will provide a vehicle by which you can build your conducting technique. Spend time with the sequential skill sets in the second half of this text. Laban's world demands that we see movement and perceive our own movement through a structured process based in both the intrinsic geometry of our bodies and the feelings of what it is to move. It also asks that we develop a movement vocabulary rooted in a system of movement recall that builds a gestural vocabulary for eventual marriage with sound. That eventual marriage will hopefully reveal an expressive world where, in the words of Parker Palmer below, the "world acts back"!

INTRODUCTION

> To be fully alive is to act. The capacity to act is the most obvious difference between the quick and the dead. But action is more than movement; it is movement that involves expression, discovery, re-formation of ourselves and our world. *I understand action to be any way that we can co-create reality with other beings and with the Spirit.* Through action we both express and learn something of who we are, of the kind of world we have or want. Action, like a sacrament, is the visible form of an invisible spirit, an outward manifestation of an inward power. But as we act, we not only express what is in us and help give shape to the world; we also receive what is outside us, and we reshape our inner selves. When we act, the world acts back, and we and the world are co-created. (p. 17)
>
> —Parker Palmer
> in *The Active Life*

One of the finest professors I encountered in my life taught me music theory at the graduate level: B. Stimson Carrow always began his theory and counterpoint classes with a simple admonition and a foreshadowing of the class to come: "System is comfort." For our purposes here, we might say, "Pedagogy is comfort." You will find that Laban will provide a "system" that will lead you to a deeper understanding at a more intuitive level of just how you can learn to move as a conductor who *both* inspires and compels musicians to reveal the miracles within the scores they study and perform. What should be our hope for a "final product" as conductors? Frank Battisti, a conductor whose very way of teaching and making music has inspired so many of us, perhaps says it best.

> A musician is musical when their music making elicits an emotional response from players and listeners. To be musical is to "make music like God makes trees"—that is, in a manner and style that is natural and consistent with the performer's personality, intellect and intimate emotional capacity. Being musical is more than juggling notes; it's liberating what's *inside* the notes. One's music making should awaken the soul.
>
> —Frank Battisti in Eugene Migliaro Corporon,
> "Principles of Achievement, Enhancing
> Musicianship and Valued Colleagues"
> from *Teaching Music through Performance in Band, Volume 8*

—James Jordan
January 2011

CHAPTER 2
The Beginnings

Laban insisted that in the human body there is a three-fold unity: body, mind and spirit. Each of these is movement related and interdependent and throughout there is a two-way process in operation: we feel, we think and that affects and effects body movement; we move in a certain way and that affects and effects outlook and thought. (p. 17)

—Hodgson and Dunlop
in *Rudolf Laban:*
An Introduction to His Work and Influence

Author's Note: *The article reprint that follows by Gail B. Poch was the first writing that established a direct connection between the work of Rudolf von Laban and conducting pedagogy. The principles put forward by Professor Poch formed much of this author's approach to the material contained in this book and started this author on the pedagogical implications through research and further study. This author is indebted to Professor Poch for his innovative insights and pedagogical ideas put forth in the article.*

Conducting: Movement Analogues through Effort ∫hape
(reprinted from The Choral Journal, November 1982)

———— Gail Poch ————

Mr. Gail B. Poch was Associate Professor of Choral Music at Temple University, College of Music, in Philadelphia, and Director of Music for the Reading (PA) Choral Society. He has presented interest sessions on this approach to conducting at the American Choral Directors Association Eastern Division Convention (February 1982) and at the state convention of the Pennsylvania Music Educators Association (January 1982).

In two editorials written in 1981, Past ACDA President, Royce Saltzman, spoke out strongly about the absence of basic technical skills on the part of many choral conductors. Why this embarrassing observation has not been made sooner is as alarming as the deficiency itself. Recognition of the problem is, however, only the first step. Is there a solution? The fact that there is such extensive evidence of this absence indicates an obvious lack of effective methodology for developing these skills. Therefore, one cannot place the blame on those who have been victimized by the pedagogical deficiencies of our instructional institutions. Rather, one should closely examine available teaching resources and determine why this vital aspect of musical training is not meeting with success. The result of such an examination reveals the factual truth—there is no source which offers a logical and meaningful learning sequence for the development of the techniques and skills of conducting. It is important to distinguish differences between the physical movement of conducting and the artistic/musicological component of the act. It is the element of physical movement which is not being recognized and properly improved, therefore the growth of these potentially articulate conductors is stunted.

Many of us have experienced frustration in teaching conducting. How does one guide a student to comprehend the relationship of gesture (movement) to music, and at the same time remain within the confines of traditional orientation and clarity? Texts on conducting deal only with the spatial reproduction of patterns, minimal introduction to cueing, dynamics, phrasing, etc. Some recognize the difference in style of beat, but none provide tangible methods for developing those differences. The problem: conducting is initially an imitative form of communication dictated by conventional patterns of movement which have evolved into a series of universally understandable gestures. It is possible for a student to learn to articulate these gestures through imitation, yet, the movement patterns fail to successfully convey the basic demands of a score. The communication of stylistic qualities or musical sensitivity is beyond the realm of possibility when a conductor is only imitating the gesture.

The connection of gesture to musical style as part of the basic technique is not adequately provided for. Some instructors have been able to devise their own individual approach to accommodate this need, but obviously, most others have not been able to find successful concepts to solidify this link.

A conductor has the responsibility to recreate an artistic product of a composer, and the accomplishment of this task involves a great deal more than simply realizing the printed symbols on the pages of a score. The conductor must be able to convey a multiplicity of nuances to his ensemble through gestures which serve as his vocabulary for this form of non-verbal communication. If the conductor does not understand movement potential and its relationship to the music, his palette is limited to monochromatic expression. If he is aware of the vast range of movement implications, he may successfully impart those qualities which elicit a genuine musical statement.

Many conductors achieve a well-defined presentation as the result of skillfully developed rehearsal procedures. However, the performance can never exceed the rehearsed level because of the conductor's inability to spontaneously create that unique atmosphere which elevates a performance to a special quality of musical excellence. This does not imply that the conductor does not desire a response of great artistic accomplishment. In many instances, he simply does not understand, or have the ability to transmit those subtleties which accompany tempo, dynamics, and phrasing in order to communicate the full essence or excitement of a score. Realizing the need to augment available resources for teaching conducting, I attempted to incorporate many different approaches in the classroom. None seemed to provide for the total demands until I was introduced to the studies of Rudolf Laban which explore movement analysis and effort shape.

Laban's principles have been applied to many other areas: dance, music therapy, physical therapy, industry, and management, but the application of these studies to conducting has never been developed in a practical form. Laban suggests that all movement is initiated from within. A conductor's interpretation shares the same origin. These two elements must emerge as a unified entity through the gesture.

Music has movement analogues—music originates from movement: the flow of a line, the weight of maestoso, the quickness of staccato, the relaxation of a cadence, the irregularity of recitative, or the ease of jazz. What a conductor must accomplish through his gesture is the recovery of these movement analogues in order to represent the expressive origins of the music. This quality of the gesture must convey the inherent movement in the music.

After becoming aware of Laban's works, I began to investigate the possible utilization of these concepts in conducting pedagogy. The correlation was astounding. After continued study, I began to introduce some of these ideas in my conducting classes and the student's response was one of immediate acceptance. I have continued extensive research and have taken classes in this field and now have devised an approach based on these principles.

As the result, students in the classroom and in private instruction have been able to realize a tangible relationship of conducting gesture to the music they are studying. This physical awareness and it association to the entire body have provided that "missing link." The students have realized the practicality of comprehending the elements of movement as a preliminary exercise to be completed before they begin to conduct in the more traditional sense. With its own vocabulary of nonmusical terminologies, movement analysis provides guidance for the students in predetermining the physical quality of a gesture so that it will accurately serve a musical idea. The analysis of movement qualities has also proven to be especially beneficial in identifying individual problems and in facilitating the correction of those difficulties. The students become extremely perceptive and are quickly able to apply these principles as an evaluative criterion for assessing the performance of others. They are able to determine why a movement is working well and are better able to employ a similar effort in their own conducting. In perceiving those movements which are less desirable, they may then choose to avoid similar activity in their gestures. When the evaluation process, either positive or negative, takes place, it is directed toward the movement of a person, not toward the person himself. This results in a non-personal criticism and consequently, the students feel much less threatened by the observations of others. The obvious result is that students are more receptive to constructive comments and are more willing to discuss their own observations of others. They are also able to adapt more readily while they are in front of the class. Because the movement skills have been developed as a separate technique, they are able to modify their movement in order to communicate more accurately or effectively. Also, the impersonalness of the evaluation provides a more relaxed classroom atmosphere. It is the psychological advantage of dealing with movement rather than with personality which has been of immeasurable value in the development of these young conductors. Movement study has also proven to be extremely useful as a remedial tool for those who do not possess in innate flair, or a natural inclination for conducting. Many of these students are vitally interested in developing effective communication skills, but they are inhibited by their apparent awkwardness. Once they have experienced the movement efforts and realize how a gesture is shaped so that it connects with the music, they gain confidence and their abilities improve rapidly. Often it is these students who ultimately become the most compelling conductors. They frequently possess a greater degree of musicality and sensitivity than their peers who were initially more demonstrative or better coordinated.

Another positive factor of this approach is that the physical activity of the conductor is totally compatible with the physical needs of the choral singer. Unlike most texts which are primarily focused toward instrumental conducting, this movement awareness is designed to complement the requirements of proper voice production. Physical empathy between conductor and singer is of optimum importance and provides for many of the demands which are unique to the choral art. Since adapting the Laban studies to conducting pedagogy, the "imitate a : pattern" concept of teaching has been proven to be ineffective as a developmental tool for thorough internalization of the required basic technical skills. How one learns is of profound importance. True learning takes place when one is able to synthesize the information and establish a foundation for continued development. Movement analysis provides such a basis and accommodates the requirements for further growth. It allows the skills and techniques to be subsumed and manipulated as either a separate component, or as an integral part of the music. Conducting skills then progress to something more than a rote procedure of retracing pattern outlines.

Copyright © 1982
American Choral Directors Association
www.acda.org.
Used with permission.

CHAPTER 3

The Consequences of Gesture

Awareness of bodily perspective will assist in the discrimination between spatial feeling and understanding the spontaneous activity of our limbs. Following trace-forms in their pure kinepheric form can be the first step towards meaningful use of the limbs. Later the faculty of discrimination between the quality and inner impulse and the outer form which is present in all movements will grow. The definite and joyful execution of an integrated movement will be the final result. (p. 114)

—Rudolf Laban
in *Choreutics*

One thought only: rhythmic problems are not primarily problems of reading—for us. We repeat things often enough so that it should be difficult for a sightless person to make more than a few mistakes. The primary problem is that of *feeling*. Now, that is a fairly indeterminate "term," but what I'm trying to say is that the "sense" of rhythm is a mighty complex thing: physical, physiological, psychological, visceral, etceteractual; and our problem as a group is not that of visual identification—two quarter-notes equal one half-note—but that of getting people to *experience* two quarter-notes simultaneously physically, physiologically, psychologically, viscerally and etceteractually. We turn the old grade school apology, "I know what it is, but I can't put it into words," all the way around. We can put rhythm into words—symbols—but we have no idea what it is. (p. 65)

—Robert Shaw
in *The Robert Shaw Reader*

It can be said that that a movement can be describe as a composite of its shapes and rhythms, both making part of the superimposed flow of movement in which the control exerted by the moving person upon the movement becomes visible. (p. 93)

A refreshing swim in the sea is a wonderful and healthy thing, but no human being could live constantly in the water. It is a very similar case with the occasional swim in the flow of movement which we call dance. Such swimming, refreshing in many aspects for the body, the mind and for that dreamy part of our being which has been called the soul, is an exceptional pleasure and stimulation. As water is a widespread means to sustain life, so is movement. (p. 95)

When we realize that movement is the essence of life, and that expression, whether it be speaking, writing, singing, painting or dancing, uses movement as a vehicle, we cannot help seeing the importance of understanding this outward expression of the living energy within, and this we can do through effort study. (p. 99)

Music or any rhythms of sounds are produced by movements of the musician which show also variations in their shape and space evolution. In musical rhythm, the Time element is used in a highly differentiated manner. (p. 92)

Rhythm, however, is only a part of music, a kind of skeleton around which the main content of the musical composition—the melodies and harmonies of tones—are built up. In dance, the melody and harmony of tones recede and the importance of rhythm increases. (p. 92)

—Rudolf Laban
in *Modern Educational Dance*

THE CONSEQUENCES OF GESTURE

Chapter 3

It may seem a bit odd to speak of the "consequences" of conducting gesture. But for those of us who have been drawn to this unusual means of expression, the more we work as conductors, the more we realize that what we do with our bodies does have profound consequences for our ensembles. Those consequences are both musical and human. Elaine Brown, also one of my teachers, often said that "choirs sing as they are able to sing." The ability to sing (or play) is dramatically affected by not only what we "do" with our bodies but also our ability to cultivate and build an expressive language with our bodies to inform our musical idea and the reality of the sounds being produced by the people who sit in front of us.

Just as every word we speak has consequence, every action we take in our daily lives has consequence. Our gestures have an immediate musical human effect upon the people we interact with in ensembles. For centuries, human movement has carried the hopes and dreams of cultures. Movement has carried life stories and has inspired entire cultures to higher levels of human experience. As musicians/conductors, I don't think any of us fully grasp the power of the intimate wedding of gesture to sound. While each alone is powerful, when combined, they form a potent alchemy of human idea transported through how we move. That movement is like a vocabulary, where each movement carries within it a silent and powerful expression of a creative idea that lives in the notes that composers write.

In my work of finding connections within the principles of Laban to what we do as conductors, it is my belief that the work of Laban holds answers for us as conductors. Laban's principles are simple and theoretically crystalline in their vivid clarity to verbally and accurately describe the feeling of moving. Many of the students I work with seem to look past the simplicity and ignore the power in these principles. It seems much more productive to them to spend time learning rehearsal technique "things" rather than accepting responsibility for the fact that what they may be doing with their bodies as conductors is sabotaging all of their good teaching.

Expressive gesture is exceedingly hard to learn, or rather, acquire, on any level. It is even more difficult for conductors because we come to it not as our first love, but as a necessity for what we do. As musicians, we are generally not skilled movers; we generally have not experienced the expressive power of movement devoid of sound. Our movement skills are usually acquired in a very narrow expressive context, within a somewhat rigid structure of "conducting patterns." We almost never study movement separated from sound to learn its communicative potential. For me, Laban has provided a tool for the study and re-awakening of movement that is fundamental to all human expression.

One of the beliefs of Laban is that *everyone* is born with a full vocabulary of movement. If you observe any preschool playground, you can see the miracle of human movement on any given day. Children are leaping, rolling, laughing, communicating…often accompanied by movement. It's a miracle to sit and watch the beauty of how they move.

So what needs to be realized from the start of your study is that we are all movers! What Laban has done is to provide a method for reawakening that movement within us. Once reawakened, it can then easily be used to discover what movements as conductors will communicate and release human ideas in the people we music with.

Developing Observation Skills and Awareness of Movement

This process is part assigning common words to describe and categorize human movement; this was Laban's gift to us. Another part of this learning process is to develop movement observation skills that will, in turn, inform and sensitize our own expressive vocabularies. Simple but effective movement observation skills is one of the skill sets presented later in this book. Both parts of the process are necessary for the acquisition of a useable and meaningful movement vocabulary. The ability to be kinesthetically aware of how you move *is* informed by how you observe movement around you. A sensitivity to your own movement and the movement of others informs your awareness of sound.

The Real Issue

The real pedagogical challenge here is to acquire an honest movement vocabulary, reawakened in you, that can be used to reflect sounds in your audiation. Just like acquiring words in spoken language, we acquire a kinesthesia of how each movement "feels." Each movement we use has a weight, time, and space factor that defines how it is spelled "kinesthetically" to our feeling of movement as we move. Acquiring those movement "words" or Efforts in Combination (covered in detail in Chapter 10) is one issue, and marrying them to sound ideas and sound created is not only a challenge, but a miracle. Psychologists have not studied the phenomenon of movement as the initiator of sound. Dancers move in tandem to sound as an expressive act; they perform to provide a deeper understanding and enhance aesthetically what we hear *and* see. Conductors birth sound through the movements they use, which is rooted in human idea and impulse. Then add to this the miracle of the breath as the igniter of musical idea, and you begin to understand the miracle of conducting in a whole new light.

The purposes of this book in your "conductor education" are severalfold:

1. To provide an education about the movement world of Laban through Effort/Shape;
2. To lead you to a re-discovery of your own movement vocabulary based upon movements you have done in everyday life;
3. To connect Effort/Shape to an aware kinesthesia, or feeling of what it is to be a "mover";
4. To begin development of movement observation skills;
5. To lead you to an understanding of how the Efforts in Combination of Laban can unlock a world of sound not only for you but also for your ensembles.

A New Pedagogy and Theory for Conducting

Any pedagogy, if it is to have legitimacy in the mind of the user, must not only detail the "how" and clearly delineate the process by which one acquires this new "skill," but it must also provide a convincing logic as to why it works, and also why we must master it if we are to become any better at our craft. Many pedagogies certainly detail a directed path for study, which this book will certainly. But I also hope the strength of this pedagogy will be deepened by an understanding of just what happens when we move as conductors. For me, the answer lies in the work of those pursuing Body Maps, specifically the work of

Antonio Damasio. His writings give explanation to what we have known for a very long time: that a conductor through gesture, connection, and vulnerability creates miracles that are manifest in sound.

> Organisms make minds out of the activity of special cells known as neurons. Neurons share most of the characteristics of other cells in our body, and yet their operation is distinctive. They are sensitive to changes around them; they are excitable (an interesting property they share with muscle cells). Thanks to a fibrous prolongation known as the axon, and to the end region of the axon known as the synapse, neurons can send signals to other cells—other neurons, muscle cells—often quite far away. Neurons are largely concentrated in a central nervous system (the brain, for short), but they send signals to the organism's body, as well as to the outside world, and they receive signals from both. (p. 17)
>
> Minds emerge when the activity of small circuits organized across large networks so as to compose momentary patterns. The patterns represent things and events located outside the brain, either in the body or in the external world, but some patterns also represent the brain's own processing of other patterns. The term *map* applies to all those representational patterns, some of which are coarse, while others are very refined, some concrete, others abstract. In brief, the brain maps the world around it and maps its own doings. Those maps are experienced as *images* in our own minds, and the term *image* refers not just to visual kind but to images of any sense origin such as auditory, visceral, tactile, and so forth. (p. 18)
>
> To explain why neurons are so special, we should consider a functional difference and a strategic difference. The essential functional difference has to do with the neuron's ability to produce electrochemical signals capable of changing the state of other cells. (p. 37)
>
> —Antonio Damasio
> in *Self Comes to Mind*

Conducting has not enjoyed the sheer discipline that other aspects of musical study have long enjoyed. For all those who play and sing, acquiring a basic technique has been the focus of our study. We know that without technique, we cannot realize any degree of performance or communicative success in music. However, we have been hasty and impatient in the study of conducting. We acquire a few basic patterns, copy a few expressive gestures, and then go about the business of cobbling together some means of expression through gesture. We have, for the most part, acquired technique "along the way," unless we have encountered a teacher with a pedagogical viewpoint such as Elizabeth Green.

THE CONSEQUENCES OF GESTURE

Chapter 3

Not only must we look toward some organized method of acquiring (or, in Laban's case, re-acquiring) a movement vocabulary and understanding how that vocabulary is built, but we must also understand and believe why it works. The intent of this book is to make you slow down and build your technique through Laban applied in a rather comprehensive fashion to the study of conducting. But the change should come in your own mind as to just what it is when you stand in front of your ensemble and conduct.

The work of Damasio, capsulated in the previous quote, tells us that pedagogy informs and builds mirror neuron activity in us. Those neurons *do* produce electrochemical activity that can be read by others. Movement learned through this sequential Laban pedagogy creates a network of neurons and maps. We have maps for sound, and maps for movement, and certain maps for human stuff that lives deep within us. We know from his theory that mirror neurons are excitable in not only ourselves, but others. We must have a pedagogy that will place *images* in our minds to be used when calling forth sound. Damasio says it more elegantly, and his words perhaps are the center of the pedagogy method *and* theory presented in this book. "We know that the most stable aspects of body function are represented in the brain, in the form of maps, thereby contributing images to the mind. This is the basis of the hypothesis that the special kind of mental images of the body produced in the body mapping structures constitutes the protoself, which foreshadows the self to be.[1]

Damasio goes on to make yet a stronger argument: "Another central idea is based on the consistently overlooked fact that the brain's *protoself* structures are not merely about the body. They are literally and inextricably *attached* to the body. Specifically, they are attached to the parts of the body that bombard the brain with their signals, at all times, only to be bombarded back by the brain and, by so doing, creating a resonant loop. This resonant loop is perpetual, broken only by brain disease or death. Body and Brain *bond*.[2]

So why then must we pursue the study of conducting technique in a sequential and somewhat tedious way. Every movement, every variation of movement, carries mirror neuron activity. We must take time for technical study to construct a network of mirror neurons of movement that can foreshadow our self to be when wedded to sound. Without the "protoself" that can be built through Laban's ideas, there is little hope for conducting that not only inspires but also illuminates. Coupled with the breath, which begins the "firing" process

---
1   Antonio Damasio, *Self Comes to Mind*, p. 20.
2   Damasio, p. 11.

in our mirror neurons, gesture can become a burden to the musicians who sit in front of us. Instead of empathetic mirror neurons firing and building an expressive journey in all of us, we move with a limited gestural vocabulary that works against all that we believe and all that we are.

Can there be any better justification for studying the technique of conducting?

CHAPTER 4

An Overview of the Psychological Research: Kinesthesia, Body Mapping, and the Influence of Mirror Neurons

Organisms make minds out of the activity of special cells known as neurons. Neurons share most of the characteristics of other cells in our body, and yet their operation is distinctive. They are sensitive to changes around them; they are excitable (an interesting property they share with muscle cells). Thanks to a fibrous prolongation known as the axon, and to the end region of the axon known as the synapse, neurons can send signals to other cells—other neurons, muscle cells—often quite far away. Neurons are largely concentrated in a central nervous system (the brain, for short), but they send signals to the organism's body, as well as to the outside world, and they receive signals from both. (p. 17)

Minds emerge when the activity of small circuits organized across large networks so as to compose momentary patterns.. The patterns represent things and events located outside the brain, either in the body or in the external world, but some patterns also represent the brain's own processing of other patterns. The term *map* applies to all those representational patterns, some of which are coarse, while others are very refined, some concrete, others abstract. In brief, the brain maps the world around it and maps its own doings. Those maps are experienced as *images* in our own minds, and the term *image* refers not just to visual kind but to images of any sense origin such as auditory, visceral, tactile, and so forth. (p. 18)

There is indeed a self, but it is a process, not a thing, and the process is present at all times when we are presumed to be conscious. We can consider the self process from two vantage points. One is the vantage point of an observer appreciating a dynamic *object*—the dynamic object constituted by certain workings of minds, certain traits of behavior, and a certain history of life. The other vantage point is that of the self as *knower*, the process that gives a focus to our experiences and eventually lets us reflect on those experiences. (p. 8)

—Antonio Damasio
in *Self Comes to Mind*

In approaching the writings of Laban, a very interesting problem becomes immediately apparent: If we make applications of Laban to conducting, are we studying the perception of how one moves (self-perception of movement), or are we studying how one perceives others as they move? Certainly, conducting utilizes both perceptual viewpoints. It is interesting to note that psychology has wrestled with these problems, and much time has been spent researching the psychology of how one perceives another moving rather than researching through experimental design how one perceives oneself as moving. The main reason for this is that it is easier to formulate research designs for the former. Perhaps this has been the case because there was no language in place to describe movement and, hence, come up with experimental designs to test hypotheses.

The intent of this chapter is to understand the movement perception issue and its history in the psychology of music as a background for the study of Laban applied to conducting. While the summary that follows is my no means exhaustive, it is meant to provide you with connections along the way in the history of psychology to the study of movement. Of all the research and ideas presented, it is the work of William James that provides the greatest preparation for the use of Laban as a beginning movement morphology for conductors.

Introduction to the Research

Studies in the techniques of teaching rhythm and the theories of rhythm, as well as studies in the techniques of teaching movement and the theories of movement, have been undertaken in an effort to define rhythm and movement. Approaches to teaching those techniques and interpreting those theories may be found in the literature of psychology, music education, and modern educational dance.

A History of the Development of the Theories of Kinesthetic Sensation for Movement Perception

Movement has been studied because it is one aspect of perceptual experience. Philosophers were concerned with whether the ability to perceive spatial aspects of the world was an innate or a learned process. Julian Hochberg stated in a study of perception that there is inter- and intra-individual variability in the relationship between the stimulus and the perceptual response. That ambiguity cannot be ascribed to the stimulus alone. It depends upon the various dimensions in which a movement response is measured.[3] Those dimensions have traditionally included vision, the perception of space, and the perception of movement. In the history of the study of space perception and movement perception, ambiguities arise as a result of different persons examining the problems.

To articulate that inter- and intra-individual variability between the stimulus and the perceptual response for the purpose of this study, the work of only those philosophers and psychologists who recognize the importance of body sensation or kinesthetic responses to movement perceptions will be discussed.

Perception as Examined by the Empiricist Philosophers and the Associationist Psychologists

Early Greek philosophers, and consequently their philosophies, were objective. The early Greek empiricists believed that the mind gains experience of the external world through the senses. Boring states that Heraclitus (fifth century, B.C.) made the early distinction that knowledge comes to man "through the door of the senses."[4] From Plato's Thaetetus, a dialogue between Socrates and Thaetetus, we are given information that knowledge and sensation are different.[5] Protagoras (485–411 B.C.) stated that the entire life of a person consists of only sensations. Consequently, the stoic philosophers first stated the tabula rasa concept: Sensations are impressions on the mind, and knowledge is gained through those impressions. Therefore, one gains knowledge through one's experience.[6]

---

3   Julian E. Hochberg, "Perception: Toward the Recovery of a Definition," in *Psychological Review*, 63 (1956), p. 404.

4   E. G. Boring, *Sensation and Perception in the History of Experimental Psychology* (New York: Appleton-Century Crofts, Inc., 1942), p. 4.

5   L. Postman, *Psychology in the Making* (New York: Alfred A. Knopf, 1962), p. 257.

6   Aristotle, "Tabula Rasa Mind," in *History of Psychology*, ed. W. S. Sahakian (Itasca, IL: Peacock Publishers, 1980), p. 14.

Empedocles (490–435 B.C.) stated that objects "give off from their surfaces or pores effluvia, which act upon the senses to furnish knowledge of the outer world."[7] Democritos (460–370 B.C.) and Epicuros (341–270 B.C.) described those projected sensations as "faint images, simulacra or eidola of the objects which, being conducted to the mind, give it acquaintance with the objects they represent."[8] It seems that the early Greeks were attempting to form hypotheses about the perceptive act through nature versus nurture. They agreed that generalized senses were used in perception gathering, yet no attempt was made to define the true nature of the sensation.

René Descartes (1596–1650) was both an empiricist and a nativist philosopher. His deductive methods classified him as an empiricist. His belief (i.e., that our knowledge about size, form, motion, and the positions of objects is a set of innate ideas) also classifies him as a nativist.

The beginning of the mechanistic tradition in France was important to Descartes and to the early history of the study of perception. That tradition explains sensation and, indirectly, perception as a mechanical process. Descartes stated that the machine-like body "can be incited by the external objects which strike upon its organs of sense to move it in a thousand different ways."[9] Descartes further hypothesized that despite those principles of mechanics, each person possesses a soul that operates through the pineal gland. The mind affects the body through sensation, emotion, and action.[10] That dualistic approach to the perception problem was later adopted by the empiricist school. Descartes, in his study of perception, is known for his belief in innate ideas. A mathematician as well as a philosopher, Descartes believed that there are certain truths basic to the acquisition of knowledge. Those truths, according to Descartes, are innate.

Descartes's ideas concerning sensation and the senses were continued through the work of Condillac, who attempted to demonstrate how the mind of a statue could be established by unlocking the senses, beginning with the sense of smell.[11] Etienne Bonnot de Condillac (1715–1780), along with his contemporary, Julien Offray de La Mettrie (1709–1751), explained perception in terms of nature. Knowledge comes from sensation, and those sensations can be obtained only through the senses.

---

7   Boring, p. 4.
8   Boring, p. 4.
9   Boring, p. 7.
10   E. Heidbredder, *Seven Psychologies* (New York: Appleton-Century-Crofts, Inc., 1933), p. 37.
11   Etienne Bonnot de Condillac, "French Sensationalism," in *History of Psychology*, ed. W. S. Sahakian (Itasca, IL: Peacock Publishers, 1980), p. 44.

The work of Descartes contributed to the development of the school of the physiological psychologists. Using Descartes's principle of matter in motion, all perception could be examined in terms of cause and effect. Behaviors are initiated by the effects of the physical world on the brain. Therefore, it became important to determine which mechanisms enabled one to gain knowledge of the world.

Empiricism was firmly established as a result of the work of Thomas Hobbes (1588–1679). Hobbes objected to Descartes's principle of innate ideas and wrote: "There is no conception in man's mind which hath not at first, totally or by parts, been begotten upon the organs of sense."[12] Pivotal to the study of space perception is Hobbes's work, which attempts to explain perception in relationship to motion. Reminiscent of Empedocles and Galileo, Hobbes stated that motion or the sensation of motion is communicated by the external object to the brain. Hobbes used the principle of associationism to explain "that just as ideas are determined by objects acting on the senses, so the transitions from one idea to another are determined by the relations they bear to each other in the original experience."[13]

Early Phenomenology

Hobbes's successor, John Locke (1632–1704), continued to maintain that all ideas must be derived from something previously experienced. Locke stated that there were two processes in perception: (1) the primary qualities that exist in the object itself (red, shape, etc.) and (2) the secondary qualities or the residues that the primary qualities leave behind (the thoughts of red, texture, etc.). Those secondary qualities may be remembered when the object is not physically present.[14] At that point, according to Locke, the laws of association govern our perceptions.

George Berkeley (1685–1753) and Locke agreed that knowledge is acquired through the senses. Bishop Berkeley, however, stated that we cannot directly perceive the characteristics of the physical world, such as spatial distance. Berkeley studied four problems: (1) abstract distance, (2) the perception of far objects, (3) convergence and near objects, and (4) the perception of size. Hochberg summarizes Berkeley's observations: "One cannot simply and completely

---

12   Boring, p. 5.
13   Heidbredder, p. 40.
14   Postman, p. 259.

specify the three-dimensional position of an object in space in terms of the two physical dimensions of a flat (static) retinal image. All the visual indications of the distance we have—linear perspective, interposition of near objects in front of far ones, size perspective, etc.—are only secondary clues or cues to an object's depth or distance."[15]

A dichotomy exists within the work of the empiricists, which is summarized in the work of Descartes and Locke. Although the empiricists established the dualism that the mind affects the body through sensation, the relationship of the senses to the perceptive process remained unclear. The empiricist ambiguity between mind and body sensation confounds what constitutes a perceptive response, and to what degree body sensations affect those perceptive processes. Although the empiricists accepted the mind/body duality, they would not accept the data of experience to support their hypotheses. A branch of psychology was needed that would (1) examine the relationships between consciousness and body sensation and (2) accept the data of experience as support for their hypotheses. In essence, psychological phenomenology was established by the ambiguities of empiricism in an attempt to clarify the role of sensation in perception.

Modern Psychological Phenomenology

Robert B. MacLeod, in discussing "psychological phenomenology," emphasizes that what was referred to as "consciousness" in the old psychologies can and should be studied.[16] The phenomenologist accepts all the data of experience. According to MacLeod, Descartes provided the foundation for modern psychological phenomenology. Descartes combined experience with deductive method in a phenomenological approach to perception. Merleau-Ponty in *The Primacy of Perception* (1964) states that "perception is thus paradoxical"[17] when discussing perception in phenomenological terms. The phenomenology of Descartes and Locke is one in which "the medium must convey similarities between the two worlds," mind and body.[18] Consequently, a dichotomy exists for the phenomenologist in the study of perception. The psychologist studying perception must now balance deductive and inductive

---

15   Postman, p. 264.
16   R. B. MacLeod, "Phenomenology: A Challenge to Experimental Psychology," in *Behaviorism and Phenomenology*, ed. W. T. Wann (Chicago: University of Chicago Press, 1964), p. 72.
17   Maurice Merleau-Ponty, *The Primacy of Perception* (Chicago: Northwestern University Press, 1964), p. 16.
18   MacLeod, p. 70.

information with the true nature of the perceptive experience, if that experience can be defined. The definition of that experience, derived from inductive and deductive information, may be described through associative principles.

The Associationists

Hypotheses concerning perception and body sensations were investigated by the associationists. The associationists hoped to reduce the complex nature of thoughts and ideas to their basic elements. David Hartley (1705–1757), the first of the associationist psychologists, stated the following process of associationism:

> Sensations may be said to be associated together, when their impressions are either made precisely at the same instant of time, or in the contiguous successive instants. We may therefore distinguish association into two sorts, the synchronous and the successive.[19]

The methods of the associationists were introspective observation and logical analysis. The early associationists recognized the ambiguity of the perception problem as later proposed by Hochberg. Moreover, the assumptions of the associationists concerning the workings of the mind determined both research problems and investigative methods. The mind/body sensation functioning of the perception could be ascribed to simple associative principles.

The work of the associationist school culminated in the work of James Mill (1806–1873). His law of frequency of repetition represents an attempt to explain how ideas are linked to one another. Mill's analysis of a house demonstrates that principle. A perception, according to Mill, is based upon the frequency of individual perceptions of a window, mortar, bricks, and glass. Mill hypothesized that the strength of those associations combined with the frequency by which they are seen compose the idea of a house.

Helmholtz studied movement perception when preparing his laws of causation and previous visualization. The law of causation establishes a kinesthetic relationship between the perceiver and space. "We can get no experience from natural objects unless the law of causation is already active in us."[20] Central to the theory of unconscious inference is Helmholtz's interpretation of previous visualization.

---

19 David Hartley, "Association of Ideas," in *History of Psychology*, ed. W. S. Sahakian (Itasca, IL: Peacock Publishers, 1980), p. 50.
20 Helmholtz, p. 32.

The image at the time awakes the memory of everything like it is experienced in previous visualizations, and likewise the recollection of everything regularly associated by special experiences with these former visual images, such as the number of steps we had to take to reach a man who appeared in the field of view to be a certain size, etc. This kind of association of ideas is unconscious and involuntary, and is produced by a sort of blind force of nature, no matter if it occurs also according to the laws of our mental being; and hence it enters into our perceptions with all the external and compelling power of impressions that come to us from outside.[21]

Helmholtz believed that the associative process provided kinesthetic sensations that were obtained from the environment to support specific perceptions. Helmholtz was in opposition to the nativist point of view held by Immanuel Kant. Kant believed that time and space were dogmatic categories of perception that were naturally endowed to man. Space and time were held to be necessary *a priori* representations.[22] Kant continued:

Space and time are pure forms of our intuition, while sensation forms its matter. What we can know *a priori*—before all real intuition, are the forms of space and time, which are therefore called pure intuition, while sensation is that which causes our knowledge to be called a *posteriori* knowledge, i.e., empirical intuition.[23]

Both Helmholtz and Kant agree, however, that sensations shape perception and that they are a part of the perceptive process.

William McDougall: Hormic Psychology and the Nature of Instincts

The hormic psychology of William McDougall (1871–1938) is an early effort to relate perceptions to kinesthesia. McDougall defines his hormic theory with reference to evolutionary psychology. He discussed instinct in terms of an

---

21 Helmholtz, p. 291.
22 Immanuel Kant, "The *A Priori* Intuition of Space," in *History of Psychology*, ed. W. S. Sahakian (Itasca, IL: Peacock Publishers, 1980), pp. 69–70.
23 Kant, p. 72.

inherited or innate psycho-physical disposition which determines "its possessor to perceive, and to pay attention to, objects of a certain class, to experience an emotional excitement of a particular quality upon perceiving such an object, and to act in regard to it in a particular manner, or at least, to experience an impulse to such action."[24] McDougall's theory of instinctive reactions objectifies movement with reference to a reaction to a perception. Through movement, then, the instinct finds expression. Those bodily expressions, however, may be modified and complicated. McDougall emphasized two additional points concerning the relationship of the instinct-perception-reactive tendency: (1) given the complexity of the ideas of perception, several "instincts" can be excited and (2) "instincts" become organized around "certain objects or ideas."[25]

Edward Bradford Titchener: Context Theory and Structural Psychology

Introspective analysis of psychological content was the necessary and sufficient method of studying perception according to Titchener (1867–1927). He stated in the context theory that the sensory core of perception was most important, and the context of the perception was secondary. "No sensation means; a sensation simply goes on in various attributive ways, intensively, clearly, spatially, and so forth. All perceptions mean; they go on, also, in various attributive ways; but they go on meaningly."[26]

Titchener believed that perception was a nurture process. Sensation was secondary to perception. Titchener's emphasis on the "kinesthetic attitude" affected the study of perception. He states: "General kinesthetic supplements, derived from our experiences of handling objects, are also exceedingly common: things look heavy or light, sound heavy or light, precisely as they look or sound here or there, near or far."[27]

> Of all its possible forms, however, two appear to be of especial importance: kinaesthesis and verbal image. The words we read are both perception and context of perception; the auditory-kinesthetic idea is the meaning of the

---

24 William McDougall, "Social Psychology and Instincts," in *History of Psychology*, ed. W. S. Sahakian (Itasca, IL: Peacock Publishers, 1980), p. 72.
25 McDougall, p. 167.
26 E. B. Titchener, *A Textbook of Psychology* (New York: MacMillan and Company, 1910), p. 367.
27 Titchener, p. 366.

visual symbols. And it is obvious that all sorts of sensory and imaginal complexes receive their meaning from some mode of verbal representation: we understand a thing, as soon as we have named it.[28]

Titchener further states a hierarchy for the perceptive process:

I conclude, then, that the affective element is constituted of quality, intensity, and duration; the sense element (sensation or idea) of quality, intensity, duration, clearness, and in some cases, extent. Quality is intrinsic and individual; intensity and clearness are "relative" characteristics; duration and extent are, very probably, extrinsic translations into structure of the lowest terms of a functional series.[29]

Although Helmholtz, McDougall, Kant, and Titchener disagreed about the "nature versus nurture" origin of kinesthetic sensation, they were in agreement about the role of kinesthesia in perception. Kinesthesia and its consequent sensations are a matter of the perceptive process. The origins of kinesthesia, however, were at that time still in question.

William James: Muscular Theory—Eccentric Projection of the Feeling

William James (1842–1910) discussed spatial experiences using the concepts of discrimination, association, and selection. James states: "Extensity becomes an element in each sensation just as intensity is."[30] According to James, all of our experiences in space form a vast objective whole. Those individual objective experiences were the foundation of his beliefs concerning space perception. James was concerned with how perceptual information is obtained for those "objective experiences."

James's "eccentric projection of the feeling" provides a way for gathering those perceptual images through the use of a muscular theory. Kinesthetic in concept, his muscular theory implies validation through surface sensibility. James discusses the question of how, if one with his eyes closed traces a geometric pattern in the air with his fingertip, he can perceive the finger's movement in

---

28 Titchener, p. 368.
29 E. B. Titchener, "The Postulates of a Structural Psychology," in *Philosophical Review*, 7 (1898), p. 465.
30 William James, *Principles of Psychology* (1891; rpt. Chicago: Encyclopaedia Britannica, 1952), p. 541.

space. According to James, one can sense not only the movements in space, but every angle and curve as if they had been seen.[31] He discusses that hypothesis further by locating the origin of those space perception signals. James states: "We indubitably localize the fingertip at the successive points of its path by means of sensations that we receive from our joints."[32] Space, and consequently the motion through that space, is perceived in the joints. The feelings of our own movement are principally due to the sensibility of our own rotating joints.[33]

According to James, primitive body feelings in young children do relay spatial qualities. For James, a child's perceptive powers develop in several space worlds. James presents the analogy of a child with a toe ache. The child is too young to yet have perceived his toe. The perception of the toe is not yet in the child's optical space. Also, the toe is not an element in the child's hand movement space, nor is it a member of his leg and foot space. The baby is void of any space perception as a newborn. The pain and the toe have no mental existence, excepting a pain space. It is through the developmental factors of discrimination, operation, and association, however, that the child relates one space world with another.[34] Consequently, James established a developmental relationship between the stimulus and perceptual response. Moreover, James established a hypothetical connection among the kinesthetic theories of Helmholtz, McDougall, Kant, and Titchener with body feeling. Through the eccentric projection of the feeling and his muscular theory, James began to formulate a learning theory based upon the kinesthetic connection of mind and body as a mechanism of learning.

Gestalt Psychology

Gestalt psychologists believe that characteristics of the whole cannot be explained using discrete and elementary sensory experiences. The Gestalt hypothesis that depth is a primary characteristic of the perception of space is opposed to the hypotheses that depth is established by the associations, themselves depthless. According to Gestalt psychologists, associative learning has little importance in the perceptive process.

Kurt Koffka published *Growth of the Mind* in 1924. In that work, Koffka presented his views of how cognitive processes are developed through perception.

---

31 James, p. 577.
32 James, p. 578.
33 James, p. 579.
34 James, p. 574.

To Koffka, total cognition was a developmental process of articulation rather than of association. For him, perceptual development was "how a picture of the world as we know it gradually arises out of the primitive and diffuses configurations of early experience."[35]

Additionally, Koffka argued that a child's perceptions are not a bundle of meaningless sensations organized by means of simple stimuli, but that unorganized sensations in perception are organized by complex stimuli, such as the voice. Koffka also stated that both maturation and learning were involved in perceptual differentiation, but that learning and the consequent maturation were not trial and error. According to Koffka, in *The Mentality of Apes* (1925), learning occurs in animals when a sudden transformation takes place in their perceptive field. For Koffka, the learning experience is a continual substitution of one's perceptual fields.

Similarly, Leeper (1935) discusses perceptual reorganization. According to Leeper, sensory reorganization is stressed by the Gestaltists. The reverse, however, that learning (perception) takes place during or after sensory reorganization, is not recognized by Gestalt psychologists. Beginning with Gottschaldt in 1926, objective experimentation was conducted, which attempted to demonstrate that past experience was an overall organizing perceptual factor.[36]

Unfortunately, specific problems relating to the study of perception offered ambiguous interpretations for researchers. Visual perception, cognitive space perception, and motion perception were treated as a single element within a stimulus, and this contributed to inaccurate interpretations.[37] Perceptual organization can be considered as necessary for both perception and learning to take place, as shown by the Gestaltists. How that perceptual organization takes place, however, remains in question.

---

35 Kurt Koffka, *The Growth of the Mind* (New York: Harcourt, 1931), p. 380.

36 The interpretation of Gestalt studies is questionable. Considerable discussion has taken place about both the true nature of the stimulus in Gestalt experiments and the ambiguities of the stimuli used. Replications of the Gottschaldt experiment in 1926 by Braly (1933), Djang (1937), Henle (1942), and Robinson (1964) offer ambiguous interpretations of perceived stimuli. Zuckerman and Rock (1957) concluded that strong structural factors could overcome familiarity with a Gestalt stimulus. Conversely, Hanawalt (1942) attempted to clarify the idea that practice in perceiving geometric figures in space would transfer to other designs.

37 Eleanor Gibson questioned the validity of the Gestalt stimuli. She emphasizes that "it is not clear whether the old perceptual experience must be an exact repetition of the new one, nor how one can weigh its effects fairly when it is pitted against some presumably conflicting factor." (*Principles of Perceptual Learning*, p. 33) Her work established that the ambiguous demonstration figures that the Gestaltists use do not provide acceptable data for perceptual study.

The Differentiation Theory of Werner

Werner's differentiation theory is primarily Gestaltist. However, it combines the Gestalt perceptual theories with the theories of the Darwinian evolutionists. Darwin's work affected all branches of psychology. It had considerable influence on the perception theories of the time, as a result of the work of Werner. Werner defined development as a function of "increasing differentiation of parts or hierarchization."[38] As a developmentalist, Werner defined physiognomic perception as a syncretic perceptual organization, which he deduced to be characteristic of children in various stages of development. Consequently, Werner was the first psychologist to imply that the development of perception occurs in small units. According to Werner, those small units of perception must be repeated by experience to become noticeably separate, and then they become part of the perception vocabulary. Werner also states that perceptual abilities are innate: "The average adult generally has a physiognomic experience only in his perception of other human beings, their faces and their bodies. The child, on the other hand, frequently sees physiognomic qualities in all objects, animate or inanimate."[39]

Werner's theory does not provide an obvious strategy with which to approach experimental research. His model is based upon an intuitive/phenomenological approach which, at best, is difficult to objectify. Evidence of this can be seen in his 1940 study of microscales and micromelodies. Gibson points out that the 1940 study is an example of Werner's work in which a model specifying mechanisms and processes can be developed.[40] Werner's hypotheses concerning the importance of the repetition of small units of a perceptive experience are of significant importance to the study of rhythm perception.

Twentieth-Century Developmental Psychology

Developmental psychologists in the early part of the twentieth century did not discuss space perception in the same way as did their predecessors. Perception was handled as a problem in sensory motor development. Although

---

38 H. Werner, *Comparative Psychology of Mental Development*, rev. ed. (New York: Science Editions, 1961), p. 41.
39 Werner, p. 72.
40 E. J. Gibson, *Principles of Perceptual Learning and Development* (New York: Appleton-Century Crofts, 1969), p. 35.

the study of perception at the beginning of the twentieth century was dominated by behaviorists, H. A. Carr and his students at the University of Chicago had an interest in space perception in the empirical tradition. Carr studied kinesthetic associations and their relationships to perception.

> Like Stratton, we shall assume for each sense department a sense of local signs…we shall assume that these signs become directly associated by contiguity with localizing movements. These localizing movements may be of the eyes, the head, the body, or the hands and arms, or symbolically represented by judgmental responses expressed in verbal terms.[41]

Using experimental evidence, Carr proposed a motor theory to explain spatial relations. Spatial relations were discussed in relation to auditory, visual, and aesthetic impressions of objects. Carr believed that the visual, auditory, and aesthetic images, all unrelated, created a sensory system, with each having its own internal spatial organization. That system became spatially related only through associative connections.

> When two diverse sense objects are associated with different localizing responses, that response will manipulate both impressions. The two impressions will thus have the same locality significance, and they will be regarded as two sensory attributes of a single object.[42]

Child psychology in America, as represented by the work of Gesell, ran contrary to the "zeitgeist" of the day. For example, a quote of Gesell's from *Developmental Psychology*, by Goodenough, demonstrates how his explanation of thought processes can be traced to Berkeley:

> Very early in life and without being aware that we are doing so, we learn to interpret this (binocular) difference in visual sensations in terms of tactual and muscular sensations we get from handling objects…. When we say the tree trunk looks rounded, we mean only that the visual sensation has the qualities that from infancy on we have learned to associate with objects that feel rounded.[43]

---

41   H. A. Carr, *An Introduction to Space Perception* (New York: Longman's Green, 1935), p. 28.
42   Carr, p. 79.
43   F. Goodenough, *Developmental Psychology: An Introduction to the Study of Human Behavior* (New York: Appleton-Century Crofts, 1934), p. 138.

Arnold Gesell disagreed with the empirical approach to perception. He employed longitudinal studies to detect developmental sequences, if any, in perception. In his book, *Vision: Its Development in Infant and Child* (1949), Gesell was not interested in the history or origin of the perception problem. Gesell had an interest in the use of direct longitudinal observation to provide experimental data for the study of perception. His descriptive longitudinal studies contained observations as follows:

> At 36 weeks, he takes a cube and pushes another cube with the one in hand; or he brings one cube against the side of another cube. He differentiates the string attached to the ring and manipulates it exploitively. By such tokens he shows a recognition of the posture and relationship of the two objects in space. He is just beginning to see them as solid envelopes.[44]

Gesell used longitudinal observation to assist him in making inferences and hypotheses. Unlike the work of Piaget, Gesell attempted to speak of perception in terms of developmental observation, rather than undocumented inference. Gesell's work documented the position that the visual world of the child undergoes a tri-dimensional differentiation by slow, but progressive, stages. In the first months of life, the child exhibits increased selectivity to stimuli. The basic components of vision, present at birth, develop in successive phases in a rank ordering of specificity and complexity.

The work of Jean Piaget presents unique designs and descriptive analyses for the study of perception in children. Piaget used both the functionalist and nativist designs, but his work is more clearly of the latter type. Piaget's perceptual categories and his references to the roles of those categories do not clarify his experimental hypotheses. Gibson states that "the elaborate detail of both description and reasoning defies coming to terms with it."[45]

From 1941 through 1962, Piaget published a synthesis of his work in *The Mechanism of Perception* (1961). Piaget's theories of perception follow two philosophies. First, Piaget presents a model in which he attempts to explain the effects of the primary perceptual field. Second, he discusses how the primary perceptive structures are of a geometric origin. Those structures are later complemented by secondary structures, which are the result of the child's reconstruction of his perceptual field. Piaget employs the term "field effect," which was borrowed

---

44 A. Gesell, F. I. Ilg, and G. E. Bulls, *Vision: Its Development in Infant and Child* (New York: Paul Hoeber, 1949), p. 96.
45 Gibson, *Principles of Perceptual Learning*, p. 409.

from Gestalt psychology. A field effect in Gestalt psychology, however, is relative only to one stimulus. According to Piaget, as soon as there is eye movement, the child takes in several stimuli, and thereby he negates the Gestalt implications of the field effect. Space is perceived by the child only in relation to himself and to his own activity. For Piaget, it is the concept of space that is developing, not the perception of the child's environment. Space expands as the child matures. According to Piaget, near or reachable space is cognized first. Consequently, as the child's movement activities expand, so too do his spatial perceptions.

Piaget's study of perception rejects the role of the kinesthetic and psychological influences on perceptual behavior. "For the task of psychology is not the explanation of the working of the nervous system in terms of conscious behavior, but rather the analysis of the evolution of behavior."[46] The movement act in space, not kinesthesia, transforms the perceptual field of the child. For Piaget, kinesthesia for each movement does not function in the perception of space or time.

Accordingly, Eleanor J. Gibson stresses that Piaget and the school of Russian psychologists emphasize that action in space is essential for the development of perception in space. In terms of perceptual learning, however, the perceptual process is not gradually assembled. James J. Gibson hypothesizes that "the ability to perceive is innate, and that perceptual learning is a process of delineation."[47]

The work of the early developmental psychologists offers information concerning the development of perceptual abilities within the maturation process. James J. Gibson recognizes the importance of moving through space as an integral part of the learning process. Like the other developmental psychologists, however, he did not examine the role of kinesthesia in movement.

Studies Concerning the Origin and Development of Movement Patterns in Young Children

Judith Kestenberg, through the use of dance and movement therapy and case studies, investigated the fluctuations in shape and flow of movement in newborn infants. Adapting the movement observation techniques of Rudolf von Laban, Kestenberg developed a complex movement profiling system to provide objective data for her case studies of movement development. Her observations found in

---

46   J. Piaget and B. Inhlder, *The Child's Conception of Space* (New York: W. W. Norton, 1967), p. 14.
47   J. J. Gibson, P. Olum, and F. Rosenblatt, "parallax and Perspective During Aircraft Landing," in *American Journal of Psychology,* 68 (1955), p. 374.

The Role of Movement Patterns in Development demonstrate how "the fluctuations in early Tension Flow have rhythmical patterns that foreshadow the later Space, Weight, Time, and Effort elements" explained by Laban.[48] Kestenberg hypothesizes that "premature, consistent interference with congenitally preferred motor patterns may retard development or enhance the early formation of rigid defenses."[49]

Contemporary developmental psychologist Esther Thelen at the University of Missouri at Columbia cites experimental studies in which the developmental origins of motor skills in infants is discussed. In a 1981 study, Thelen found that the movements of infants in their first year of life are "intrinsic oscillations of functionally related muscle groups. They are seen in infants as transition behaviors between early coordinated activity and the development of full voluntary control."[50] Thelen refers to those movements as rhythmical stereotypes. Previous explanations of Thelen's "rhythmical stereotypes" can be found in earlier research. Gesell, in a 1954 study, found rocking in infants as a specific stage in prone progression. He warned that persistent stereotypy was a sign of developmental delay or impoverished environment. In a 1952 study, Piaget called kicking and waving "secondary circular reactions," a stage of sensorimotor development when infants attempt to repeat an interesting effect within their environment. Conversely, Thelen found that stereotypies were a function of individual differences related to specific caregiving practices. According to Thelen, "Infants who performed many stereotyped movements received comparatively less rocking, bouncing, and carrying from their caregivers, and probably less vestibular stimulation. These infants were also more likely to be placed in locations that restricted their own movements."[51] Consequently, Thelen concluded that the individual differences in stereotypy seen in the first year of life are a direct result of caregiving practices. For the infant, stereotypies were used to provide necessary vestibular stimulation to compensate for the lack of movement in their lives provided by caregivers.

In a later study, Thelen investigated the origins of the newborn stepping reflex. According to Thelen, when held upright, newborn infants show well-coordinated walking movements that cannot be elicited after two months

---

48   Irmgard Bartenieff, *Body Movement: Coping with the Environment* (New York: Gordon and Breach, 1980), p. 85.
49   Judith Kestenberg, *The Role of Movement Patterns in Development*, I (New York: Dance Notation Bureau, 1971), p. 6.
50   Esther Thelen, "Kicking, Rocking and Waving: Contextual Analysis of Rhythmical Stereotypes in Normal Human Infants," in *Animal Behavior*, 29 (1981), p. 9.
51   Thelen, "Kicking, Rocking and Waving," p. 10.

of age. In contrast, spontaneous kicking in the supine position increases in frequency during the first six months. Thelen suggests that the disappearance of stepping "is a result of the biodynamic consequences of upright posture due to asynchronous development of muscle mass and concomitant strength."[52] In her conclusions, Thelen suggests that the disappearance of the stepping reflex in movement development may be a direct result of Western infant-care practices that do not optimize the development of infant motor strength. Thelen's research implies that a newborn infant is equipped with the motor and nervous system development from birth that is necessary for upright movement, but because of rapid changes in bodyweight, the child loses those locomotion abilities. Those abilities are re-acquired through one or a combination of the following: (1) self-movement in the horizontal position, (2) child caregiving practices that are culturally influenced, and (3) environmental conditions. Consequently, depending upon the combinations of that re-acquisition, individual differences in movement potential are found in infants.

The work of Kestenberg and Thelen emphasizes the importance of early movement experience upon the movement development of the young child. Their experimental work places the descriptive and observational studies of Piaget and Gesell in question. Moreover, hypotheses can be formulated using the work of Kestenberg and Thelen concerning the importance of moving and the effects of the early movement experience upon both developmental and stabilized rhythm aptitude.

James J. Gibson; Gunnar Johansson

James J. Gibson, in studies published in 1959, 1965, 1966, and 1968, places increasing importance on transformations of the motion perspective. Gibson's work was experimentally clarified in 1974 by Gunnar Johansson. Johansson stated that although authors of most previous studies of the motion perception problem discussed the concept of time, they did so on a limited basis. According to Johansson, "A more efficient theory has to include change over time, or rather, must be founded on studies of the perception of spatial changes."[53] Johansson's

---

52 Esther Thelen and Donna M. Fisher, "Newborn Stepping: An Explanation for a Disappearing Reflex," in *Developmental Psychology*, 18 (1982), p. 760.

53 Gunnar Johansson, "Projective Transformations as Determining Visual Space Perception in Perception," in *Essays in Honor of James J. Gibson*, ed. Robert B. MacLeod and Herbert L. Pick (Ithaca, NY: Cornell University Press, 1974), p. 118.

work is unique to psychology because he is the first to use a model based upon a kinetic/projective geometry of the body to study, and consequently describe, the movement perception processes as they relate to both mover and observer. Additionally, the work of both Gibson and Johansson treat the movement perception problem from two opposing viewpoints: (1) the viewpoint of the mover sensating his own movement and perceiving it (Gibson) and (2) the perceptions of the skilled movement observer (Johansson). The work of Gibson and Johansson has provided initial experimental validation for the movement theory of Rudolf von Laban.

Behaviorism

James B. Watson, in *Behaviorism* (1925), addresses the "nature versus nurture" argument. Watson denies the existence of instincts and native intelligence. Instincts are the result of environment and training. According to Heidbredder, the subject matter of the behaviorists after Watson "is behavior; not conscious contents, not mental functions, not psychological processes of any sort, but movement in time and space."[54]

The behavioral processes, according to Watson, are laryngeal habits and manual habits. The laryngeal habits, or the thinking processes, are acquired by random, unlearned vocalization. The manual habits include skills such as writing, painting, etc. Those habits are built upon random movements of the trunk, arms, legs, hands, and fingers. Consequently, the behaviorist measures perception in terms of behavior. The process of thinking, according to the behaviorists, is exclusively a product of language mechanisms.

Contemporary behaviorist B. F. Skinner admits that behaviorists have difficulty with discussions of perception dealing with both conscious and unconscious content. For Skinner, the question is not how to perceive an object, but rather, how to perceive an object when it is not present.

Skinner's work incorporates the perception theories of the Greeks. The Greeks believed that in order to know, the mind gathered sensory material from the environment. Behaviorists believe that the initiating action is taken by the environment rather than by the perceiver. Skinner states that "in both theories, the environment penetrated the body: in the mentalistic view, it was taken in by the

---

54   Heidbredder, p. 243.

perceiver; in the stimulus-response view, it battered its way in."[55] Consequently, Skinner believes that behaviorists must deal with the stimulus, the response, and the consequences of the perception. Consequence and the environmental history of the perceiver, he claims, will determine what will be perceived.

In his book, *About Behaviorism* (1974), Skinner presents the observation that animals carried about in an environment do not move as well as animals who have been allowed to move on their own within their own environment. Both animals have had the same visual stimuli, but the consequences are different. According to Skinner, the reason for the different responses of the animals is "that they have not acquired behavior under the control of the setting."[56] The implications for space perception are parallel. We must move in space in order to perceive it. Skinner reinforces that belief by giving brief attention to the Gestaltists. He states that there is no "need to postulate structural principles to explain these characteristics. Contingencies of reinforcement also contribute to irresistible perceptions...."[57]

Skinnerian psychology is often criticized for its failure to recognize "how a situation looks to a person." According to Skinner, "We must examine his behavior with respect to it, including descriptions of it, and we can do this only in terms of his genetic and environmental histories."[58]

Skinner continues to emphasize the importance of conscious content. The importance of content was weakened when methodological behaviorism questioned the usefulness of kinesthetic sensations as scientific data. Consequently, psychologists examined only the processes of discrimination. Skinner summarizes the problem: "To argue that the layman and the scientist are simply looking at two aspects of the same thing is to miss the point, because aspect is what causes trouble; people see different contingencies of reinforcement."[59] Further, Skinner states that a copy theory of perception is not in operation. A person is changed by the contingencies of reinforcement, but he does not store "copies" of those contingencies.

Skinner proposes that behaviorists and those studying perception analyze the contingencies that control our behavior, taking into account individual environmental and genetic backgrounds. To paraphrase Skinner, "Seeing does not require a thing seen," and movement does not require a thing moved.[60]

---

55 B. F. Skinner, *About Behaviorism* (New York: Alfred A. Knopf, 1974), p. 73.
56 Skinner, p. 75.
57 Skinner, p. 77.
58 Skinner, p. 77.
59 Skinner, p. 79.
60 Skinner, p. 86.

Skinner's work supports the developmental studies of Kestenberg and Thelen. Rhythm aptitude, and consequently rhythm achievement, may be influenced by specific contingencies of reinforcement. Those contingencies, according to Skinner, Kestenberg, and Thelen, may be most effective at an early age, yet they may affect rhythm learning that involves movement at a later age.

Music Education

Carl Seashore, in *Psychology of Musical Talent* (1919), presents a discussion on rhythm based upon perception and action. According to Seashore, rhythm contains the elements of personal, subjective, and objective characteristics, which are dealt with through free and regulated actions. He continues by delineating the five factors that define the rhythmic sense: (1) sense of time, (2) sense of intensity, (3) auditory imagery, (4) motor imagery and (5) a motor impulse for rhythm.[61]

Music aptitude has been researched and discussed by Edwin Gordon. In discussing the construct validity of the *Musical Aptitude Profile,* Gordon states that "in order to assess basic rhythmic aptitude, a rhythm aptitude test must arouse a kinesthetic rhythmic feeling in the student which is itself a musical reaction."[62] The role and development of that aptitude and consequent achievement through effective rhythm and movement pedagogy, however, has not been studied. Gordon discusses music aptitude in the following way:

> Music aptitude is a product of nature and nurture: both contribute in unknown proportions to a child's music aptitude. Thus, music aptitude is developmental, that is, it fluctuates during the most important years of a child's life, from birth to age nine, the first three years being the most crucial. Music aptitude becomes stabilized after age nine and remains stabilized throughout adulthood. Regardless of the level of music aptitude a child is born with, unless early informal environmental influences are favorable, that level will never be realized in achievement. Conversely, regardless of how favorable informal environmental influences are, a child's music aptitude will never reach a higher level than that with which he was born. The level of developmental music aptitude a child reaches at age nine becomes his stabilized level of music aptitude throughout his

---

61 Carl Emil Seashore, *The Psychology of Musical Talent* (New York: Silver Burdett and Co., 1919), pp. 116–117.
62 E. E. Gordon, *Musical Aptitude Profile* (Boston: Houghton-Mifflin, 1965), p. 10.

life. That statement should not be interpreted to mean that after age nine a child cannot learn music. What it does mean is that a child cannot be expected to reach in music achievement a level higher than that at which his potential to achieve in music has stabilized.[63]

Little is known of the factors that contribute to the development of consistent tempo or steady beat in the developmental music aptitude stage. Furthermore, less is known concerning the effect of informal instruction upon those elements of rhythm in terms of music achievement. Gordon has theorized how rhythm is audiated.[64] He states: "Rhythm is correctly audiated by musicians who fortunately were not taught to memorize standard non-functional definitions of measure signatures or the arithmetic values of notes before they received informal and formal guidance in moving their bodies to music."[65]

Additionally, although Gordon does not theorize about the importance of rhythm techniques in music achievement, he does discuss, based upon observation, informal rhythm instruction. Instruction in the developmental music aptitude stage contains implications for rhythm achievement.

Like the adult, the young child must depend upon movements to grasp the meaning of a steady beat, consistent tempo, and meter. Only the young child understands the rhythm babble of his movements and chant. As with his tonal activities, no attempt should be made to correct "mistakes" or to correct him if he has not moved or chanted as the parent or teacher thinks he should have done. He should be given total freedom in exploring and expressing himself rhythmically. Indeed, a relaxed feeling for rhythm is the best basis upon which formal instruction and rhythm aptitude are developed.[66]

---

63 E. E. Gordon, *Learning Sequences in Music* (Chicago: GIA Publications, 1984), p. 25.
64 According to Edwin Gordon, "Audiation takes place when one hears music silently, that is, when the sound is not physically present. One may audiate in recalling music or in composing music. In contrast, aural perception takes place when one hears music when the sound is physically present. Although the term 'aural imagery' rather than aural perception is sometimes used to describe the audiation process, it is not recommended, because the word 'image' is associated with the visual, not the aural, sense. To use the term 'imagery' is to suggest the audiation of music which is seen in notational form. The term 'notational audiation' is more appropriate than aural imagery, and further, the distinction between audiation and notational audiation is clear." Edwin E. Gordon, *Learning Sequences in Music* (Chicago: GIA Publications, 1984), p. 11.
65 Gordon, *Learning Sequences in Music,* p. 102.
66 Gordon, *Learning Sequences in Music,* p. 29.

Gordon, unlike Kodaly, Orff, and Dalcroze, continually emphasizes a pedagogy for rhythm that uses a multidimensional concept of movement. It implies sensitivity beyond the dimensions of perceptual time and space through the encouragement of free body movement. The following is an excerpt from Gordon's discussion of measure (meter) signatures:

> It follows that the meter of a piece of music is most appropriately determined through kinetic response, in terms of audiation, rather than by an inadequate and misleading definition of the meter signature. Meter was correctly determined in that way long before notation and incorrect definitions began to contradict audiation. Once a piece of music is kinetically understood, it will be found that a measure signature can indicate the meter of the notation it precedes according to whether the numerals in the measure signature refer to macro beats or micro beats, not just to "beats" in general.[67]

The importance of the kinesthetic feeling of what Gordon terms the macrobeat can be seen throughout his discussions about rhythm content learning sequence. The ability to kinetically feel macrobeats in audiation is fundamental to rhythm performance. The rhythm syllable system Gordon developed is the only one that systematizes rhythm in terms of audiational understanding.[68]

Modern Educational Dance

The work of Rudolf von Laban (1879–1958) has been used as the basis of several descriptive studies; his theories, however, have not been used as a basis for experimental design and analysis in *Modern Educational Dance* (1980). One such descriptive study, *An Examination of Rudolf Laban's Theory of Modern Educational Dance to Derive Implications for Program Development in the Elementary School* (1983), by Maristela de Moura Silva, is a collection of Laban writings from diverse sources designed for practical use in movement curriculum development. To the writer's knowledge, the theories of Laban have not been applied to rhythm pedagogy in music education.

---

67 Gordon, *Learning Sequences in Music,* p. 113.
68 For a detailed explanation of the development of rhythm syllable systems for pedagogical use, the reader is referred to Edwin E. Gordon's *Learning Sequences in Music* (Chicago: GIA Publications, 1984), pp. 234–239.

Rudolf von Laban

Rudolf von Laban was born in 1879 in Bratislava, Hungary, the son of an army general. His early years were preoccupied with observing movement. As a child, he spent considerable time drawing and visualizing patterns in space. His desire to understand both physical and mental effort led him to a lengthy course of study in painting, sculpture, and stage design in Paris, Berlin, and Vienna. As part of his training, he studied various cultures, particularly the natives of Africa, the people of the Near East, and the Chinese.

In 1910, he founded his first dance group and school in Munich, where he developed one of his favorite genres, the movement choir. During World War I, he lived in Switzerland and continued to develop his ideas. In 1919, he formed a stage dance group, the Tanzbuhne Laban, which specialized in expressive dance. Through that ensemble, he created many full-length dance compositions (*The Swinging Cathedral, Die Geblendeten, Gaukelei, Don Juan,* and *Die Nacht*).

In 1926, he founded the Choreographic Institute in Wurzburg, which he later moved to Berlin. That institute specialized in the development of a dance notation system, originally known as Eukinetics, which was published in 1928 as *Kinetrography*. In the United States, his work is known as *Labanotation*. He became Director of Movement at the Berlin State Opera in 1930, and subsequently was recognized as one of Europe's most famous choreographers.

Unable to continue work under the Nazi regime, Laban and some of his pupils sought sanctuary in the United Kingdom. Laban introduced modern educational dance into the schools as a new creative subject. In Manchester, England, where he lived from 1942 to 1953, he helped establish the Art of Movement Studio with Lisa Ullman. Concurrently, he established the *Laban-Lawrence Industrial Rhythm,* which developed the effort graph as a means of recording the kinesthetic quality of individual performance in industry.

In 1946, the Laban Art of Movement Guild was formed. That guild supported the movement training center for movement study and educational dance based upon Laban's concepts. Laban lectured on a regular basis at his studio, and at the same time he lectured at colleges and universities.

In 1953, Laban moved to Addlestone, Surrey, where he established archives for his own work and the work of the Art of Movement Studio. In 1954, the Laban Art of Movement Centre was formed as an educational trust to perpetuate his work and to promote and provide education in the art of movement. He continued to work at Addlestone until his death in 1958.

Philosophical Basis of the Work of Laban

Many disciplines use the work of Laban: personality assessment for management and industry, dance therapy, modern educational dance, mime, acting, sociology, child development, anatomy, education for the handicapped, and music therapy. Moreover, various training institutes offer instruction in Laban's teachings. Few disciplines or training institutes, however, offer formal comprehensive studies for the understanding of the philosophy that established the foundation of his work. An understanding of Laban's philosophy is necessary for an accurate re-creation of his work and ideas.

Laban's writings consistently integrate the body and the mind. For Laban, movement is a combination of phenomenological experience with a highly specialized kinesthetic perception for self and environment. Movement is the link between those two worlds. The understanding of that mind-body duality is a lifetime process, which can grow only through observation and direct experience.

> But what are symbolic actions? They are certainly not just imitations or representations of the ordinary actions of everyday life. To perform movements, as if chopping wood or as if embracing or threatening someone, has little to do with the real symbolism of movement. Such imitations of everyday acts may be significant, but they are not symbolic. Man in those silent movements, pregnant with emotion, may perform strange movements which appear meaningless, or at any rate inexplicable. Yet, and this is the curious thing, he moves with the same actions he uses in chopping, carrying, mending, assembling or doing any everyday operation; but these actions appear in specific sequences having shapes and rhythms of their own. Words expressing feelings, emotions, sentiments or certain mental and spiritual states will but touch the fringe of the inner responses which the shapes and rhythms of bodily actions are capable of evoking. Movement can say more, for all its shortness, than pages of verbal description.[69]

---

69   Rudolf Laban, *The Mastery of Movement*, ed. Lisa Ullman (London: MacDonald and Evans Ltd., 1980), p. 87.

Throughout his life, Laban attempted to document his thinking. It is through his writings that movers gain a clearer image of the interaction of mind and body. Further, as one reads Laban, a philosophy of life based upon moving and observing movers becomes apparent. For Laban, movement is the basic impulse of man and life.

> What one experiences through movement can never be expressed in words; in a simple step there may be a reverence of which we are scarcely aware. Yet through it something higher than just tenderness and devotion may flow into us and from us.[70]

> ...It is impossible, of course, to describe the essence of the movements. But sometimes one can experience the same sort of impulse to move, for example, in a fight, in danger, in ecstasy and in passion, in short, in times of excessive emotion.[71]

> ...Movement is first and fundamental in what comes forth from a human being as an expression of his intentions and experiences. One must remember that all sound productions, such as speaking, singing, shouting, spring from physical actions, or in other words, from movements. Whether I bang a table or make it resound, or vibrate the air with shouts, it is always the same thing—movement made audible.[72]

> ...Is it possible to express all this through movement, through dance? Only if the participants know and believe that dance has ethical life and only when they have become able to let this experience infiltrate their demeanour and movement drive.[73]

> ...But the main aim of the movement choir must always be the shared experience of the joy of moving. Actually, the expression "joy of moving" does not fully describe the fundamental idea. It is to a great extent an inner experience and, above all a strengthening of the desire for communion.[74]

---

70 Rudolf Laban, *A Life for Dance* (London: MacDonald and Evans Ltd., 1975), p. 35.
71 Laban, p. 51.
72 Laban, p. 87.
73 Laban, p. 137.
74 Laban, p. 157.

Looking at the whole range of innate and acquired impulses of man, one is tempted to search for a common denominator. In my opinion this denominator is not mere motion, but movement with all its spiritual implication.... What has to be done today—and our time seems to stand on the threshold of a new awareness of movement—is to acknowledge movement as the great integrator. This involves, of course, the conviction that movement is the vehicle which concerns the whole man with all his physical and spiritual facilities. To be able to see this great unity is not the privilege of the artist alone. Everybody, every single human individual, has this unity at the basis of his natural tendencies and impulses, which can be lifted out of the treasure of forgotten truth and cultivated in all the various ramifications of life.[75]

Effort

Body movement is a complex event in which many changes occur simultaneously. The different aspects of those changes of movement can be studied by organizing movement through the framework developed by Laban. That framework, for the first time, permitted the documentation of movement from subtle moment-to-moment changes to the larger impressions of movement. The study of Laban movement analysis allows for a rich understanding of, and sensitivity to, the movement event. Effort/Shape analysis further substantiates, through specific documentation, the complexity of movement.

> An observer of a moving person is at once aware, not only of the paths and rhythms of movement, but also of the mood the paths in themselves carry, because the shapes of the movements through space are always more or less colored by a feeling or an idea. The content of ideas and feelings which we have when moving or seeing movement can be analyzed as well as the forms and lines in space.[76]

The basis for Laban's broad theory is what he refers to as "movement thinking." Movement thinking is defined as an acquisition and perceptual storage of movements and their uses, even though a "nomenclature" is lacking.

---

75 Rudolf Laban, "Movement Concerns the Whole Man," *The Laban Art of Movement Guild Magazine*, No. 21 (November 1958), pp. 12–13.
76 Bartenieff, *Body Movement*, p. 181.

Movement thinking does not necessarily provide mental agility with developing movement inferences, but it does provide a person with the ability to "think" or imagine the kinesthetic sensation for a particular body motion.[77]

Those kinesthetic sensations are acquired through the movement of one's body and through one's observation of others. According to Laban, training in movement sensation must help the mover to "bodily feel the difference" among and between the movements of both his natural and newly acquired movement vocabulary, and to consequently recognize them in the movement of the world around him.[78] The term that Laban employs to describe those sensations which are the result of the expenditure of energy is "effort." Effort, in the purest sense, is the inner impulse from which movement originates. Effort is the mind/body combination of a mental image combined with a physical activity that manifests itself in a movement act. A definition and discussion of effort by Laban, however, can lead to some ambiguity, and it is subject to personal interpretations.

> In order to discern the mechanics of motion within living movement in which purposeful control of the physical happening is at work, it is useful to give a name to the inner function originating such movement. The word used here for this purpose is *effort*. Every human movement is indissolubly linked with an effort, which is, indeed, its origin and inner aspect. Effort and its resulting action may be both unconscious and involuntary, but they are always present in any bodily movement; otherwise they could not be perceived by others, or become effectual in the external surroundings of the moving person. Effort is visible in the action movement of a worker, or a dancer, and it is audible in song or speech. If one hears a laugh or cry of despair, one can visualize in imagination the movement accompanying the audible effort. The fact that the effort and its various shadings can not only be seen and heard, but also imagined, is of great importance for their representation, both visible and audible, by the actor-dancer. He derives a certain inspiration from descriptions of movements that awaken his imagination.[79]

---

77 Laban, *The Mastery of Movement*, p. 15.
78 Rudolf Laban and F. C. Lawrence, *Effort* (London: MacDonald and Evans, 1947), p. 35.
79 Laban, *The Mastery of Movement*, pp. 20–21.

The Effort Elements

Laban discusses the effort elements of Space, Weight, Time, and Flow as movement variables. Those efforts can have different attitudes, variations, intensities, qualities, or elements that are dependent upon the immediate mind/body condition. Consequently, a mover will have an attitude toward a particular effort factor. The quality of those attitudes for each effort will fluctuate between two extremes and, thus, indicate how the effort will be performed. The extreme ranges of elements for each effort are illustrated in Figure 1. The indulging elements offer no resistance to the efforts of Flow, Weight, Time, and Space, but they are considered as active or energy-containing by Laban. The fighting elements move against Flow, Weight, Time, and Space. Consequently, continua are established for each effort. For example, there exists a continuum for space between indirect and direct, a continuum for weight between light and strong, a continuum for time between sustained and sudden, and a continuum for flow between free and bound. Consequently, every effort must include at least two elements: one with an "indulging" quality and one with a "fighting" quality. In all cases, combinations of efforts with their particular elements occur in spatial paths and shapes within a kinesphere or one's personal space.

Figure 1. Effort elements continua.

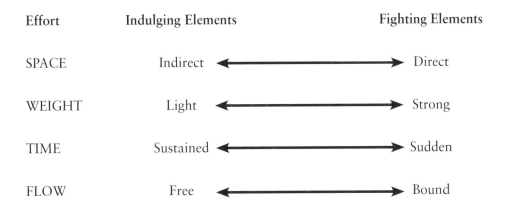

The efforts and their elements may be described in the following manner. *Flow* is the variation in the quality of bodily tension, which underlies other effort elements. *Free flow* is allowing energy to flow through and out beyond the body boundaries. Free movements are difficult to stop instantly. *Bound flow* forces the mover to contain energy within the body boundary. Bound movements are controlled and restrained, and can be stopped easily at any point in the movement.

Weight is the sensation of force or pressure exerted in a movement. *Lightness* can be described as delicate, fine, or soft. Lightness overcomes or rarifies the sensation of body weight. *Strength* can be described as a movement that is forceful or one that has increased pressure. Strength actively uses the sensation of body weight to make an impact.

Time is an attitude toward the expenditure or duration of time in a movement. *Sustained time* can be characterized as stretching, prolonging, lingering, or decelerating. Conversely, *suddenness* contains a sense of urgency, instantaneousness, and quickness.

Space is the manner in which energy is focused in an action. *Indirectness* is a multi-faceted attention to the environment; it is flexible and can be all-encompassing. *Directness* is a channeled, singularly focused awareness of the environment.

Effort elements frequently occur in combinations of two, referred to as states by Laban, and combinations of three, referred to as drives or actions. Combinations of the four effort elements appear in extremes of expression where an apparent dissolution of the movement takes place. According to Laban, it is the addition of Flow that provides for the extremes of expression.

The Effort Elements in Combination

Laban identified the basic effort actions as a result of observing the movement patterns of workers in the British war industry. Laban combined one element each from Space, Weight, and Time to obtain the eight combinations that appear in Figure 2.

Figure 2. The eight effort actions.

FLOAT	WRING	PRESS	GLIDE
Indirect	Indirect	Direct	Direct
Light	Strong	Strong	Light
Sustained	Sustained	Sustained	Sustained

DAB	FLICK	SLASH	PUNCH
Direct	Indirect	Indirect	Direct
Light	Light	Strong	Strong
Quick	Quick	Quick	Quick

Laban discovered that a worker is often required to attend to Weight, Space, and Time simultaneously. Consequently, Flow is subsumed in those combinations. Simultaneous concentration on the three factors of Weight, Space, and Time are known as the basic effort actions, or the full efforts. Laban did not specifically assign names to each of the eight combinations. He felt that language could be more exacting about the action than it could be for the more subtle shades of experience. Transitions occur when one moves between effort actions by changing one of the effort elements, For example, one may progress from punching (strong/direct/sudden) to pressing (sustained/direct/strong). Transitions often involve the changing of a simple component; it is possible, however, to change two and three components simultaneously.

The combinations of elements attended to simultaneously are difficult to name. Laban referred to combinations of two factors, however, as an incomplete effort. Those combinations are also referred to as the inner attitudes because the combinations of only two efforts suggests that the movement is not yet externalized but, instead, expresses states of feeling. Laban states: "It is difficult to attach names to these variations of incomplete effort as they are concerned with pure movement experience and expression."[80] Again, the verbal descriptions are not precise, and they are subject to movement validation. For each combination of two factors, the mover can combine the elements in four different ways.[81] All possible combinations of the six groupings are illustrated in Figure 3.[82]

---

80 Rudolf Laban, *The Mastery of Movement*, ed. Lisa Ullman (Boston: Plays, Inc., 1975), p. 86.
81 Marion North, in *Personality Assessment through Movement* (Boston: Plays, Inc., 1975), described in detail those externalized drives and inner attitudes. The reader is referred to that source for additional information.
82 The chapter later in this book, by Giselle Wyers, deals in great detail with what Laban refers to as "States and Drives."

Figure 3. Combinations of two effort elements.

SPACE & TIME	WEIGHT & TIME	WEIGHT & FLOW
(awake)	(near rhythm)	(dream)
Indirect/slow	Light/slow	Light/free
Indirect/quick	Strong/slow	Strong/free
Direct/slow	Light/quick	Light/bound
Direct/quick	Strong/quick	Strong/bound

SPACE & FLOW	FLOW & TIME	SPACE & WEIGHT
(remote)	(mobile)	(stable)
Indirect/free	Free/slow	Indirect/light
Indirect/bound	Free/quick	Indirect/strong
Direct/free	Bound/slow	Direct/light
Direct/bound	Bound/quick	Direct/strong

Laban summarizes the efforts in the following manner:

> In conclusion, it may be repeated that effort, with all its manifold shadings of which the human being is capable, is mirrored in the actions of the body. But bodily actions performed with imaginative awareness stimulate and enrich inner life. Therefore, mastery of movement is not only of value to the stage artist, but to everyone since we are all concerned, whether consciously or subconsciously, with perception and expression. The person who has learnt to relate himself to Space, and has physical mastery of this, has Attention. The person who has mastery of his relation to the Weight factor of effort has Intention, and he has Decision when he is adjusted to Time. Attention, intention and decision are stages of the inner preparation of an outer bodily action. This comes about when through the flow of movement effort finds concrete expression in the body.[83]

---

83 Laban, *The Mastery of Movement* (1975), pp. 88–89.

The Projective Geometry of Laban

To objectify the movement observation process for both the mover and the observer of movement, Laban describes movement with reference to the geometric spaces the body creates while moving. Richard Kraus and Sarah Chapman summarize Laban's hypotheses:

> According to his theory of *eukinetics*, all movement may be divided into two major categories: "outgoing" and "incoming." Laban developed a number of theories relating to *centrifugal* movement (movement originating in the center of the body and radiating or spreading out to the periphery) and *peripheral* movement (beginning with the extremities and moving to the center of the body). He carefully analyzed movement as to intensity, speed, and direction, making use of the object known as the *icosahedron*, the twenty-faced geometrical form which is a midpoint between a cube and a sphere. The essential concept of the icosahedron was that man's movements are both spherical and related to the three dimensions of space which are represented by the cube. Thus, movement takes place in three dimensions, and also on diagonals and inclines, limited only by the anatomical possibilities of the body; Laban used imaginary points in space dictated by the icosahedron to develop a complicated movement scale that provided a systematic basis for dance training.[84]

The Rhythm of Movement and Phrasing in the Theories of Laban

According to Laban, the elements of movement, arranged in various sequences, constitute rhythms. Those rhythms can be discussed in three categories: (1) space-rhythms, (2) time-rhythms, and (3) weight-rhythms. Laban states: "In reality these three forms of rhythm are always united, though one can occupy the foreground of an action."[85] Space-rhythm is a term used by Laban to discuss the use of movement in directions that result in shapes in space. There are two aspects of space-rhythm: "(a) the one in which there is successive development of changing directions, and (b) the other where shapes are produced through simultaneous actions of different parts of the body."[86]

---

84 R. Kraus and S. Chapman, *History of the Dance in Art and Education* (Englewood Cliffs, NJ: Prentice-Hall, Inc., 1981), p. 138.
85 Laban, *The Mastery of Movement* (1975), p. 134.
86 Laban, *The Mastery of Movement* (1975), p. 134.

Of particular significance to the present research, however, is Laban's hypothesis concerning the rhythm of movement in time.

> The significance of the time-rhythms of movement can be observed in individual dancers who have clearly discernible preferences for special rhythms. While one dancer will be more tempted to interpret music in which the sharp metricality of regular beats prevails, another might be repelled by the exact metricality and prefer the free, irregular unfolding of time-rhythm. The precision of the metrical dancer is in strong contrast to the expressiveness of the dance-mime-actor preferring free rhythm. There exist many shades between the two extreme contrasts of regular and irregular rhythm. To a certain degree it is true that the dancer's legs and feet prefer metrical function; but feet, arms, and hands should equally be able to express the qualities of a free time-rhythm. In fact, the whole body should be able to express the regular and irregular vibrations and waves of movement. Although an understanding and appreciation of music, which is an abstract expression of movement, can help the actor in his grasp of rhythm, it is not in itself sufficient. Even the dancer, who interprets music, has to translate it into the effort sequences from which his or her expressive steps and gestures arise. In dance, the rhythm of movement is mainly expressed by the steps, and this is particularly true of traditional ballet which uses a number of basic steps and characteristic combinations of these.[87]

Laban encouraged dancing without music as he worked with his early movement choirs. According to Laban, the "rhythm" of movement could be perceived in many ways. Consequently, the perception of "rhythm" is the result of individual differences among movers. For Laban, the transference of "rhythm" to music is an outgrowth of the total movement experience.

Laban's theories of rhythm should not be thought of as simply a duration of time accentuated by various stresses. They should be considered as the interactions of various effort combinations with various spatial patterns that create rhythm. Rhythm then becomes the experiences of body tension that provide points of reference that we commonly refer to as meter. Rhythm, experienced and discussed in those terms, could possibly assist and improve discrimination among and between various rhythms and rhythm modes in audiation and performance.

---

87 Laban, *The Mastery of Movement* (1975), p. 135.

*S*ummary

Psychology has established the importance of kinesthesia in perception. Developmental psychologists have shown that kinesthesia develops as part of the physical and mental maturation process in the child through descriptive longitudinal and experimental studies. In music education, Orff and Kodaly have recognized the importance of the early developmental stages of the child and have developed techniques to assist in music rhythm development. Those techniques, along with the techniques of Dalcroze, emphasize movement in Time and Space. Gordon encourages the use of free body movement using elements of Weight and Flow to establish an associative auditional kinesthesia for the discrimination of meter and specific rhythm patterns.

Gordon has hypothesized the importance of auditional kinesthesia for rhythm learning and teaching. He does not discuss, however, specific techniques or pedagogies for teaching auditional kinesthesia. Nor does he discuss the possible magnitude of that kinesthesia. *Modern Educational Dance*, through the Effort/Shape theory of Laban, acknowledges the importance of kinetic sensitivity while one engages in movement or the observation of that movement. Laban additionally provides a vocabulary for organizing movement experiences. The elements of Time and Space employed in Dalcroze, Orff, and Kodaly, and the elements of Weight and Flow as implied by Gordon, coexist within Laban's theories. Time, Space, Weight, and Flow can be combined or experienced in dyads or triads as an experimental adjunct to the teaching of rhythm. More importantly, Laban's Effort/Shape provides a framework by which one could organize and describe movement for specific pedagogical purposes. It should also be noted that because of the theories of Effort/Shape developed specifically for his book, *Modern Educational Dance*, a basis for a morphology for conductors exists in its beginning form for use as a pedagogical framework for applications to conducting and conducting pedagogy.

The Importance of the Body Map and the Theories of Antonio Damasio: Connections with William James and "Feelings of Knowing"

As with any pedagogy or suggested pedagogy, there is at the very roots a kernel of an idea that not only fuels the pedagogy but also gives it educational imperative. While many have theorized and have made practical applications of the work of Laban to many areas, and have attested to its effectiveness, there has been little information as to "why" it works or even what should be the focus of a pedagogy that employs it.

Earlier in this chapter, the thoughts of William James and his "eccentric projection of feelings" was discussed. This theoretical discussion held in the nineteenth century did not have the benefit of computers or MRI technology to validate any part of the theory. The work of neurologist Antonio Damasio makes a connection between what James calls "feelings of knowing" and what our brain actually maps. These "feelings" operate at many levels, according to Damasio, but they are integral to the development, in this case, of the communicative human power of gesture.

As conductors, we have long known about the power and influence that gesture has upon musical sound. Heretofore, we have accepted its magic and used our ears to inform our decisions. That paradigm must certainly continue. But at another, perhaps deeper, level we must understand that the study of movement through the kinesthetic of Laban's world is the way to these "feelings of knowing" as a conductor.

All of Laban's work provides conductors a way—a clean and distinct pedagogy—to explore an expressive movement world that becomes, for lack of a better term, *our* "expressive body map." Body maps allow us to associate gestures with sounds of the scores we study, but more importantly, Damasio's theories tell us that these movement feelings that exist in our maps can be read instantaneously and intuitively via mirror neurons that are cast off of us like a static-ridden cloth in the dry winter air. It is mirror neurons that evoke sound. It is mirror neurons that are coded within our gestural world that are read and deciphered by musicians in sound. Mirror neurons are of many types; they are sounds in our audiation, they are colors, they are human emotions. But make no mistake about it: it is gesture that releases them to the musicians who are in front of it. Gesture, if acquired in a sequential fashion, provides a framework for those "feelings of knowing" of which William James speaks. We, in fact, do project onto others through mirror neurons through gesture all that is about the music we create through the symbiotic relationships of human being to human being. It is these mirror neurons that make up our gestural body map that are the means of communication.

The Pedagogical Mandate of This Book

This book attempts to set out, for the first time, the use of Laban's Effort/Shape as the vehicle for the structuring and nourishing of mirror neurons in conductors. The theories of our mind "body maps" complete the overall pedagogical structure to give both legitimacy and imperativeness to Laban's work. For those of us who have wrestled with this material for years, both "mind maps" and the actions of mirror neurons explain as much as we can hope for now the "why" of the miracle of human expressive gesture when wedded to the creation of musical sound.

It is truly gesture that starts an incineration and firing of neurons in others—those things that are intuitively read. It now becomes our responsibility as conductors to build a pedagogically logical vocabulary of gesture based upon Laban's clairvoyant sight into the elegant structure of movement. It is this author's hope that you will invest yourselves in this very potent idea. While we may debate the particulars of the pedagogy for years to come, I do not think that the idea of both our "mind maps" and mirror neurons should be debated; rather, we should accept the theory as just present and move forward into this new pedagogical journey for conductors.

How Movement and Conducting Affects Ensembles: Understanding the Power of Body Mapping and Mirror Neurons

> So-called mirror neurons are, in effect, the ultimate as-if body device. The network in which those neurons are embedded achieves conceptually what I have hypothesized as the as-if body loop system: the simulation, in the brain's body maps, of a body state that is not actually taking place in the organism. The fact that the body state simulated by mirror neurons is not the subject's body state amplifies the power of this functional resemblance. If a complex brain can simulate someone else's body state, one assumes that it would be able to simulate its own body states. A state that has already occurred in the organism should be easier to simulate since it has already been mapped by precisely the same somatosensing structures that are now responsible for simulating it. (p. 103)

> Explanations of the existence of mirror neurons have emphasized the role that such neurons can play in allowing us to understand the actions of others by placing ourselves in a comparable body state. As we witness an action in another, our body-sensing brain adopts the body state we would assume were we ourselves moving, and it does so, in all probability, not by passive sensory patterns but by a preactivation of mirror structures—ready for action but not allowed to act yet—and in some cases by actual motor activation. (pp. 103–104)
>
> —Antonio Damasio
> in *Self Comes to Mind*

> The essential thing is that we should neither have preference for nor avoid certain movements because of physical or psychical restrictions. We should be able to do every imaginable movement and then select those which seem to be most suitable and desirable for our own nature. These can be found only by each individual himself. For this reason, practice of the free use of kinetic and dynamic possibilities is of the greatest advantage. We should be acquainted both with the general movement capacities of a healthy body and mind with the specific restrictions and capacities resulting from the individual structure of our own bodies and minds. (p. 112)
>
> —Rudolf Laban
> in *Choreutics*

> The distinctive feature of brains such as the one we own is their uncanny ability to create maps. Mapping is essential for sophisticated management, mapping and life management going hand in hand. When the brain makes maps, it *informs* itself. The information contained in the maps can be used nonconsciously to guide motor behavior efficaciously, a most desirable consequence considering that survival depends on taking the right action. But when brains make maps, they are also creating images, the main currency of our minds. Ultimately consciousness allows us to experience maps as images, to manipulate those images, and to apply reasoning to them.
>
> Maps are constructed when we interact with objects, such as a person, a machine, a place, from the outside of the brain toward its interior. I cannot emphasize the word *interaction* enough. It reminds us that making maps, which is essential for improving actions as noted above, often occurs in a setting of action to begin with. Action and maps, movements and mind, are part of an unending cycle.... (pp. 63–64).
>
> —Antonio Damasio
> in *Self Comes to Mind*

AN OVERVIEW OF THE PSYCHOLOGICAL RESEARCH

Chapter 4

We can have our body in mind, at all times, providing us with a backdrop of feeling potentially available at every instant but noticeable only when it departs significantly from relatively balanced states and begins to register in the pleasantness or unpleasantness range. We have our body in mind because it helps govern behavior in all manner of situations that could threaten the integrity of the organism and compromise life. That particular function draws on the oldest kind of life regulation based on a brain. It harks back to simple body-to-brain signaling, to basic prompts for automated regulatory responses meant to assist with life management. But we simply have to marvel at what has been accomplished from such humble beginnings. Body mapping of the most refined order undergirds *both* the self process in conscious minds *and* the representations of the world external to the organism. The inner world has opened the way for our ability to *know* not only that very inner world but the world around us.

The living body is the central locus. Life regulation is the need and the motivation. Brain mapping is the enabler, the engine that transforms plain life regulation into minded regulation and, eventually, into consciously minded regulation. (pp. 106–107)

—Antonio Damasio
in *Self Comes to Mind*

To be fully alive is to act. The capacity to act is the most obvious difference between the quick and the dead. But action is more than movement; it is movement that involves expression, discovery, reformation of ourselves and our world. *I understand action to be any way that we can co-create reality with other beings and with the Spirit.* Through action we both express and learn something of who we are, of the kind of world we have or want. Action, like a sacrament, is the visible form of an invisible spirit, an outward manifestation of an inward power. But as we act, we not only express what is in us and help give shape to the world; we also receive what is outside us, and we reshape our inner selves. When we act, the world acts back, and we and the world are co-created. (p. 17)

—Parker Palmer
in *The Active Life*

The quotes above continue to present persuasive argument for you to consider the power of both your "body map" carried within your mind and the mirror neurons that transfer wordlessly those "feelings of knowing." In *The Musician's Breath* (2011), I make a plea to trust what the breath can carry. Gesture that emerges out of the breath incites mirror neurons in the ensemble members we conduct. But just as we must trust in the breath and what it carries, we must also trust in the body maps we have "planted" through sequential study of movement through Laban.

Kinesthetic language is like any other language. Language is most efficiently acquired when it is taught in an orderly and organic process. Laban's approach to the complex world of movement allows us to self-experience movement that can then be stored for future use. Laban is the vehicle by which we create kinesthetic body maps for recall. While mirror neurons are instinctually read by musicians, it is the kinesthetic maps that allow us a vocabulary of gesture that will both reinforce intuitive mirror neuron reading and serve to support and bring alive the sounds of the composer in our audiation. Our conducting gesture acts in the same way that friction acts when starting a fire with two sticks. Oxygen must be present for fire; mirror neurons, always present, are ignited (or rather excited) by conducting gesture. That gesture, to reinforce the complex world of mirror neurons, must have a wide range of expressivity to be both profound and expressive. While I realize that the scale of these ideas cuts a wide swath, I also feel that such theories only have legitimacy in the larger, practical world if they do articulate a wide and far-reaching idea.

CHAPTER 5

A Morphology of Conducting: Outlining the Laban Path through Spatial Imagination and Projective Geometry

Space is a hidden feature of movement and movement is a visible aspect of space. (p. 4)

—Rudolf von Laban
in *The Language of Movement*

The basic elements common to all movements may be categorized under three broad headings: (1) the use of the body, (2) the use of space, and (3) the use of dynamic energy. (p. 187)

—Carol-Lynne Moore
in *Beyond Words*

We should be able to do every imaginable movement possible and then select those which seem to be most suitable and desirable for our own nature. These can be found only by each individual himself. For this reason, practice of free use of kinetic and dynamic possibilities is of the greatest advantage. We should be acquainted both with the general movement capacities of a healthy body and mind and with the specific restrictions and capacities resulting from the individual structure of our own bodies and minds. (p. 17)

—Rudolf Laban
in Irmgard Bartenieff,
Body Movement

I thought it might be helpful to detail in somewhat broad terms the organization of what I refer to as the "morphology of conducting." With any pedagogy, decisions must be made. For me, Laban has made all those decisions, and what I have attempted to do is to relate my movement act as a conductor to Laban's perceptive and pedagogical genius. This process of experiencing and describing movement is one of the most valuable links that has allowed me to communicate not only with my students, but also with myself. As musicians, while we realize that physical movement and perception of that movement is a strong element in our musicing, there has been little other than our own trial and error and Dalcroze to awaken the movers within us.

When I studied at the Laban Institute, the instructors called everyone (not just dancers) "movers" regardless of their artistic calling! I found that very liberating and would like to apply that here by asking you to change your mental paradigm and view yourself as a mover.

There is a pivotal idea that Laban placed forward in his development of modern educational dance. Laban had a passion for developing dance curricula for children. His passion was to develop movement curricula for children that would re-acquaint them with the movement world he believed we were all born with. To Laban's thinking, as human beings we are born with a full world of movement at our fingertips. Just watch children at any playground; they run, tumble, jump and leap. Movement, part of their play world, is a vital part of their expressive world. As Laban observed, that full world of movement begins to disappear for many reasons, so he believed that movement sense need only be re-awakened.

The same is true for conductors! We possess a full range of expressive movement that we practiced as young children and throughout our lives. We either have forgotten that expressive movement *or* do not realize or understand how to re-connect that movement world back into our adult lives! The genius of Laban is that he provides a way to re-awaken movement that can then be bonded to the sounds we hear as musicians. Conducting gesture, then, becomes part of a movement world that already exists in us rather than something we "apply" to the music we must conduct. This is the morphology I am speaking of....

What is the genesis of movements that we use as expressive and humanly communicative devices? Those "movements" as conductors, if they are to have any honesty, must come from a place that is deep within a movement core formed at birth. Thus, morphology of conducting gesture begins by way of Laban; it begins with movement experienced in the course of life that is expressive and directly relates to our own physical world. We use such movement to navigate the physical world every day. That movement is the very foundation of our expressive vocabulary as conductors.

Through Laban, movement as conductors is not something we apply to our musicing to become "expressive"; it is the expressive movement we use every day that we bring to our musicing tasks! When you read the material that follows, you will see that how our movement is birthed, lived, and ends as conductors throughout the entire life of a piece of music has everything to do with how we move in life. For me, an understanding of my own impulses to move have come from revisiting the way I move in life. I then relate and connect that way of movement "thinking" to the music I hear and audiate. It is that connection between body and ear that makes Laban's ideas so powerful and immediately useful for all who wish to live a life communicating though conducting.

The Morphology: A Movement Learning Theory

As a result of my work with Music Learning Theory and my study of Laban Effort shape over the past twenty-five years, I propose the following morphology for the development of movement awarenesses that could be connected to one's audiation of music. After all these years of conducting and teaching conducting, I confidently suggest the following as a *movement* learning theory for conductors based upon the theories of Laban. I believe that many of us who teach conducting would perhaps be more efficient if we adhere to a sequence of acquiring a movement vocabulary that coordinates physical technique acquisition with the geometric framework and effort framework that is suggested by Laban. The theory is detailed in Figure 4.

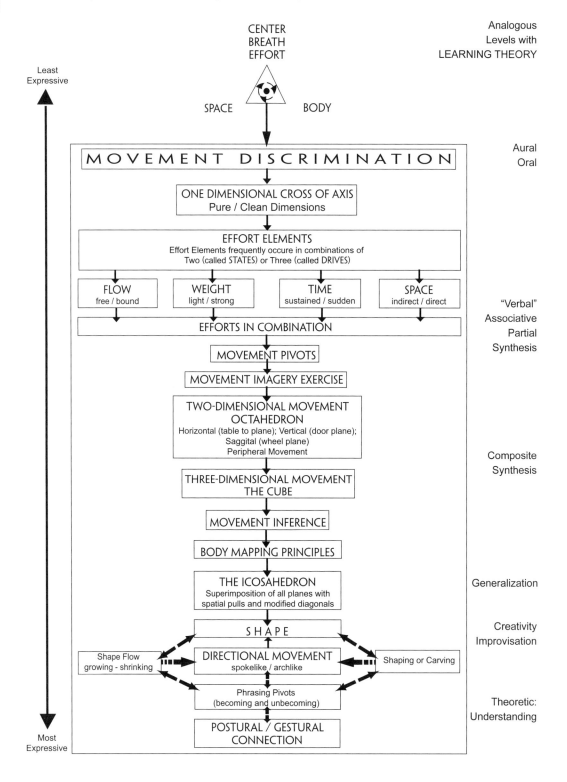

Figure 4.
A suggested movement acquisition theory based on the theories of Laban.

An Explanation of the Morphology

What I have attempted to do is combine the theories of Rudolf von Laban that are presented in *Modern Educational Dance* (Plays, 1976) with principles from Labanotation to arrive at a theory that will take conductors through a process that includes awareness of body architecture followed by acquiring a sequential understanding through the Efforts in Combination of not only how they move, but how it feels to move. The feeling of how to move is the movement vocabulary for any conductor, which needs to be available to associate with musical sounds a conductor hears in audiation.

This book is not about how to acquire sound biases through study; rather, it is about how to develop a movement vocabulary that is available for use as one audiates. From this author's perspective, we have not developed an efficient pedagogy by which a comprehensive movement vocabulary can be awakened, retrieved, and applied to our musicing. I believe this sequence does exactly that, and remains true to some basic principles of learning. Acquiring a gestural vocabulary is similar to the processes we use to acquire an aural vocabulary. Consequently, I have applied a template similar to the approach to Music Learning Theory that was introduced over thirty years ago by Edwin Gordon. In considering Dr. Gordon's approach to Music Learning Theory, it seems that his paradigm derived from language acquisition warrants use here. Just as we acquire language in a specific pedagogical sequence when we are learning in an efficient manner, so, too, do we acquire our musical vocabulary. However, we have not taken the time to propose a learning sequence for the kinesthetic learning of music, yet it seems that the principles are all contained in the work of Laban. The major tenets of the sequence shown in Figure 4 are Laban's, but the specific sequencing is from this author's viewpoint. In looking at this sequence, you will find a valid starting point for consideration for a kinesthetic skill and technique acquisition sequence by those who wish to both acquire conducting skills and enhance their expressivity.

Because this sequence views movement from its initial perceptual conception to its association and binding to musical sounds, I refer to it as a *morphology* of movement rather than a *method*. (The difference between those words is subtle, but pedagogically profound.) This morphology attempts to specifically define how the perception of self-movement (not the perception of others moving)[88] is acquired and used.

---

88 The inclusion of all of the research in the Psychology of Movement perception was included in detail in this volume to clearly define that the perception of personal movement is a different psychological problem than the perception of movement as a movement observer. The self-perception of movement is the overall focus of this book.

Specifics of the Morphology

In beginning to study the morphology, consider the following points. Refer to the morphology chart in Figure 4 when examining the points below. Also note that the specifics of each of these points are explained in more detail in other parts of this text. In essence, this morphology is a self-cntained learning theory for movement.

The morphology is arranged beginning with least expressive and moving to most expressive, from top to bottom. Also, any impulse to move must have at its roots and genesis an audiated musical sound in all its dimensions (e.g., dynamic, color, musical phrasing, etc.), all acquired through score study.

- **Effort Affinity Triangle** – This beginning part of the morphology should not be underestimated. Laban believed that various movement tendencies are genetic. Most musicians, especially conductors, have the triangle affixed in the position in the diagram, with effort in the dominant position, and space and body as secondary areas. While a conductor tends to be gifted in terms of the perception of effort, the triangle in this position clearly identifies that conductors need to pay close attention to how they perceive personal space and how their body moves in that personal space. All three elements must be perceived together for movement to be truly expressive. All three elements must be developed as skills sequentially and in tandem with each other. The problem with most conductors and conducting pedagogy is that one of the levels is developed without the other two levels, which inadvertently retards or restricts the acquisition of expressive conducting technique.

- **Breath** – An understanding of breath is central to the functioning of this morphology. Later in this book I present why and how the breath contains all things musical.

In examining the right side of the morphology, one encounters parallels of Music Learning Theory with the acquisition of movement understanding:

- **Aural/Oral** – At this level of learning, kinesthetic knowledge of movement is acquired in the broadest sense possible. One needs to move in the broadest possible way to acquire the perception of the total sphere of one's movement. This is the basic architecture of movement.

- **Verbal Association** – This is where the types and qualities of movement are labeled, like words in language. It is the acquisition of the Efforts in Combination (Press, Flick, Glide, Punch, Press, Slash, Dab, and Punch) that is central to this morphology. The labeling of movement using movements experienced in life is key.

- **Partial Synthesis** – Partial synthesis in this morphology is achieved when one chains the Efforts in Combination together through the movement imagery exercises suggested later in this text. By chaining the Efforts in Combination, one learns to adapt quickly to changes in body feeling. Without acquiring these changes in body feeling, one cannot develop an expressive conducting technique. Partial synthesis is learned phrase by phrase at beginning levels of experience.

- **Composite Synthesis** – Composite synthesis in movement learning occurs when the Efforts in Combination are experienced throughout an *entire* piece of music.

Inferential Movement Learning:

- **Movement Inference** – After one acquires a basic movement vocabulary, movement to conduct a new musical style or new harmonic syntax of a composer takes place by knowing what something is by what it is not. Movement inference is the highest level of movement understanding and is pivotal to the development of expressive conducting technique.

- **Body Mapping Principles** – It is at this stage of the morphology that Body Mapping principles should be studied and acquired. In *Evoking Sound*, the principles of Body Mapping (i.e., the understanding of how one's body is used in movement) is discussed in detail. The use of the *Anatomy of Conducting* DVD (GIA, 2008) is central to this process.

- **Movement within the Icosahedron and Shaping** (generalization) – At this level, the Efforts in Combination acquired are applied to accepted conducting patterns, but with a perception of how one moves in one's total personal space or icosahedron.

- **Creativity/Improvisation** – Conducting, ultimately, is an improvisatory act. This movement improvisation responds immediately to sound that is heard and immediately reacted to.

- **Postural Gestural Connection** (theoretical understanding) – This is where, after moving to sounds heard, one can objectively describe how one arrived at decisions on how to move as a conductor for a specific passage or a specific piece. At this stage, because of the way in which the movement learning was acquired, one can analyze why certain conducting gestures did not achieve the desired musical result and make adjustments in conducting technique to achieve a different musical reaction in the ensemble.

CHAPTER 6
Toward an Understanding of Effort

The Effort elements are the attitudes of the moving person towards the motion factors of Weight, Space, Time and Flow. (p. 8)

—Rudolf Laban
in *Modern Educational Dance*

Laban called the dynamic aspect of movement "effort," and discerned four motion factors that may be varied in any given action. We can change the focus, the degree of pressure, the timing, and the degree of control or kind of flow with which a motion is done. Laban believed that the dynamics of effort are derived from the inner attitudes of the mover towards these four motion factors. (p. 197)

—Carol-Lynne Moore
in *Beyond Words*

In order to discern the mechanics of motion within living movement in which purposeful control of the physical happening is at work, it is useful to give a name to the *inner function* originating such movement. The word used here for this purpose is effort. Every human movement is indissolubly linked with an effort, which is, indeed, its origin and its inner aspect. Effort and its resulting action may be both unconscious and involuntary, but they are always present in any bodily movement; otherwise they could not be perceived by others, or become effectual in the external surroundings of the moving person. Effort is visible in the action of a worker, or a dancer, and it is audible in speech or song. (p. 24)

—Rudolf Laban
in *The Mastery of Movement*

I would like to encourage you never sing to anyone, and you certainly never sing at anyone. You do, however, sing for them in the sense that you let them hear what you are thinking. And what you're thinking is what you're re-creating, which has already been thought.

It just gets less and less about you every minute, doesn't it? It isn't about us…EVER. It's about what we're singing. You should never come out on stage with something to say. They have come to be part of your life.

—Thomas Hampson
from a Masterclass at Westminster Choir College
(November 18, 2009)

A deep and abiding belief in something is usually at the core of great teaching and great musicing. I have seen it time and time again in great artists. That deep belief is usually embedded in a single word, a single thought. It is the utter simplicity of the idea that makes it deeply powerful, moving, expressive, and life changing. For Laban, "Effort" was and is such a word.

In understanding any theory or pedagogy, there always seems to be at the core a single, broad concept that is the foundation of all that is to follow. For example, in Music Learning Theory, an understanding of audiation is at the central core of understanding not only the philosophy but also the teaching procedures. For those studying Laban, an understanding of Effort is central to launching one's mind into Laban's perceptual movement world.

The problem is that as musicians we take movement for granted. Because sound is our language, it dominates all that we do and believe. But as conductors our horizon must broaden; we must somehow marry the sounds we hear to gesture that can evoke honest sounds from our musicians and be an honest representation of the composer's intent. It is often difficult for us as conductors (especially inexperienced ones) to come to an understanding that the music is not about us; in fact, it is never about us. It may be influenced by our lives, but it is never about us.

TOWARD AN UNDERSTANDING OF EFFORT

Chapter 6

Physical gesture, if left unattended, has a tendency to be self-gratifying and a bit self-indulgent. Used in a state of unawareness, gesture becomes an outgrowth of feelings of moving *to* music rather than movement that grows out of profound human idea. The incendiary device that allows an idea to birth gesture is the breath.

By understanding Effort, we come to honor and respect our movement as a language. Effort is the umbrella term used by Laban to house the specific qualities of Flow, Weight, Time, and Space. Strictly defined, Effort is the observed and kinesthetically felt by-product of the myriad of interaction of Weight, Time, and Space that we perceive and *feel* as Flow. In the quote at the beginning of this chapter, Laban stunningly defines Effort as "the inner function originating movement."

Effort and the movement that grows out of Effort is a reflection and manifestation of one's inner musical functioning—not the reverse! We do not move as we hear music; rather, our conducting movement must be an intuitive response to hearing an idea. That process encapsulates what Effort is to a conductor: the immediate and spontaneous impulse to move, which is prepared by an awakening process that causes a conductor to be aware of a vast vocabulary of movement at his disposal to birth musical ideas. Effort language can be developed through an understanding of Weight, Time, Space, and Flow in theory, and one's movement vocabulary can be acquired and re-awakened through life experience using the Efforts in Combination.

So what is the overriding objective for conductors? To gain an intellectual *and* a kinesthetic understanding of Effort, and how those efforts are communicated through body architecture.

In looking at the rest of this book, presented first is a translation of Laban's movement ideas and theories, followed by practical application (Skill Sets) that develop specific movement perception and analysis skills, followed by basic exercises on how to marry sound with gesture.

We are all movers…we just don't realize it as musicians! For me, Laban has been the most exciting musical and pedagogical journey of my life. I hope that I can convince all who read this book of the same!

CHAPTER 7

An Overview of the Importance of Breath and Its Relationship to Movement[89]

Inspirit 1. To put spirit, life, or energy into; to quicken, enliven, animate, to incite, stir.

—*The Compact Edition of the Oxford English Dictionary*

I would like to encourage you never sing to anyone, and you certainly never sing at anyone. You do, however, sing for them in the sense that you let them hear what you are thinking. And what you're thinking is what you're re-creating, which has already been thought.

It just gets less and less about you every minute, doesn't it? It isn't about us…EVER. It's about what we're singing. You should never come out on stage with something to say. They have come to be part of your life.

Now the interesting thing about singing is when we have the need or the desire to make audible this thing that goes on forever. I promise you, *technically*, ALL you want to think about is inhaling. Just keep the feeling of drawing in the breath while you are singing, and make your thoughts audible. *Three things I want you to know today*. The first is your mantra for the rest of your life: Hear it; I mean hear it exactly how you want it to be heard in every aspect.

You hear THAT, you breathe into THAT, and you make THAT audible.

—Thomas Hampson
from a Masterclass at Westminster Choir College
(November 19, 2009)

---

89   This chapter is meant only as an introduction into the importance of breath as *the* vehicle by which audiation and movement and musical expression are brought together. The reader is also encouraged to read *The Musician's Breath* (GIA).

> You must work out of your own silence. Not knowing and trusting simultaneously.
>
> —M. C. Richards
> in *The Fire Within*

Out of deep breathing issue physical and psychic energies. (p. 17)

> —Wilhelm Ehmann
> in *Choral Directing*

The building blocks of text, rhythm, and pitch we have been discussing are here woven into one whole: the song itself. The basic unit of the combination is the phrase, the smallest element of musical thought. Just as in the English language, the phrase expresses an idea, and several phrases make up the equivalent of a sentence or a paragraph.

   Phrases begin and end with an intake of breath, and their length is often determined by this physical limitation. Breath is to the singer as the floor is to the dancer. There is no way to escape this human necessity. It is woven into the fabric of all song. (p. 67)

> —Alice Parker
> in *The Anatomy of Melody*

Mirror neurons in your mind have "emotional" content. I must fire your neurons as a conductor and that can only be done through the breath! We have not even begun to discover the treasures in our breath as conductors.

> —Weston Noble
> from The Westminster Conducting Institute
> (June 29, 2010)

The connections which I want particularly to celebrate here today are those between the inner invisible realm of the "force" and the outer visible realm of the "flower," the inner realm of nature and the inner realm of man, connections between the invisible life of man and the invisible life of the universe, invisible that is to ordinary eyesight. Connections between human beings, between fields of study and work, the fabric of a common spiritual community. Artists are sometimes particularly attuned to these connections, scientists too, mystics too, soul-brothers too. (p. 171)

> —M. C. Richards
> in *The Crossing Point*

> Therefore, the basic trick is in the preparatory upbeat. It is exactly like breathing: the preparation is like an inhalation, and the music sounds like an exhalation. We all have to inhale in order to speak, for example; all verbal expression is exhaled. So it is with music: we inhale on the upbeat and sing out a phrase of music, then inhale again and breathe out the next phrase. A conductor who breathes with the music has gone far in acquiring a technique. (p. 272)
>
> —Leonard Bernstein
> in *The Conductor's Art*

Allow me a small digression and a bit of introspection. I have always been deeply concerned, and a bit puzzled, when I encounter musicians who do not breathe during their musicing. What I hear is music that not only lacks a sonic dimensionality and richness, but also carries a muted or very murky interpretative message. Without the engagement of the breath in the musicing process, the sounds that follow always seem to be a bit labored and thin, and the sounds seem handicapped and unable to carry meaningful human emotion or to communicate anything to anyone. Moreover, conductors who do not breathe usually are severely limited in the colors they can achieve with their ensembles. In most cases, the sound of those ensembles is monochromatic, robbing the conductors of an expressive device. Changes in style, therefore, can only be accomplished by focusing only on articulation, instead of articulation *and* color.

Elaine Brown always asked her students to make music that was "meaningful." As a young conductor, I thought meaningful music was that music born out of intense and sequestered score study—understanding phrase structure, harmonic motion, and such. Those elements of a musician's preparation are indeed important. But the meaningful issue is: How does one makes one's music making meaningful? M. C. Richards, in her book, *The Moral Eye*, speaks of the importance of authenticity and honesty in artistic creation. She says she knows that art will live with those characteristics when there is true "spiritual presence" in sound, word, or sight. It seems the challenge for all of us who conduct, teach, and perform is how to ensure that these mystical, almost clairvoyant qualities are in our musicing. Emphasis on the delivery system for all things human does not, in most cases, occupy a significant part of our creative thought, creative psyche, or creative doing.

In a *New York Times*[90] review of a performance of *The Wound Dresser* (1988) for orchestra and baritone, composer John Adams is quoted as saying, "In an astute description of the poem in a program note, Mr. Adams calls it the most intimate, graphic and profoundly affecting evocation of the act of nursing he knows of, a text 'astonishingly free of any kind of hyperbole or amplified emotion,' yet filled with imagery 'of a procession that only could be attained by one who had been there.'"

The review continues:

> Bearing the Bandages, water and sponge, Straight and swift to my wounded I go," he sings. As the description of the scene becomes rawer, the music shifts from meditative restraint through restless agitation to controlled intensity. Now and then you hear a consoling battlefield trumpet. The music is driven by Whitman's words, set with a deft blend of achieving lyricism and conversational naturalness. Mr. Hampson brought myriad colorings to his singing—an almost spectral tone to convey the image of blood that 'reddens the grass, the ground,' and the plaintive beauty touched with longing when the poet describes the 'burning flame' he feels as he tends to soldier amputees who dare not look at their stumps. (p. C7)

Considering the review above and the music the composer wrote to carry the text, how then is it that we as musicians arrive at an "interpretation"? How is it that we set about doing what the composer has charged us with?

All music, if it is worth "doing," carries profound human messages within its words sung or its sounds played. Those messages, when understood by performers and teachers, give interiority to art….profound human expression. Those messages must be sought and studied both through the words and the notes of the composer. Then after what I call a moment of clairvoyance, where one understands in the most profound human way the "meaning," it is the job of the performers to transport that message to others.

Many believe that an understanding and "interpretation" of the text is sufficient. I also believed that for many years and used that as my mode of operation. I thought that the sheer act of study allowed me to somehow, magically,

---

[90] Anthony Tomasini, "Poetry for Times of Calamity and War", C1, *The New York Times,* January 16, 2010.

transport the message. What I failed to see was that while my understanding is an important step in the interpretative process, if I do nothing further, then the message is held within me. The experience of the performance in this case would be solely mine. The listeners would somehow distill what I had been feeling, but just knowing a translation or "knowing" an interpretation of the words does not magically communicate those ideas to an ensemble or an audience. How does one first have a point of view, and further, how does one *convey* that point of view?

What I failed to understand for so many years is that the only vehicle for the transport of the deepest and most profound musical idea is breath. After one understands the physical process of breathing, and one understands that breath is taken during a state of intense vulnerability, then one must buy into the concept that it is only through breath that human spirit can be transported into the musicing process. Breath is the only way to carry the message. You cannot inflict interpretation of message while executing a phrase. *The phrase must be uploaded before any sound is made through and in the breath.* Breath transports idea from conductor to ensemble, and breath likewise transports the idea from player or singer to listening audience. Every breath in a piece must be viewed as an opportunity for expression and transmission of the idea at the moment. You cannot will a musical idea—you must breathe the idea, and then the musicing takes care of itself.

We must hold ourselves to a higher standard as artists to breathe ideas, not just think them. It is your breath that will make your musicing honest, even meaningful. The intention of your breath is far more important than any physical gesture or facial expression. Through your breath, you can achieve and experience musical clairvoyance. If you can recall a musical performance where you felt the music dull, listless, and its message veiled, most likely you did not empower your breath to do its work. When you overlook the power of the breath, you try to will the sounds you make; we tend to *make sound* instead of *allowing sound to happen*. Breaths are taken because they must be taken, but they are never empowered or *inspired*. In essence, breath is the birthing point of movement, and subsequently sound.

Don't underestimate the power of your breath to transport, transform and, at times, even be redemptive for your expressive lives. Breath, when viewed from this perspective in the musicing process, will refine your awareness and bring you into a deeper, more profound, and more meaningful relationship with the composer's intent.

CHAPTER 8

The Dimensional Architectures of Movement

> Dynamic space, with its terrific dance of tensions and discharges is the fertile ground in which movement flourishes. Movement is the life of space. Dead space does not exist, for there is neither space without movement nor movement without space. All movement is an eternal change between binding and loosening, between the creation of knots with the concentrating and uniting power of binding, and the creation of twisted lines in the process on unifying and untwisting. Stability and mobility alternate endlessly. (p. 101)
>
> —Rudolf von Laban
>   in Irmgard Bartenieff,
>   *Body Movement*

It can be said that that a movement can be described as a composite of its shapes and rhythms, both making part of the superimposed flow of movement in which the control exerted by the moving person upon the movement becomes visible. (p. 93)

A refreshing swim in the sea is a wonderful and healthy thing, but no human being could live constantly in the water. It is a very similar case with the occasional swim in the flow of movement which we call dance. Such swimming, refreshing in many aspects for the body, the mind and for that dreamy part of our being which has been called the soul, is an exceptional pleasure and stimulation. As water is a widespread means to sustain life, so is movement. (p. 95)

When we realize that movement is the essence of life, and that expression, whether it be speaking, writing, singing, painting or dancing, uses movement as a vehicle, we cannot help seeing the importance of understanding this outward expression of the living energy within, and this we can do through effort study. (p. 99)

Music or any rhythms of sounds are produced by movements of the musician which show also variations in their shape and space evolution. In musical rhythm, the Time element is used in a highly differentiated manner. (p. 92)

Rhythm, however, is only a part of music, a kind of skeleton around which the main content of the musical composition—the melodies and harmonies of tones—are built up. In dance, the melody and harmony of tones recede and the importance of rhythm increases. (p. 92)

—Rudolf Laban
in *Modern Educational Dance*

One of the pedagogical stumbling blocks for conductors is that it is impossible to "conduct" if there is no rhythm impulse within that gives birth to movement. For musicians, the physicalization of rhythm is often problematic, and it is often overlooked as a step in the development of conducting technique.

Rhythm Impulse and Conducting Are Inseparable

To show movement through physical gesture, one must first perceive that movement by moving in a larger, more physical way. Not only does Laban provide a framework for describing in very specific terms the movements we make as conductors to reflect sounds we hear in our audiation, but he provides a framework by which we can reawaken the full sensation of movement in *all* its dimensions. His approach using movement within various geometric shapes helps us to organize and perceive our own movement, and practice and experience the body moving in a much larger physical space than what we normally do as conductors. Before conductors can expressively react to sound, they must first acquire an "architectural vocabulary" of movement!

The material in this chapter, which draws from Laban's seminal work, *Modern Educational Dance,* provides the perfect model for both movement exploration and movement organization and self-perception. Just as conductors acquire rhythm patterns to become musically "literate," there is a movement "literacy" that must be acquired and/or revisited as well.

Eugene Corporon, my colleague and friend, has discussed the need for a basic regimen of exercises to keep one's technique clean, fresh, and expressive. One way to do this is to practice and move through and between the diagonals in Laban's cube to remain aware of one's movement space and to provide a beginning morphology for a larger world of movement. Even though our gestures as conductors occur on a smaller scale, the perception of ourselves moving in a larger movement world must always be perceived and felt for our gestural vocabulary to have any meaning.

Kinesthetic Oral/Aural

Given the history of research in movement perception and the self-perception of movement, the material presented in this chapter will quite likely be unfamiliar to most musicians. Musicians generally perceive music rhythm as a segmentation of division in time. And for most intents and purposes, that is an appropriate model. However, given the research and writings of Laban, we must as musicians alter our educational paradigm. If we are truly interested and committed to a pedagogy of rhythm, then we must begin outside ourselves in a larger movement and rhythm world, experience rhythm in a larger context, and then internalize that movement experienced through fantasy, imagination, and the music to be performed at hand.

I was recently asked about what movement activities one should do with an ensemble. Most pedagogies encourage us to do movement activities within one's personal space. Those personal movement pedagogies are crucial for the development of coordination (i.e., the work of Phyllis Weikart), but they do not create the world for a truly expressive rhythm vocabulary, either as an individual musician or a music ensemble. I had always stressed this type of personal movement in a somewhat *confined* personal space! But after revisiting the original writings of Laban, it is now clear to me that there can be no rhythm understanding without gathering a vocabulary of moving through a *larger* space.

The teachings and theoretical constructs of Laban encourage, and perhaps insist, that without teaching a larger architecture to move within, spatially limited pedagogies will have limited reward. Exploring one's personal space and moving through it could be considered as the *kinesthetic aural/oral* that must precede the oral/aural level of learning in rhythm teaching and learning. *Kinesthetic Oral/Aural must be experienced so musicians can associate the perceived space of their movement and associate that movement with harmonic movement.* Then and only then can rhythm performance achieve a level of honest and authentic expressivity.

Teaching the Architecture of Sound

> Sequences of movements can be performed so that each movement is directed to a certain point in the space round the body and change from one point to the next is harmonious and flowing, forming definite patterns. This means with a definite space orientation. These patterns may extend chiefly in the air around the body, when they are known as peripheral, or they may pass close to the body, and are more central in character. Patterns most frequently combine with central and peripheral movements. (p. 35)
>
> Dance as a sequence of movement can be compared with spoken language. As words are built up of letters, so are movements built up of elements; as sentences are built up of words, so are dance phrases built up of movements. This language of movement, according to its content, stimulates activity of the mind in a similar but more complex manner than the spoken word. (p. 26)
>
> —Rudolf Laban
> in *Modern Educational Dance*

If musicians are aware and listening, harmonic motion creates a vibrant architectural framework for rhythm. The aural realization of that remarkable framework can only be sounded in performance if one believes that rhythm exists in such a framework. Many persons have described architecture as music "frozen in time." Louis Kahn, the great American architect, once described all honest architecture as being first born in a dream and then realized by an architect in physical materials of mortar, stone, and steel. However, Kahn also said that if the architecture has any merit, in its constructed state, it returns the human experience to the original dream—hence, honesty and authenticity in architecture.

For rhythm to achieve such a state of honesty and authentic human expression, it must be dreamed and imagined in a larger architecture outside your inward self. Rhythm is propelled and shaped by the harmonic forces acting upon it. If you adopt this paradigm, then it follows that in considering a rhythm pedagogy, you must find as many ways as possible to conceptualize the space that rhythm occupies in your musical fantasy, and then bring that vocabulary of spatial fantasy to bear upon the harmonic message of the composer. Finally, it is the shape and trajectory of the very melody (both text and tune). itself that adds the final "element" to the performance of any rhythm.

Laban has made the teaching of this first architectural framework of rhythm stupendously simple and accessible. He describes this in No. 11 of his sixteen movement themes: *Themes concerned with space orientation*. His model allows musicians to conceptualize the space, or rather the dynamic architecture, of the musical phrase. One's perception of space and the perception of moving in and through space is fundamental to being able to associate a harmonic movement to a specific rhythm pattern or series of rhythm patterns. Viewed this way, rhythm pedagogy is able to teach the inherent multi-dimensional architecture of rhythm. In doing so, rhythm becomes an authentic, organic, and honest manifestation of the composer's intent! Laban clearly states these principles:

> Sequences of movements can be performed so that each movement is directed to a certain point in the space round the body and the change from one point to the next is harmonious and flowing, forming definite patterns. That means with a definite space orientation. These patterns may extend chiefly in the air around the body, when they are known as peripheral, or they may pass close to the body, and are more central in character. (p. 35)

Always Moving in Cross Dimensions: Space Orientation

In his book, *Modern Educational Dance* (1948), Laban clearly puts forth the principle that for any movement to be kinesthetically valid as a movement experience, body movements should involve diagonal movement that crosses at least two planes. This is a pedagogical game changer, because Laban clearly alludes that shifts in weight can only be "experienced" when we move in diagonals within his representational cube. Laban further writes:

> The themes of space orientation can be performed in small medium and large extension. The moving person can stop at any point on the way from the center to the most distant point he can reach. There exist, for example many points *bf,* distributed along the line *c* to *bf*. The distinction of a narrow *bf* (level with shoulders), a medium distance *bf* (level with forehead), and a wide *bf* (reaching as far as possible), will suffice for training purposes. The rhythm of the movements along orientation patterns can be chosen as one wishes, but it is advisable to start with regular time intervals, each stretch in space have the same time duration. (p. 37)

If you perceive yourself being placed within a cube, the space that surrounds you is organized in a clearly geometric arrangement.

Figure 5. Representation of self in the dimensions of a cube.

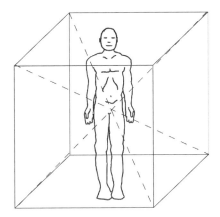

Using this geometric model, if one conceives of the possibilities of diagonal movement, the illustration in Figure 6 vividly represents the paths of *possible* movement.[91]

Figure 6. The paths of possible movement.

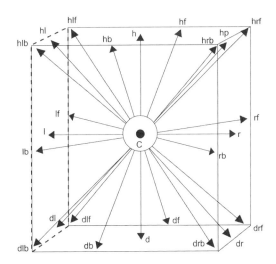

---

91   This illustration appeared in *Modern Educational Dance* (1948), on p. 36.

If one lists all of the possibilities for movement within the cube, the following list is the result:

Key to Abbreviations in Laban Diagonal Movement Path Cube

h = high d = down l = left r = right
b = backward f = forward c = center

hr	=	high right
db	=	down backward
lf	=	left forward
dr	=	down right
hb	=	high backward
rf	=	right forward
dl	=	down left
hf	=	high forward
rb	=	right backward
hl	=	high left
df	=	down forward
lb	=	left backward
hrf	=	high right forward
dlb	=	down left backward
hlf	=	high left forward
drb	=	down right backward
hlb	=	high left backward
drf	=	down right forward
hrb	=	high right backward
dlf	=	down left forward

CHAPTER 9
The Theory Underlying the Perceptions of Personal Space

The Distal Cross of Axis

The Door Plane

The Wheel Plane

Perceiving Your Personal Icosahedron

One of the challenges for anyone studying conducting is to not only gain an awareness of their body but to also acquire a geometric perception, if you will, of the space the body occupies and moves within. DaVinci was fascinated by the symmetries the body occupied in his rendering of the Virtruvian Man standing in both a square and a circle. DaVinci was preoccupied with Plato's idea that in three-dimensional space there were only five regular and perfect solids or crystalline figures in all of nature. Using both the ideas of Plato and DaVinci, Laban envisioned what the geometric space surrounding our bodies would be. He named that geometric shape as represented by the icosahedron (discussed below) as the *kinesphere*. The icosahedron, is, in effect, a cognitive map of the parameters of our movement. Without that map firmly in our perception, expressive conducting can never achieve a full range of movement based upon body use. The perception of the space one occupies in all its dimensions empowers and expands the possibilities of gesture that does, in fact, evoke sound.

Figure 7. Virtruvian Man (da Vinci).

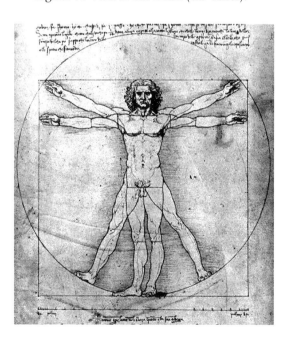

The Line of Embrace

Let us again consider the geometry, or rather the implied geometry and geometrical logic of conducting patterns. What should be the width of any conducting pattern at its widest and most *forte* point? Using an open embrace to mark the widest parameters of the width of a pattern, the line of embrace is clearly defined for each body type. You will notice on each conducting pattern the dotted lines that note the left and right parameters of the line of embrace. Aside from the human implications the line of embrace implies, the width of a conducting pattern that is maintained within these parameters helps maintain vowel colors. Conducting beyond the line of ictus, especially when both hands are involved, causes vowel sounds to become open and spread. Also, the roundness of this gesture tends to mirror an appropriate ribcage for singing, while the spaciousness under the arms encourages appropriate inhalation, exhalation, and breath support and usage by singers.

Figure 8. The widest point for any conducting pattern: the line of embrace.

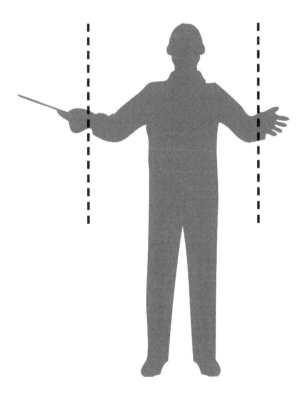

The Sound Membrane or Door Plane

Laban, when discussing the geometric delineations of the space we move in, defined one of the planes as a door plane. If you imagine a vertical surface in front of you similar to the height and width of a door, at a comfortable welcoming distance from your body, that imaginary vertical surface was called a *door plane* by Laban. For conductors, however, you must envision that door plane not as a solid mass, but rather as a flexible, large membrane that represents the sound itself.

It is important to conceptualize the vertical plane (or what I call the "membrane plane") directly in front of you. In the diagram below, the line represents a wall that can be likened to a flexible membrane, which represents sound. By visualizing such a vertical plane, you can begin to establish both a direct and an intimate connection with the sound, and hence, each singer in the ensemble.

Figure 9. Side view of embrace with the sound membrane or door plan.

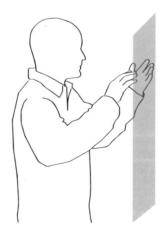

Simultaneous Conducting Planes: The Three Dimensional Planes

> The person who has learnt to relate himself to Space, and has physical mastery of this, has attention. The person who has mastery of his relation to the Weight factor of effort has Intention and he has Decision when he is adjusted to time. Attention, intention and decision are the stages of inner preparation of an outer bodily action. This comes about when through the Flow of movement, effort finds concrete expression in the body. (p. 251)
>
> —Rudolf von Laban
> in Jean Newlove and John Dalby,
> *Laban for All*

THE THEORY UNDERLYING THE PERCEPTIONS OF PERSONAL SPACE

Perception, or rather awareness, must be everything to a conductor. Awareness of body, awareness of the space in which one moves, and awareness of sound must function as simultaneous awarenesses. To acquire such an awareness, you must *want* to acquire that awareness. Awareness is truly a state that must be desired to be acquired. Of all the awarenesses that seem to be problematic for conductors, space seems to pose the most serious perceptual problems. Once understood, conducting "technique" can achieve fluidity, breadth, and expansiveness.

The illustration below shows in three dimensions the three planes that must be part of one's geometric perceptual apparatus at all times, as conceptualized by Laban and generalized here to conductors. One of Laban's unique gifts was his ability to summarize all movement possibilities into what he called a *dimensional cross* (shown below). The vertical plane should be perceived as the six points of balance comprising the core of the body. The horizontal, or table plane, is the line of ictus.

Figure 10. The three dimensional planes.

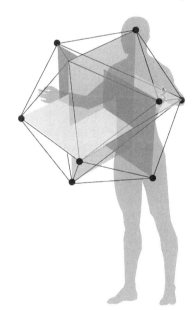

Once the perception of these three planes is understood, it is important for conductors to not only perceive the space in front of them but all of the space around them. When this is in place, the body's farthest points of exterior boundaries form a twelve-cornered geometry known as the *icosahedron*. The icosahedron represents the space possible for movement.

Figure 11. Icosahedron with door plane highlighted.

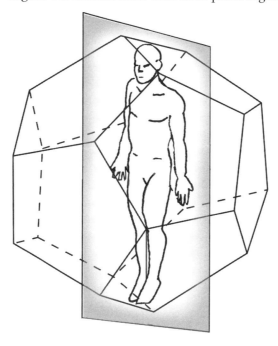

Figure 12. Icosahedron with wheel plane highlighted.

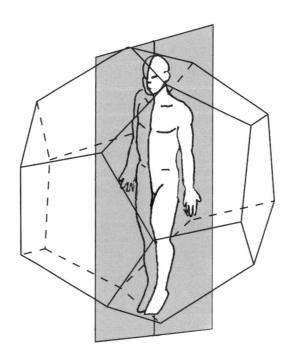

THE THEORY UNDERLYING THE PERCEPTIONS OF PERSONAL SPACE

Figure 13. Icosahedron with table plane highlighted.

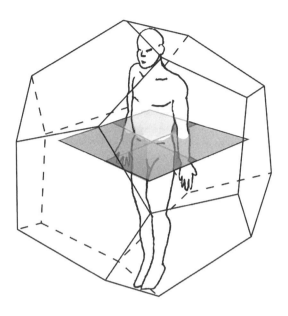

Figure 14. Icosahedron showing all three planes.

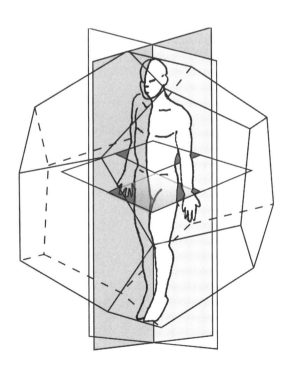

101

I have often observed conducting students who had great conducting facility and, in fact, good coordinative skills. But as I observed them, there was lack of cohesion in the conducting gesture. So I would always talk about becoming more "grounded," "connected to the earth," or being more "centered." While all those concepts improved the "gesture," there was always something eluding the pedagogy. There was an important connection that needed to be established between one's center and one's groundedness to the movement of one's arms. Center establishes a certain rootedness that gives some integrity to the gesture. Center and groundedness become a given rather than an exception in this pedagogical approach. But the truth of any conducting gesture ultimately lies in its spiritual core and the connectedness to the "inside" and "physical center to the hands through the arms via one's body. The concept that clearly connects and relates all movement into a functioning whole is the powerful concept of distal connection.

Connecting Core to the Distal Relationships of the Body

Gesturally, conductors function in the world of distal connections. That is, if their gesture has any meaning to the ensemble, they are somehow able to connect their "extremities (i.e., hands via the arms) to their core. Alexander Technique has taught us imagery that allows for a more direct connection of the arms to the core of the body[92] For example, Alexander Technique has taught us to perceive our arms as having no joints and that those arms connect to our bodies in the small of the back. While this image is extremely valuable in connecting our arms "to" our bodies, it generally is unable to ultimately connect our arms to the core of our bodies. Until that connection to core is made, gesture cannot be empowered to communicate directly to any ensemble.

The Starfish Connection

To understand this principle, envision the structure of your body like a starfish. Orient the starfish in your mind, with one point at the top and the other

---

92 This is assuming that the conductor has himself/herself correctly mapped using the principles of Body Mapping. Fundamental to all conducting gesture is an intimate understanding of one's body map, as presented on the *Evoking Sound* DVD (GIA, 2002) and in chapters devoted to those concepts in this text.

THE THEORY UNDERLYING THE PERCEPTIONS OF PERSONAL SPACE

points of the star being both arms and legs. Starfish move distally—that is, all of their locomotion grows out of their center, or rather through their center.[93] The starfish moves through what Laban calls a *dimension cross of axis*. In other words, the upper right hand should always be perceived as being connected with the lower left foot passing through the core of the body. The upper left hand should always be perceived as being connected to the lower right foot, establishing a connection to the core of the body by passing through it. Many conductors perceive their own movement as each arm connected to the trunk of their body. Their legs are attached in similar fashion to the trunk of the body. Because of this misconception, the limbs, especially the arms, look like moving appendages. Visually, this concept of the "X" of distal connection of opposite limbs can be depicted in the following way:

Figure 15. Distal connection of opposite limbs.

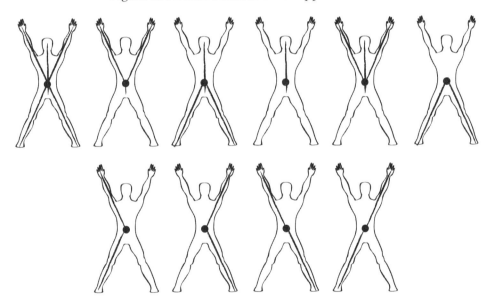

While the above representations are important to gaining an understanding of the interrelationship of our limbs to the core of the body, the image that is most powerful follows. This image represents one of the foundational concepts for conductors.

---

93 I wish to thank Lisa Billingham of James Madison University for introducing me to this concept. Dr. Billingham has completed a textbook for conductors, *The Complete Conductor's Guide to Laban Movement Theory* (GIA, 2009) that explores in depth this connectivity and others pertinent to the development of conducting technique.

Figure 16. Composite representation of distal connections.

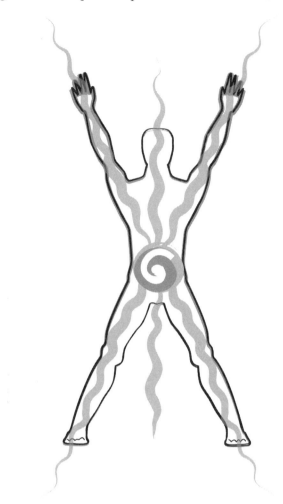

CHAPTER 10

Laban's Conceptions of Spatial Architecture Applied to Conducting

Motion comes from emotion. Children use kinesthesia to learn about their world. But Western education attempts to train the mind, and pays little attention to the kinesthetic sense.

—Robert M. Abramson
in *Dalcroze Eurhythmics,* video

While it has lately been popular in certain quarters to equate body movement with the "natural" and the "authentic" in human behavior, there is actually very little instinctive about the way we move. Due to the nature of the human brain, as mentioned earlier, voluntary movement must be learned through interaction with other human beings within a social context. Consequently, body movement is a highly structured, culturally-coded form of symbolic communication, equivalent in its sophistication to the better-known extension systems of language, music, mathematics, and so on. As part of the extended world, human movement has become an abstraction of the real, biological world. Paradoxically, body movement is at once natural *and* contrived, visceral *and* symbolic, personal *and* social, ever present *and* constantly disappearing. (pp. 84–85)

—Carol-Lynne Moore, Kaoru Yamamoto
in *Beyond Words*

Looking at the whole range of innate and acquired impulses of man, one is tempted to search for a common denominator. In my opinion this denominator is not mere motion, but movement with all its spiritual implication...What has to be done today—and our time seems to stand on the threshold of a new awareness of movement—is to acknowledge movement as the great integrator. This involves, of course, the conviction that movement is the vehicle which concerns the whole man with all his physical and spiritual facilities. To be able to see this great unity is not the privilege of the artist alone. Everybody, every single individual, has this unity as the basis of his natural tendencies and impulses, which can be lifted out of the treasure of forgotten truth and cultivated in all the various ramifications of life. (pp. 12–13)

—Rudolf von Laban
in *The Laban Art of Movement Guild Magazine*

What one experiences through movement can never be expressed in words; in a simple step there may be a reverence of which we are scarcely aware. Yet through it something higher than just tenderness and devotion may flow into us and from us. (p. 35)

—Rudolf von Laban
in *A Life for Dance*

Laban's use of the word *weight* has special significance to rhythm. To perform a crusis with appropriate weight, we need to prepare the crusis in audiation. Just as we need to shift the weight in our body to prepare for a jump, so we must shift the weight in our body in the preparation of a crusis, that is, in our performance of the anacrusis. Unless we can effect this kind of rhythmic jump with our body weight, we will not be able to audiate or to properly perform an anacrusis, and consequently, a crusis, because an anacrusis must incorporate the same feeling for a crescendo, an upward shift of weight, that is characteristic of a jump. Moreover, without a feeling for relative weight and the ability to shift our weight at will, we would not be able to sustain movement appropriately, and without sustained movement there can be no feeling for space and flow. To engage properly in bound sustained flow in performance, we must be audiating unbound sustained flow. (p. 177)

—Edwin E. Gordon
in *Learning Sequences in Music*, 1997

Chapter 10

LABAN'S CONCEPTIONS OF SPATIAL ARCHITECTURE APPLIED TO CONDUCTING

> From its birth, music has registered the rhythms of the human body of which it is the complete and idealized sound image. It has been the basis of human emotion all down the ages. The successive transformations of musical rhythms, from century to century, correspond so closely to the transformations of character and temperament that, if a musical phrase of any typical composition is played, the entire mental state of the period at which it was composed is revived; and, by association of ideas, there is aroused in our own bodies the muscular echo or response of the bodily movements imposed at the period in question by social conventions and necessities. If we would restore to the body all rhythms it has gradually forgotten, we must not only offer it as models the jolting, rioting rhythms of savage music, but also gradually initiate it into the successive transformations which time has given to these elementary rhythms. (p. 7)
>
> Musical rhythmic movement consists of linking up durations, geometry consists of linking up fragments of space, while living plastic movement links up degrees of energy. (p. 10)
>
> *Economy and balance:* such should be our motto. We must economize our nervous expenditure, which expresses itself in angry starts, sudden, irregular, impatient movements, depression, hypersensitiveness. We must economize our time, cease work before the point of fatigue is reached, anticipate the moment when rest becomes necessary. And we must economize our will to progress, moderate our appetites, and balance our desires of creation with the means at our command. (p. 12)
>
> —Emile Jaques-Dalcroze
> in *Eurhythmics, Art, and Education*

It goes without saying that conducting is movement, and vice versa. As conductors, our movements relay our innermost rhythm, musical line, and textural colors. At times our movement courts the singers to move their sound in response to our gesture, and at other times, our conducting mimes the sound that is in our inner musical fantasy world. The ability to move freely is a prerequisite for the study of conducting. The ability to reacquaint oneself with the infinite vocabulary of movement is an essential readiness for conducting. The body must be reacquainted with its full movement potential so that through movement one can elicit, evoke, excite, awaken, mirror, court, and reflect the sound of each piece.

As children, each one of us experienced the *entire* world of movement. In our play, we ran, we jumped, we swung. We leaped and rolled and tumbled, skipped and hopped. We moved by ourselves and with others. We played circle games. Play was movement. Serious play was on the playground and in the home. Life was play, and play was movement. Movement was our lives. As we grew older and more mature, we began to move less and less. Play became a less prominent part of our life. Movement no longer "felt" natural and spontaneous. As our bodies grew, we moved less and less. The world we grew into did not encourage movement. Consequently, we settled upon a limited, yet efficient movement vocabulary that would get us through our day-to-day life.

Can that spontaneous movement of early childhood be rediscovered? Yes! Is that rediscovered movement world necessary for the development of the beginning conductor? Yes. The work of Rudolf von Laban can reawaken life movement experiences so they can be used in conducting.

Rudolf von Laban

Rudolf von Laban was born in 1879 in Bratislava, Hungary, the son of an army general. His early years were preoccupied with observing movement. As a child, he spent considerable time drawing and visualizing patterns in space. His desire to understand both physical and mental effort led him to a lengthy course of study in painting, sculpture, and stage design in Paris, Berlin, and Vienna. As part of his training, he studied various cultures, particularly the natives of Africa, the people of the Near East, and the Chinese.

In 1910, Laban founded his first dance group and school in Munich, where he developed one of his favorite genres, the movement choir. During World War I, he lived in Switzerland and continued to develop his ideas. In 1919, he formed a stage dance group, the Tanzbuhne Laban, which specialized in expressive dance. Through that ensemble, he created many full-length dance compositions (*The Swinging Cathedral, Die Geblendeten, Gaukelei, Don Juan,* and *Die Nacht*).

In 1926, he founded the Choreographic Institute in Wurzburg, which he later moved to Berlin. That institute specialized in the development of a dance notation system, originally known as Eukinetics, which was published in 1928 as *Kinetography*. In the United States, his work is known as *Labanotation*. He became director of movement at the Berlin State Opera in 1930 and subsequently was recognized as one of Europe's most famous choreographers.

Unable to continue work under the Nazi regime, Laban and some of his pupils sought sanctuary in the United Kingdom. Laban introduced Modern Educational Dance into the schools as a new creative subject. In Manchester, England, where he lived from 1942 to 1953, he helped establish the Art of Movement Studio with Lisa Ullman. Concurrently, he established the Laban-Lawrence Industrial Rhythm, which developed new approaches for the selection, training, and placing of workers, in addition to developing working processes based upon the movement of man. Through that work, Laban developed the effort graph as a means of recording the kinesthetic quality of individual performance in industry.

In 1946, the Laban Art of Movement Guild was formed. That guild supported the training center for movement study and educational dance based upon Laban's concepts. Laban lectured on a regular basis at his studio, and at the same time he lectured at colleges and universities.

In 1953, Laban moved to Addlestone, Surrey, where he established archives for his own work and the work of the Art of Movement Studio. In 1954, the Laban Art of Movement Centre was formed as an educational trust to perpetuate his work and to promote and provide education in the art of movement. He continued to work at Addlestone until his death in 1958.

Philosophical Basis of the Work of Laban

For Laban, the act of moving was a link between the physical and mental experiences of life. He believed that through the act of moving, one experienced an interaction of mind and body. He also believed that movement was everywhere; movement could be seen, organized, and understood in a still leaf, in a child at play, in a simple walk, and through all aspects of our daily lives.

To Laban, the central issue underlying the understanding of movement was that persons needed to visually, physically, and internally experience the energy of movement, and then develop the ability to describe those movement experiences. He believed that after helping a person recall experiences from his or her "movement thinking," that person could enrich his or her movement vocabulary by experiencing similar experiences. For example, Laban believed that a person could recall movement experiences from earlier in life. The person could (a) be helped to recall the total experience of skipping, (b) be guided to make a self-analysis of his or her skipping, and (c) provide a vocabulary that describes the experience of skipping to heighten the skipping experience. Laban believed that everyone experiences all the subtleties and complexities of movement during early childhood, but that not everyone recalls all of those movements in later life.

Part of the Laban Movement Analysis is to identify which specific movement experiences a person is not recalling and then provide prescriptive movement instruction to reawaken those movements in that person. Those who instruct and guide movement must have experiences in a comprehensive variety of movement themselves to effectively diagnose, prescribe, and teach movement. Moreover, to teach movement with meaning, movement experiences should be guided through the use of specific movement themes, known as the *Efforts in Combination.*

But considering the Efforts in Combination, it is important to understand the theories of Laban concerning how the body is organized geometrically. Part of our awareness as conductors begins with understanding our own use of space as we move, and the parameters of our personal movement space, or kinesphere.

Using the Architecture of the Body to Conducting Advantage

One of the challenges for anyone studying conducting is to not only gain an awareness of the body but also acquire a geometric perception, if you will, of the space the body occupies and moves within. Leonardo da Vinci was fascinated by the symmetries the body occupied in his rendering of the Virtruvian Man standing in both a square and a circle. He was preoccupied with Plato's idea that in three-dimensional space there were only five regular and perfect solids or crystalline figures in all of nature. Using both the ideas of Plato and da Vinci, Laban envisioned what the geometric space surrounding our bodies would be. He named that geometric shape as represented by the icosahedron, the *kinesphere.* The icosahedron is, in effect, a cognitive map of the parameters of our movement. Without that map firmly in our perception, expressive conducting can never achieve a full range of movement based upon body use. The perception of the space one occupies in all its dimensions empowers and expands the possibilities of gesture that does, in fact, evoke sound.

Simultaneous Conducting Planes: The Three Dimensional Planes

> The person who has learnt to relate himself to Space, and has physical mastery of this, has attention. The person who has mastery of his relation to the Weight factor of effort has Intention and he has Decision when he is adjusted to Time. Attention, intention and decision are the stages of inner preparation of an outer bodily action. This comes about when through the Flow of movement, effort finds concrete expression in the body. (p. 251)
>
> —Rudolf von Laban
> in Jean Newlove and John Dalby,
> *Laban for All*

Perception, or rather awareness, must be everything to a conductor. Awareness of body, awareness of the space in which you move, and awareness of sound must function as simultaneous awarenesses. But to acquire such awareness, you must *want* to acquire it. Awareness is truly a state that must be desired to be acquired. Of all the awarenesses that seem to be problematic for conductors, space seems to pose the most serious perceptual problems. Once understood, conductors can achieve fluidity, breadth, and expansiveness in their conducting technique.

In looking at Figure 17, you can see in three dimensions the three planes that must be part of one's geometric perceptual apparatus at all times (as conceptualized by Laban and generalized by this author for conductors). One of Laban's unique gifts was to be able to summarize all movement possibilities into what he called a *dimensional cross*. The vertical plane should be perceived as the six points of balance. The horizontal, or table plane, is the line of ictus.

Figure 17. The three dimensional planes.

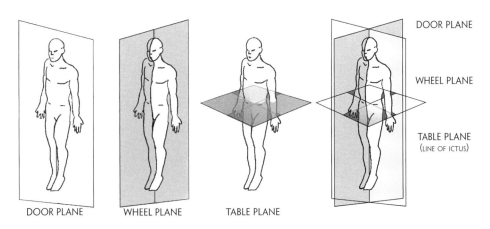

Once the perception of these three planes is completed, it is important to perceive those planes not only in front of you but also cutting through you to the back. When this is in place, the body's farthest points of exterior boundaries form a twelve-cornered geometric known as the *icosahedron*. (See Figure 18.) In other words, it is important to perceive not only the space in front of you but all of the space around you that forms your space for movement when conducting. The icosahedron represents the space possible for movement.

Figure 18. Icosahedron showing all three planes.

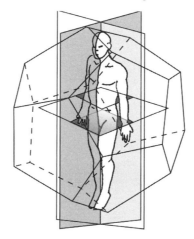

A simpler perception for awareness of space for conductors is to visualize the icosahedron simplified into the dimensions of a cube. (See Figure 19.) Imagine the potential for movement by exploring all spaces within the cube. This awareness allows for a more inclusive use of space when conducting.

Figure 19. The dimensions of the cube as a precursor to a perception of icosahedron.

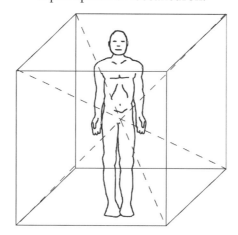

LABAN'S CONCEPTIONS OF SPATIAL ARCHITECTURE APPLIED TO CONDUCTING

Chapter 10

The Laban Effort Elements: Flow, Weight, Time, and Space

Movement is more than a change of location of the body or a change in the position of the body limbs. There are changes in speed, changes in direction, changes in focus, and changes in the energy associated with different movements. Consequently, there is constant fluctuation in levels of exertion. Laban defined exertion in movement as the interrelationship of Flow, Weight, Time, and Space, which he called the *Effort Elements*. For each of the four Effort Elements, Laban identified a pair of extremes, which he called "qualities," with the idea that the quality of each element of a given movement could be described in relation to its placement on a continuum that extends between those two extremes.

Flow is the variation in the quality of bodily tension that underlies all of the Effort Elements. The extremes of Flow are free and bound. *Free Flow* allows body energy to move through and out beyond the body boundaries without any restriction. Ideal free Flow movement is difficult to stop. A person experiencing total free Flow would be difficult to stop; that person would be weightless and unhampered by tension. *Bound Flow* movement is restrained and can be stopped easily; it forces a person to contain energy within the body boundary. A person experiencing extreme bound Flow would be tense to the point of being motionless. Between the two extremes of free Flow and bound Flow are infinite gradations of tension.

Weight is the sensation of force or burden exerted in a movement. The extremes of Weight are light and strong. *Light Weight* can be described as delicate and overcomes the sensation of body weight. *Strong Weight* is forceful and uses the sensation of body weight to make an impact. People must sense the quality of their movements as being either light or strong. Central to a person's understanding of their movements, and consequently rhythm, is the ability to sense involuntary changes in one's own body weight, as well as the ability to change Weight at will.

Time relates to the expenditure or duration of time in a movement. The extremes of Time are sustained and quick. *Sustained Time* is prolonging, lingering, or decelerating. *Quick Time* contains a sense of urgency and rapidity. For musicians, the Effort Element of Time is closely related to tempo.

Space is the manner in which energy is focused in a movement. The extremes of Space are either direct or indirect. *Indirect Space* involves a flexible but all-encompassing attention to the environment. *Direct Space* involves a channeled, singularly focused awareness of the environment. The element of Space is closely related to the concept of focus. Is the space in which a movement takes place focused or spread? Do all body parts focus to a central point, or are they dispersed?

Finally, one might think of the Effort Elements of Flow, Weight, Time, and Space as the how, what, when, and where of movement.

Experiencing the Efforts in Combination

It is easiest to gain an understanding of the Effort Elements through their various combinations, as suggested by Laban. It is difficult to experience Flow, Weight, Time, or Space separately. By adjusting the relative intensities of Flow, Weight, Time, and Space within an activity, you can relate an infinite variety of movement possibilities.

Laban assigned an action verb to each combination of three Effort Elements. Central to his theory is the simultaneous concentration on the three elements of Weight, Space, and Time taking over, or predominating, changes in Flow. Laban's action verbs, which describe combinations of the Effort Elements, along with movement examples for each verb, are shown in Figure 20. The abbreviations denote S = Space, W = Weight, and T = Time.

For each of the Efforts in Combination, the elements of Time, Space, and Weight interact to produce the illusion of Flow. That is, the perception of one's rhythmic and gestural Flow is a by-product of the interaction of Time, Space, and Weight. Flow cannot exist alone. It is the result of infinite combinations of Time, Weight, and Space, which produces an infinite variety of movement. The genius of Laban is the ability to observe how the combinations of Time, Space, and Weight can be varied to produce what is perceived as Flow. These principles are important for conducting to make you aware of the infinite potential of your own movement, to reawaken movement within yourself that may not have been used since childhood, or to reawaken movement that may not be part of your current life experience.

Figure 20. Laban Efforts in Combination to describe movement.

LABAN ACTION VERB	QUALITIES (ELEMENTS)	MOVEMENT EXAMPLES
FLOAT	indirect (S) light (W) sustained (T)	• treading water at various depths
WRING	indirect (S) strong (W) sustained (T)	• wringing a beach towel
GLIDE	direct (S) light (W) sustained (T)	• smoothing wrinkles in a cloth, • ice skating
PRESS	direct (S) strong (W) sustained (T)	• pushing a car
FLICK	indirect (S) light (W) quick (T)	• dusting off lint from clothing
SLASH	indirect (S) strong (W) quick (T)	• fencing • serving a tennis ball
DAB	direct (S) light (W) quick (T)	• typing • tapping on a window
PUNCH	direct (S) strong (W) quick (T)	• boxing

Laban did not specifically assign names to each of the eight combinations. The names of *flick*, *dab*, etc., have grown from the wide body of Laban practitioners who have found these labels useful and in keeping with the integrity of Laban's philosophical beliefs. Laban did believe that language could be more exacting about the action than it could be for the more subtle shades of experience. Transitions occur when a person moves between Effort actions by changing one of the Effort Elements. For example, one may progress from *punch* (direct/strong/quick) to *press* (direct/strong/sustained). Transitions often involve the changing of a single component; it is possible, however, to change two or three components simultaneously.

Laban believed that to become adept with movement, a person should develop a daily routine of exploring the Efforts in Combination. In the initial stages of movement exploration, the "labeling" and understanding of the Effort Element content in everyday life activities provides the foundation of movement understanding because it grows out of one's personal experience. Laban believed that we all experienced a complete spectrum of movement possibilities as children, but we have forgotten those movement experiences because the routine of our daily lives has minimized our daily movement experience. For each of the Efforts in Combination, there are suggestions for life activities that would reawaken that particular Effort Combination within conductors. (See Figure 21.) Mime each of the suggestions for each category and discover how a change in one or more of the individual Effort Elements changes the movement. Add your personal experiences to each list.

Figure 21. Experiences of Efforts in Combination.

FLOAT

indirect (Space)
light (Weight)
sustained (Time)

- tracing a picture with a pencil
- floating in a pool on your back
- vaulting over a high bar by means of a pole
- using a bubble wand
- spraying a room with air freshener
- lying on a waterbed
- falling into the first moments of sleep
- reaching for an unfamiliar cat
- staggering
- swinging on a rope swing
- blowing bubbles
- Other:

WRING

indirect (Space)
strong (Weight)
sustained (Time)

- twisting a washcloth dry
- twisting sweater dry
- twisting hair in the morning
- twisting a face cloth
- drying out a sponge
- twisting off a bottle cap
- opening a cardboard can of prepackaged cookie dough
- washing socks
- playing with a hula hoop
- drying your hands under a blower
- tightening a jar cap
- turning over dirt with a trowel
- squeezing juice from an orange
- twisting a twist tie on a garbage bag
- using a screwdriver
- pulling out the stem of an apple
- spinning a dreidel
- opening a can of sardines
- using a melon baller
- opening a stuck faucet handle
- massaging a muscle
- Other:

PRESS

direct (Space)
strong (Weight)
sustained (Time)

- kissing a child gently
- pushing a shopping cart loaded with groceries
- ironing a shirt
- pressing a button on a drink machine
- pushing a child on a swing
- squeezing a tennis ball
- pressing on the floor when doing a handstand
- closing an overloaded suitcase
- pushing a lawnmower in high grass
- pushing a lawnmower uphill
- using a paper cutter
- using a hole punch
- pushing in a laundromat coin cartridge
- moving a piano
- pedaling a mountain bike uphill
- applying the brakes on a car
- kneading dough for bread
- removing a childproof cap
- walking with an umbrella against the wind
- washing a window with a squeegee
- stapling papers
- using a clothespin
- ringing a doorbell
- pushing in a thumbtack
- using a screwdriver
- packing trash in a filled garbage bag
- using a mechanical hand drill
- going through a revolving door
- closing a car trunk lid when the trunk is very full
- making mashed potatoes
- buckling a seat belt
- Other:

GLIDE

direct (Space)
light (Weight)
sustained (Time)

- reaching to shake hands
- wiping up a spill with a paper towel
- pushing off from the side of a pool and moving forward
- ice skating
- erasing a blackboard
- dusting or wiping off a table
- drawing a violin bow across one string
- spreading butter or jelly on toast
- gently scratching your arm
- sliding down a banister
- coasting down a hill on a bicycle
- roller blading or roller skating
- throwing a paper airplane
- sliding in socks on a newly polished floor
- painting a wall with a roller
- opening a sliding glass door
- smoothing sheets when making a bed
- dusting furniture with a feather duster
- putting a ring on your finger
- closing a zip-lock sandwich bag
- turning a page in a book
- smoothing cement with a trowel
- water skiing or snow skiing
- icing a cake
- drawing a circle with a compass
- playing a glissando on a piano
- dusting
- sliding on an icy sidewalk
- shaving
- Other:

DAB

direct (Space)
light (Weight)
quick (Time)

- putting the final touches on the frosting of a cake
- tiptoeing
- playing darts (moment the dart is released from the hand)
- using a paintbrush to make dots
- poking someone's arm with a finger
- dipping a cloth in a pail of water
- breaking a balloon with a pin
- knocking ash off a cigarette
- dotting an "i"
- applying antiseptic on a small cut
- tap dancing
- pushing a button on a remote control
- typing
- finger-painting
- using touch-up paint
- testing hot water with your finger
- cleaning cobwebs from the ceiling
- powdering on make-up
- using white glue
- cleaning a child's sticky mouth
- placing a cherry on a sundae
- Other:

FLICK
indirect (Space)
light (Weight)
quick (Time)

- removing an insect off the table
- turning a light switch on or off
- leafing through the pages of a book
- lightly keeping a balloon in the air
- brushing debris off your desk or table
- shooing a fly
- wiping sweat from the brow
- shooting marbles
- touching a hot stove
- throwing a frisbee
- snapping your fingers
- opening "flip top" toothpaste
- brushing snow from a windshield
- lighting a cigarette lighter
- taking a basketball foul shot
- striking a match
- folding egg whites
- throwing rice
- popping soap bubbles
- Other:

SLASH

indirect (Space)
strong (Weight)
quick (Time)

- swinging a baseball bat
- fencing
- casting a fishing line
- golfing
- opening a cardboard carton with a utility knife
- wielding a knife like a butcher
- tearing a piece of paper
- using an axe to chop wood
- slamming a door
- shaking catsup from a new bottle
- employing self-defense maneuvers
- sweeping a sandy floor with a push broom
- beating a hanging rug clean
- cutting vegetables
- Other:

PUNCH
direct (Space)
strong (Weight)
quick (Time)

- plumping a pillow
- boxing
- using a punching bag
- applauding loudly
- hammering a nail
- pounding a fist on a table
- striking a stapler to get the staple in a hard wall
- digging a hole
- Other:

Notice that a variation of one or more of the qualities will result in a different intensity of the movement experience. After experiencing the Efforts in Combination shown in Figure 21, perform the imagery exercise below. Without pause, perform quickly each pair of movements shown. If the exercises are performed correctly, you will feel a sudden shift of energy between the two movement experiences of each pair. Perform each exercise first with external body movement and then with no external body movement so you can internalize the various combinations of movements and, more important, the changes in energy between the two movements in each combination.

Movement Imagery Exercise:

Punch / Press
Punch / Slash
Punch / Dab
Slash / Wring
Slash / Flick
Wring / Float
Wring / Press
Float / Flick
Float / Glide
Glide / Dab
Glide / Press
Dab / Flick

The combinations of Elements attended to simultaneously are difficult to name. Laban referred to combinations of two factors (Elements), however, as an *incomplete effort*. Those combinations are also referred to as *inner attitudes* because the combination of only two Elements suggests the movement is not yet externalized but, instead, expresses a state of feeling Laban refers to in *The Mastery of Movement* (MacDonalds and Evans, 1960): "It is difficult to attach names to these variations of incomplete Effort as they are concerned with pure movement experience and expression." (p. 92) The verbal descriptions are not precise, and they are always subject to movement validation. For each combination of two factors, a person can combine the Elements in four different ways. These combinations are known as *states,* or *drives*. All possible combinations of the six groups are shown in Figure 22. The italicized labels beneath the Elements are the commonly used labels for the states, or drives. Remember that the descriptive terms in italics attempt to generally mirror internal feelings—not movements.

Figure 22. Combinations of two Effort Elements into states, or drives.

SPACE & TIME (*Awake*)	**WEIGHT & TIME** (*Near Rhythm*)	**WEIGHT & FLOW** (*Dream*)
indirect/slow indirect/quick direct/slow direct/quick	light/slow strong/slow light/quick strong/quick	light/free strong/free light/bound strong/bound
SPACE & FLOW (*Remote*)	**FLOW & TIME** (*Mobile*)	**SPACE & WEIGHT** (*Stable*)
indirect/free indirect/bound direct/free direct/bound	free/slow free/quick bound/slow bound/quick	indirect/light indirect/strong direct/light direct/strong

Whether you are just beginning your conducting study or you have considerable experience, the movement categorizations of Laban can provide valuable assistance in solving many issues. If you experience and understand the Efforts in Combination, then you begin to experience and re-experience various feelings of weight. To be able to provide gestures that evoke sound, you must be able to "extract" weight from your gestures at will. The feeling of weight in one's body is produced from an overexertion of the musculature on the bone structure. This overly muscular effort restricts your natural rhythm impulse, which translates to retarded or impeded airflow (support) within the singers. Most importantly, however, muscle rigidity and tenacity (weight) negatively affects one's ability to hear. The ability to remove weight from your conducting gesture by relaxing your muscles is a valuable tool for conducting.

Connecting Sounds to Gesture: Sounding Musical Line

The chart shown in Figure 23 will also be referred to the next chapter. When used in that chapter, the skills and associations built upon its use at this stage of the conductor's development will be found to be of great importance.

Once you have gained a theoretical understanding of the Efforts in Combination and have further related those Effort Elements to movement experiences in your life, you have assembled a valuable "vocabulary" of gesture to be associated with musical sounds. Understand that what I am advocating here is *not* to mime the music you conduct, but rather to apply an alive kinesthetic vocabulary that is the kinesthetic quality of the sound being produced by your ensemble. As you begin to learn (or refine) conducting patterns using the Swiss ball, it is vitally important that you make sounds with your body that are living, sounded examples of how the sound moves forward for that particular Effort! The sounding of the musical line using the syllables shown in Figure 23 creates an indelible bonding of gesture to sound. When conducting gesture is learned in this way, an intimate bonding (or rather, an alchemy) of sound to gesture is created. That bond of kinesthesia through these voiced syllables will create an alive and meaningful vocabulary of conducting gesture that will forever be connected to sound and kinesthesia. It is important to understand that gesture learned devoid of sound voiced by the conductor will never have the desired reaction upon an ensemble.

When practicing your conducting gesture, start with the Effort pairings shown in Figure 22, and associate the appropriate voiced sound with that Effort. Then arbitrarily apply the Efforts to the pattern. For example, take a legato four beat and do two beats of *glide* (represented by the sound "ss") followed by two beats of *dab* (represented by the sound "t"). Take the framework of a marcato pattern and perform two beats of *punch* (represented by the "CH" sound) followed by two beats of *press* (represented by the "v" sound).

Figure 23.
Laban Efforts in Combination to describe movement and resulting sound.

Laban Action	Time	Gestural Conducting Translation	Weight	Descriptive Syllable	Musical Sound Analogies
Float	Sustained	Indirect	Light	f	Whole tone No weight Repetitive passages.
Wring	Sustained	Indirect	Heavy	zh	Diminished chords Chopin Prel., Op. 28, No.20
Glide	Sustained	Direct	Light	s	Line Phrase
Press	Sustained	Direct	Heavy	v	Bagpipes Feminine Cadence
Flick	Quick	Indirect	Light	~ pft	Grace notes Textures requiring lightness
Slash	Quick	Indirect	Heavy	z	sfz Accents
Dab	Quick	Direct	Light	t fast tempo p slow	Staccato
Punch (side-arm)	Quick	Direct	Heavy	CH phy	with some degree of sustainment that is not tenuto
Dab/ Press*	Sustained briefly	Direct	Light-Heavy	m	Tenuto
Punch/ Press*	Sharp attack, sustained	Direct	Heavy	hwh *a la* Lamaze breathing	Marcato

* Hybrid combination of Laban efforts to simulate movements needed to play tenuto and marcato.

Summary

Laban's theories of movement can help conductors reacquaint themselves with their movement potential. Rhythm, which comes from a source within us, can be manifest as external movement. That external movement can be labeled to help us appreciate the infinite possibilities and experiences of rhythm manifest as movement. Rhythm is a manifestation of tension and release that provides point of reference commonly referred to as *meter*. Rhythm phrases, then, are movement manifestations of the Efforts in Combination. But more importantly, a realization of the energy of the Effort Elements within us is actually a manifestation of color through rhythm.

The vocal color of a choir is directly affected by one major factor: the *breath* of the conductor. Within that breath, the rhythmic life of a piece is transferred to the choir. The rhythmic nature of the breath transfers the conductor's rhythmic opinion directly to the choir. That rhythmic (movement) vocabulary can be expanded through the conductor's facility with the Efforts in Combination.

Other Laban Organizations

The Dance Notation Bureau
New York

The Language of Dance Centre
London

LABAN
London

Laban/Bartenieff and Somatic Studies Canada
Toronto

Laban-Related Organizations

Center for Kinesthetic Education (CKE), NYC, coordinated by CMA Martha Eddy, www.WellnessCKE.net

Dance Education Laboratory of the 92nd St. Y, coordinated by CMA Jody Arnhold

Motus Humanus, coordinated by CMA Carolyn-Lynne Moore

Moving on Center, Oakland, CA, www.MovingOnCenter.org

School of Body-Mind Centering®, coordinated by CMA Bonnie Bainbridge Cohen's

Laban-Related Programs and Projects

Associazione Laban/Bartenieff Italy – coordinated by CMAs Maria Consagra and Lorella Rapisarda, www.labanbartenieff.it

European Laban/Bartenieff Program – coordinated by CMA Antja Kennedy

Integrated Movement Studies – coordinated by CMA Peggy Hackney

Istituto Laban/Bartenieff Italy – program coordinated by CMA Richard Haisma, www.istitutolabanbartenieff.it

Motivating Moves, CMA Janet Hamburg's work with a variety of populations, including people with Parkinson's

CMA Suzi Tortora's work with young children

Lims' Partner Organizations

Danspace Project, an international leader in the commission and presentation of contemporary dance/ Partners with LIMS for the presentation of MOSAIC.

CSV Cultural Center collaborates with LIMS for the development of the PERFORMANCE ATELIER.

NASD is an organization of schools, conservatories, colleges, and universities that establishes national standards for undergraduate and graduate degrees and other credentials. LIMS is an accredited institutional member.

NDEO is an organization dedicated to promoting standards of excellence in dance education. LIMS is an institutional member.

The CMA List is an online meeting point for CMAs from all over the world. LIMS strongly advises you to join the list and be current with the last theory discussions, events, and programs. http://listserv.cc.denison.edu/wws/info/cmalist

About LMA, Wikipedia entry on **Laban Movement Analysis.**

PART 2
The Impulse to Move:

Harmonic Rhythm

CHAPTER 11

Harmonic Progression: The Genesis for Movement

Marcel Tabuteau said: "I have always been in favor to play as I think. Of course, the ideal combination would be to play with *thinking* and *intelligent feeling*."

—Marcel Tabuteau
in David McGill,
Sound in Motion

I have often heard people say that music making is "intuitive." And to a certain degree, I would tend to agree. However, I have begun to think that music making is, to a large degree, "intelligent feeling." For conductors, there is a lurking danger within the melodic rhythm of what we conduct. I often see my conducting students gravitate toward the "rhythm of the melody" to arrive at information that may inform their conducting gesture. For conductors who remain in that realm, the conducting is certainly adequate, and some respects could be considered expressive.

This book is devoted to making an interpretive application of the work of Laban to the art of conducting gesture. Laban is certainly a way to expand our expressive vocabulary. But that vocabulary will have little use unless we couple it with musical thought or, as Marcel Tabuteau stated, "intelligent feeling."[94] For conductors, what qualifies as "intelligent feeling"?

To begin to process this, there are several important issues to consider.

The Importance of Harmonic Rhythm

Melodic rhythm and harmonic rhythm engage in a kind of dance in every piece we conduct. While you can certainly hear one without the other, conducting gesture must find its roots in harmonic rhythm. Harmonic rhythm as a term of study and focus has differing emphasis depending on the teacher. Walter Piston first brought our attention to the inherent magnetism and direction inherent in chord progression. Hindemith and Schoenberg also wrote about its power, and actually based much of their compositional approach on the structuring of what was called *harmonic rhythm*. In teaching conducting, I have found that the key to conducting gesture that evokes the composer's intent is the conductor's ability

---

94   For those unfamiliar with the name of Marcel Tabuteau (1887–1966), he was the principal oboist of the Philadelphia Orchestra from 1915–1954. He taught at the Curtis Institute for over thirty years. His influence to this day over countless musicians is based upon the system of musical phrasing he taught, which is carried on to this day by his students and succeeding generations of students. His teachings are best described in a wonderful book by David McGill, *Sound in Motion*.

to audiate harmonic rhythm first, and then also audiate melodic rhythm. The two are like partners in a musical dance; they must be heard concurrently by the conductor. But it is the harmonic rhythm that gives us clues as to what Laban Efforts will lead to the forward motion of phrases as well as their appropriate tension and release. It is, as Tabuteau said, "intelligent feeling."

So what is felt? In Chapter 4, Watson illuminated for us the theory that rhythm is perceived through movement in our joints. To carry this idea one step further, that "motion" in our joints is informed directly by the harmonic rhythm in the pieces we conduct. If we do not audiate harmonic rhythm, then our gesture will lack a certain degree of expressivity that relates to the music at hand. If we audiate harmonic rhythm, then we can consider the vocabulary of gesture we have acquired through experiencing the Efforts in Combination and select those movement energies that will cause the sound to move forward in a musical way. Yes, it is a type of "intelligent feeling" where we audiate the harmonic rhythm, perhaps illuminated through score study, and then intelligently apply Laban Efforts into our conducting technique. The proof of the success of our audiational interaction with our Laban gestural imaginative vocabulary is the sound created in our rehearsals and performances. But make no mistake about it…it *is* the harmonic rhythm that informs and *musically validates* our movement as conductors. Our perceptual system within our bones and muscles is complex and sophisticated. To truly audiate harmonic rhythm, we must make choices about which Efforts might best evoke the composer's intent from our ensemble.

> Three forces important to harmonic progression are the linear motion and outline of outer voices, the pull of harmonic or tonal centers and the relationships of chords, and the time duration of stressed and unstressed chords. Coupled with these forces are graded tensions of texture and pitch and the rhythm created by phrasing, bowing, and tonguing indications. (p. 212)
>
> Harmonic rhythm is the underlying rhythm that plays a large part in controlling and stabilizing musical flow. (p. 212)
> A melodic line, whether an inner or outer voice, often acts as a directional guide for harmonic progression. (p. 185)
> Harmonic progression is affected by the degree of dynamic nuance in which it is conceived. (p. 226)
>
> —Vincent Persichetti
> in *Twentieth Century Harmony*

> A true musician believes only in what he hears. No matter how ingenious theory is, it means nothing to him until the evidence is placed before him in actual sound. (p. 156)
>
> —Paul Hindemith
> in *The Craft of Musical Composition, Vol. 1*

With all the necessary components in place—rhythm patterns performed and audiated, a kinesthetic envelope established, and movement to those rhythm patterns learned and audiated by movement through diagonals—now "phrasing" can be added, almost as another layer to any rhythm pattern.

Harmonic progression is what holds all the messages for us as musicians. In Laban terms, harmonic progression informs our decisions on when to Press, when to Glide, when to Dab, and when to Flick. If rhythm is motion personified in sound, then it seems to follow that harmonic progression holds the inherent kinetic formula for all phrasing decisions. It is our awareness and sensitivity to the miracle of harmonic progression that holds the essences for us as musicians of the "how" of musical phrasing.

Hierarchy of Chord Progressions
(as suggested by Arnold Schoenberg)

At the beginning of the twentieth century, Arnold Schoenberg suggested that there is an hierarchical structure of chord progressions; some progressions strike our audiation stronger than others. Obviously, the hierarchy of strength he suggests affects the phrasing intent of the rhythm that occupies those progressions. Schoenberg calls upon the acoustic properties of sound to support his strength hierarchy. My friend Gerald Custer, a composer, conductor, and theorist, shared a bit of a lecture on the subject and offered it to be used as part of this discussion:

> One of the greatest musical minds of the twentieth century, Arnold Schoenberg said that melodic harmonization is one of the hardest assignments in music theory, and one of the most artificial, because in real life composers seldom write melodies and harmonies apart from one another. Schoenberg, himself a noted theorist and teacher, was absolutely right: we don't.

So why do some sequences of chords strike our ears as satisfying, while others do not? What is it that allows a particular series of sonorities to balance the need for music to remain interesting over time but still somehow hang together, meeting the competing demands of diversity and unity?

Part of the answer is found in the Harmonic Series, a practical application of the law of physics known as the *principle of vibrating strings*. If you sound the note C, for example, it will generate a rising series of harmonics or overtones that will always be the same: C, G, C, E, G, B-flat, and C. In other words, the intervallic movement this series outlines is: up an octave, up a fifth, up a fourth, up a major third, up a minor third, and up a second. In scale degree terms, it moves from ^1 to ^1, ^1 to ^5, ^5 to ^1, ^1 to ^3, ^3 to ^5, ^5 to ^b7, and then back to ^1. The Harmonic Series is purposeful…goal-oriented…not random. It goes somewhere. All music follows this pattern, flows from this order.

Said another way, music is fundamentally intentional. It starts out somewhere, moves away from the point of origin, and ultimately returns to where it started. Sequences of chords that reflect this reality and map onto the order of the universe given in the Harmonic Series are called "progressions" because they make forward progress; they go somewhere. We have been hard-wired by thousands of years of evolution to expect this pattern. When we hear sequences that match it, they're normally more satisfying to our ears than ones that don't.

Alongside this underlying structural order, consider a second reality: there are only three ways to connect two chords. They will either be related to one another by root motion of a fifth or a fourth, by root motion of a third, or by root motion of a second (just like the intervallic order in the Harmonic Series). No matter where we transpose things or which inversions of triads we use, in the end there are just three choices: up or down a fifth or fourth, up or down a third, and up or down a second.

Root motion by a fifth (or its inversion, the fourth) is the favored choice among these three because it offers the best balance between unity and diversity—since it always has one common tone. It can be found in a variety of places in the scale, and is called a "strong" progression by Schoenberg. Here are some examples of strong progressions:

I–V	vi–iii		I^6–V	I–V^6
ii–vi	I–IV	and	I^6_4–V	I–V^6_4
IV–I	ii–V			
V–ii	iii–vi			

(as are all their transpositions, like ii^6–vi, ii^6_4–vi, and so forth)

and I^6–V^6
     I^6_4–V^6
     I^6–V^6_5 (and all their transpositions)

Don't miss this point: regardless of what inversion you use, the motion of the *roots* of each of these progressions is by a P5 or P4. Therefore, they are all "strong" progressions. It doesn't matter whether they're written in root position or some inversion; it's the relationship between the roots of the chords that is determinative.

Now consider root motion by a second. Schoenberg calls this a "super-strong" progression because the second chord completely obliterates the first. When the second is sounded, nothing remains in the mind's ear of the first sonority. Said another way, root motion by the interval of a second has no common tones. It's all diversity and no unity. There's nothing in common, no carryover. That's what makes this progression so powerful (and why it should be used less frequently—sparingly, in fact).

Here are super-strong progressions in a major key:

I–ii	IV–V
ii–iii	V–vi
iii–IV	VI–vii°

As before, it doesn't matter which inversion (or inversions) you happen to use: as long as the roots are a second apart, they still create a super-strong progression. So these are also super-strong progressions:

I–ii^6	I^6_4–ii
I^6–ii	I^6–ii^6
I–ii^6_4	I^6–ii^6_4

and so are all the transpositions that start on other degrees of the scale:

$$\text{iii}^6\text{–IV, etc.}$$

Finally, there is the progression where the two thirds are a third apart (higher or lower). These sequences have not one but two common tones: more unity than diversity here. In fact, they are almost the same chord, with only one note actually different. That's why jazz musicians typically think of them as "substitution" progressions (a term I prefer to "semi-strong," which is what Schoenberg calls them):

$$\begin{array}{ll} \text{vi } \textit{for } \text{I} & \text{ii } \textit{for } \text{IV} \\ \text{iii } \textit{for } \text{V} & \text{vii}° \textit{ for } \text{V} \end{array}$$

And because it is the root relationships that matter (not the inversions), these are all substitution progressions as well:

$$\begin{array}{ll} \text{vi–I}^6 & \text{vii}^6_4\text{–I} \\ \text{vi–I}^6_4 & \text{vi}^6\text{–I}^6 \quad \text{and so on} \\ \text{vi}^6\text{–I} & \text{vii}^6_4\text{–I}^6_4 \end{array}$$

The Intentionality and Imperatives of Harmonic Progression

Harmony has clear directional intention. That directional intention determines and interacts with the phrasing of the rhythm that is part of that musical whole. In some ways, musicians take harmonic progression for granted, many times as an afterthought because of the power of the melody and text upon us as musicians. Authentic musical phrasing must take all of these elements into account. Phrasing of rhythm mirrors the intent of the harmonic structure, the architecture of the melody, and the implied movement in sound of the entire composite! But those decisions begin with acknowledging the message buried within harmonic progression. The ebb and flow, tension and release, color and dissonance all should contribute strongly to a conductor's first phrasing inclinations. Harmonic structure and the awareness of its messages hold many of the musical messages from the composer who conceived the music you perform. An intimate and immediate awareness of harmonic progression is everything in a world of honest, authentic, and beautiful musical phrasing.

So for Laban to be used with musical meaning, gestural decisions must grow out of harmonic rhythm. Harmonic rhythm, if studied and audiated, gives definitive information to how the music moves forward. Armed with that information, conductors can then choose from their Laban gestural vocabulary to make the music live. The integrity that grows out of the marriage of harmonic rhythm and the Laban Efforts in Combination should not be underestimated.

Explanation of Exercises in Skill Set Eight

Later in this text, you will find musical exercises set out for your use. The exercises in Skill Set Eight were designed so harmonic movement would determine what specific Effort in Combination could possibly be used when conducting the exercises. The pedagogical purpose of those exercises is to begin your own audiation of harmonic progression, and harmonic "weight," and to see how that audiation influences the choice you make about which Laban Effort or Efforts to use. The exercises were specifically designed to train you to arrive at an Effort choice that grows out of the harmonic language and harmonic syntax of what you are to conduct. These exercises are invaluable for linking sound with conducting gesture and providing a solid introduction to the harmonic/gestural relationship conductors must adopt.

PART 3
States and Drives

CHAPTER 12

Portal to Expressivity: Laban's States and Drives for Conductors

GISELLE WYERS

> Designing trace-forms in the air with only the extremities can lead to a kind of external form of writing. (p. 49)
>
> —Rudolf von Laban
> in Irmgard Bartenieff,
> *Body Movement*

This chapter serves as an introduction to Laban's states and drives. Laban's *states* are defined as a combination of two effort elements, and *drives* are a combination of three effort elements. To review, effort elements consist of Weight (strong or light), Time (quick or sustained), Space (direct or indirect), and Flow (bound or free). In this chapter are exercises designed to help conductors explore each effort element separately, and then combined within states and drives. In addition, the chapter presents a guide to score study and listening, with the goal of identifying likely states and drives to be utilized.

A Preface to This Chapter

Geoffrey Boers

At 3:30 in the afternoon, it is time to open the door to my office as that marks the beginning of our University Chorale rehearsal, led by Dr. Giselle Wyers, just down the hall. Beautiful, healthy vocalise gives way to phrases of music sung by the choir, all seasoned with joyful noises of knowing laughter and active learning. Her rehearsals are a joy to behold and that to which we all aspire—engaged faces and joyful spirits at every point in the rehearsal process, from sight-reading to performance. Her singers describe the process as "transformational."

How does she do this? And how can each of us create this dynamic and expressive learning environment? Giselle Wyers, one of our nation's leading proponents of the application of Laban technique in rehearsal, provides compelling insight into this process in this chapter. An exploration of efforts leads to a greater awareness of how our "signatures of movement" hold meaning and reveal identity. To learn Laban is to discover self. To uncover the deeper layers of Laban's system becomes a psychological and emotional journey, a path that can lead toward transformation.

PORTAL TO EXPRESSIVITY

Chapter 12

Laban technique is proving to be a profound tool to assist choral conductors and teachers in many ways. In this chapter, Wyers describes how she is able to diagnose a student's movement "signature," build students' awareness of how they move, and help students unlock new ways of expressing themselves. Laban's language can help beginning conductors, instrumental and choral alike, to create an organic sense of connection between movement and sound, helping them to communicate music even amidst their first awkward gestures.

Laban seeks to dissect movement patterns and the associated mental and emotional states we all share. Teachers can use Laban's system to diagnose movement defaults and behaviors in students' (or our own) conducting, and help find ways to move that build musical and expressive ideas in the ensemble. Much is being written by leading researchers and pedagogues about Laban efforts—that is, the basic building blocks of movement that describe sound and sensation in a physical way. Wyers uses this knowledge as a point of departure to lead us into a deeper understanding of the combining of these efforts, first by twos, then by threes, and even suggests four (!) to help us explore deep application of this method in teaching of conducting and choral singing.

This method is powerful and densely layered, and Wyers is an ideal writer to lead us through a potentially thorny path. She helps us negotiate the layers and combinations of understanding with an easy pace and clear logic. After a brief review of the basic efforts and their combinations into drives and states, she quickly leads us into thinking about the psychological and emotional states attached to these efforts and their combinations. She explores each aspect of these states by experience. She gives us suggestions and personal anecdotes, questions, and images to lead us to experience Weight, Flow, Space and Time—experience that leads to a physical, emotional, and musical *knowing*.

The experiential knowing of the efforts then leads us into an easy introduction of states (two efforts) and drives (three efforts). This is a moment in the Laban journey that some might find challenging, but Wyers again allows us to easily experience states as we learn them with her colorful language, helpful listening exercises, and games she has gleaned from a certified Laban instructor.

Most importantly, Wyers then applies this learning to our experience on the podium. She gives us tips for score study, introducing our choir to varied states and efforts, and moving "beyond the pattern" into deeper levels of expressivity. She addresses the need for our choral culture to consider moving into more expressive conducting, yet in a disciplined and technical way. She helps give shape to our listening, to not just hear the choir or the music but to listen for these efforts and combinations—to hear deep layers of expression and meaning.

Studying, moving, listening, and being—Giselle Wyers is leading us to be more complete conductors. We can hear in her rich language and see in her vibrant teaching that she has been impacted by these techniques to the core of her being, not only as a conductor but as a human. May we all be inspired and moved toward this kind of transformation.

—G.B.

Review of Single Effort Elements

Laban conceived of effort as the inner intent of the mover. Effort is affective in character, bringing a certain quality of feeling to the person moving and those who are watching the movement. For Laban, movement was always about meaning. Along with Warren Lamb, the creator of Movement Pattern Analysis (or Action Profiling), Laban created a description of the "idea" behind each effort element. These ideas help stretch meaning beyond the movement itself and into the perspective of the mover.

Effort Elements:
Weight, Space, Time and Flow

Weight (strong or light):
- Is concerned with intention
- Asks the question: What?

Space (direct or flexible/indirect):
- Is concerned with attention
- Asks the question: Where?

Time (quick or sustained):
- Is concerned with commitment (or decision making)
- Asks the question: When?

Flow (bound or free):
- Is concerned with progression (or continuity)
- Asks the question: How?

Direct, strong, quick, and bound movements are identified by Laban as "fighting" motions. Indirect, light, sustained, and free movements are identified as "indulging" motions.

Later in the twentieth century, Jungian concepts were ascribed to Laban efforts to suggest a psychological function for each effort element.

> Weight is about Sensing (bodily)
> Space is about Thinking
> Time is about Intuiting
> Flow is about Feeling

Effort States

Effort States combine two elements. There are eight possible combinations in each state.

Awake: Space and Time
Direct Space/Quick Time, Direct Space/Sustained Time, Indirect Space/Quick Time, Indirect Space/Sustained Time

Dream: Flow and Weight
Light Weight/Bound Flow, Light Weight/Free Flow, Strong Weight/Bound Flow, Strong Weight/Free Flow

Remote: Space and Flow
Direct Space/Free Flow, Direct Space/Bound Flow, Indirect Space/Free Flow, Indirect Space/Bound Flow

Rhythm: Time and Weight
Quick Time/Strong Weight, Quick Time/Light Weight, Sustained Time/Strong Weight, Sustained Time/Light Weight

Mobile: Time and Flow
Quick Time/Free Flow, Quick Time/Bound Flow, Sustained Time/Free Flow, Sustained Time/Bound Flow

Stable: Space and Weight
Direct Space/Light Weight, Direct Space/Strong Weight, Indirect Space/Light Weight, Indirect Space/Strong Weight

Effort Drives

Effort Drives combine three elements. The Action Drive is considered the most basic of the three drives, while Passion Drive, Vision Drive, and Spell Drive are "transformations" adding Flow and removing one of the other elements.

Action Drive: Weight, Time and Space (lacks Flow):
Dab, Flick, Slash, Punch, Glide, Float, Wring, Press

Passion Drive: Weight, Time, Flow (lacks Space)

Vision Drive: Time, Flow and Space (lacks Weight)

Spell Drive: Flow, Space, Weight (lacks Time)

Full Effort Action

A full effort action would combine four effort elements simultaneously. It occurs in rare, highly dramatic circumstances.

Reviewing Single Effort Elements: Suggested Exercises

During effort training, it is crucial that the conductor *move*. Laban's system was conceived for dancers to explore a wide palette of movement possibilities and was never intended to exist only as a mental abstraction. Just as conductors cannot master baton technique through imagination alone, effort elements must be experienced physically in order to be useful.

Consider this quote from Neal King Bartee as inspiration as you embark on your training:

Doing movement creatively stimulates the mind. When the conductor practices movement for its own sake or practices imaginatively in response to musical patterns, his awareness of the possibilities of expressive movement can be increased."[95]

Experiencing Weight: Strong and Light

Weight is primarily about "sensing," and that "sense" is physical, based on experiencing an inward awareness of the muscles of the body working, and emotional, moving with a quality of self-conviction and intent. There are three kinds of Weight sensation:

1. **Light Weight** – where weight is present but in a light, delicate fashion

2. **Passive Weight** – where the conductor is not actively engaging the muscles much and is less aware of them, and

3. **Strong Weight** – where pressure and exertion are present

In my experience, young conductors often have trouble differentiating between strong Weight and bound Flow, or between passive Weight and strong Weight. The following exercises focus on these differences.

Strong Weight

Strong Weight is experienced as pressure executed with the muscles or with the actual physical weight of the body. It should be felt as energy being expended *outwards,* as opposed to inbound flow, where the energy is sensed to be pulling *inwards.* Feel strength, assertion, or willpower. Stay focused on the physical sensations more than on the space around you.

Using strong Weight can be extremely useful for conductors whose movement signatures include swaying back and forth, leaning forward and back frequently for non-musical reasons, or for conductor personalities who are less

---

[95] Neal King Bartee, "The Development of a Theoretical Position on Conducting Using Principles of Body Movement as Explicated by Rudolf Laban" (PhD diss., University of Illinois at Urbana-Champaign, 1977), 152.

likely to be comfortable asserting their ideas on the podium. Strength can be exhilarating to experience when linked to a specific musical intent. Weight is not always "strong" and does not always have to be present in the arm muscles (it may be more perceptible in the legs).

> **Strong Weight Exercise:**
> - Close your eyes to access a personal inward focus on the muscles in your body.
> - Bend your knees and exhale your air with urgency and depth, feeling the pressure of your leg muscles as you work with gravity in exertion.
> - Focus on your feet, push your hands down. Imagine sending energy through your pelvic girdle, your legs and feet.
> - Push something heavy, such as a shopping cart filled with groceries, a lawn mower, or a piece of furniture.
> - Pick something up that is heavy, such as a full suitcase.
> - Dig a hole in the ground, turning over heavy clumps of soil.
> - Intensify the dynamic in the chorus by using strong Weight.

Light Weight

Light Weight is experienced as being "inside the body's sensation," but in a delicate, graceful, or even fragile way. Let your hands be loose at your side, for a second using Passive Weight. Then allow them to slowly "float" upwards, feeling fluid, light, without heavy pressure, with a sense of buoyancy, as though you are suspending something very fragile from your wrist. Imagine picking up a hummingbird, or a goose down feather. Imagine how lightness of pressure executes the skill more usefully than any heavy motions.

All conductors should experiment with "going into lightness." Too often conductors tend towards executing strong Weight on a steady basis or using passive Weight with bound Flow. Light Weight opens up a kaleidoscope of possible sensations, among them good humor, joy, gentleness, excitement, anticipation, trust, innocence, and openness to fully experiencing the physical sound of the music.

Light Weight Exercise:
- Imagine you are carbonated, full of little bubbles.
- Fan imaginary smoke from in front of your face (slowly).
- Pick up a robin's egg.
- Brush the fine hair off of a child's face.
- Pet a kitten.
- Feel soft fabric.
- Reach for a pebble in a pool of water, feel the smoothness of the stream.
- Look at a leaf blowing in the wind and imagine what it would feel like to be that leaf.
- Blow the seeds off a dandelion; notice the lightness of the seeds as they scatter loosely in the wind.
- Feel yourself being compliant, *allowing* sensation rather than attempting to consciously *create* sensation.

Experiencing Flow: Bound and Free

Flow is related to intuition, feeling, and continuity. Because conductors early in their training often cannot distinguish between Weight and Flow, I have juxtaposed their descriptions. Notice just how different these sensations are from one another. When you practice, attempt to move quickly from Weight to Flow. This subtle difference will take time to feel, but it is well worth the effort.

Flow exists along a continuum of free Flow to bound Flow. It would be rare to linger at either edge of the continuum. A completely free Flow sensation would be that of an object unimpeded by gravity (for instance, riding a bike down a steep hill without using brakes), while a fully bound sensation would be that of a person curled fearfully in fetal position. Conducting gestures exist in the middle of the continuum, and the following examples should be interpreted as being near the middle but slightly to the left or right of center.

Bound Flow

Bound Flow is associated with the need to feel in control and is characterized by a quality of withholding energy or resisting something or someone. Using bound Flow brings a quality of caution or restraint to movement.

Bound Flow Exercise:
- Delicately thread a needle, trying to get the thread through the tiny eye.
- Draw a line precisely in a mechanical diagram. Imagine you are an architect preparing a diagram and the proportions need to be perfect.
- The next time you are outside and are very cold, notice how you tend to hold yourself tightly by pulling your muscles close together.
- Imagine you are trying to open a tightly screwed peanut butter jar or loosen a rusty bolt.
- Carefully measure some chemicals in a lab, knowing that if you add too much or too little the experiment will fail.
- Anything that must be done in a contained amount of space begins to feel like bound Flow (controlling your movements in a tight space).
- Put a large dog on a leash while it is excitedly moving about (they are in mobile state, a combination of Weight and Flow). Although the dog is in strong Weight and *free* Flow, you could match strong Weight with *bound* Flow to successfully attach the leash to its collar.
- Withhold words in an argument. You want to say something but choose to be discrete.
- Try to not cough or sneeze; pull your energy inwards.
- Peel an orange.
- Carry something really full without spilling it (bound Flow, strong Weight).
- Lift a spoonful of soup to your mouth (bound Flow, light Weight).
- Help the soprano section to control the volume of an exposed, soft melodic line.

PORTAL TO EXPRESSIVITY

Free Flow

Free Flow is momentum unchecked in movement or emotion. It should feel simple, relaxed, and open, as though you are willingly yielding to the gesture without care or concern. For example, a dancer in free Flow is speeding across a stage, opening his/her arms, spinning in circles.

> **Free Flow Exercise:**
> - Ride a bike or skateboard down a steep hill without the brakes! Feel the exhilaration!
> - Fling your arms around quickly and shake your hands lightly. Free gestures lack tension, so if you are moving slowly there is still a sense of looseness in the movement.
> - Swing slowly up and down on a swing. Notice the free Flow on the way down.
> - Walk down the street with an easygoing manner. You're feeling fine today and there is nothing to worry about.
> - It's the first day of summer vacation! Run down to the lake and jump in!

Combinations of Bound and Free Movements

In everyday life and conducting, free and bound sensations often occur in close proximity. These exercises suggest how one aspect gives way to another.

> **Combined Movements Exercise:**
> - Swing a bat (bound Flow on the swing back, released into free Flow on the swing itself).
> - Prepare for a race (you are bound, then you quickly burst into motion).
> - Shake a small rug to get the dust out (combination of binding and freeing to create momentum in the shaking).
> - Walk a tightrope carefully (bound); jump off to the ground (free).
> - Conduct a fermata with *piano* dynamic. You are lightly bound as you hold the chord, freeing with the cutoff.

Experiencing Space: Direct and Indirect

Space refers to our orientation to the world around us, and is about thinking or paying attention. Most conductors are trained to be in "direct Space" at all times. However, there are times when the music may suggest a wider, more disparate focus (indirect Space) or require us to briefly abandon our focus on Space.

Space is concerned with a conductor's various planes of movement (what Laban termed the *wheel, door,* and *table planes*) but can also suggest inner space in our imagination as they sense dimension or texture in the music and bring that out in the gesture. Some music is very pictorial, conjuring three-dimensional images with little coaxing, while other music feels more abstract or two-dimensional.

Direct Space is about clarity in thinking or movement. It is useful when cueing a section, focusing an articulation, or demanding an ensemble's heightened attention. Indirect Space attempts to encompass an entire room at once to bring the group to the conductor. Remember that direct Space signifies *resisting,* while indirect or flexible Space signifies *indulging.*

Direct Space Exercise:

- After intense concentration, you have solved the math problem! Aha!
- Scrape a small speck of toothpaste off the bathroom mirror (direct, light, quick).
- Cue a single instrument in the orchestra.
- Focus your eye on the clock in the back of the rehearsal hall to see how much time is left.
- Refine your ictus as you approach a tempo change (direct).
- Magnify your inner concept of the sound as you conduct. Try to make it louder inside your ears.

PORTAL TO EXPRESSIVITY

Indirect Space Exercise:
- Daydream; allow your mind to fog up for a minute.
- Draw circles and curves with your arms (cheironomy is in indirect Space).
- Move freely across a room as you swing your arms.
- Pan a wide landscape with your eyes.
- Attempt to bring every member of the choir into your gaze all at once.
- With strength and sustainment, stretch your arms out into the kinesphere, as though you are royalty addressing a large group in a speech.
- Sweep your arms using curves of motion to encourage fluidity and forward momentum in your singers.
- Open up your ears to what you hear around you; soften your focus visually to allow aural acuity to improve.

Combined Space Exercise:
- Draw the entire choir into your gaze before beginning a piece (indirect). Cue the pianist to start (direct).
- Swing your head around to respond to a sound you heard (indirect movement). Key into that sound with your visual focus (direct).
- Using your finger, scan a bookshelf while searching for specific title (indirect). Point to the one you found (direct).
- Try to remember where you left your keys (indirect). Now you remember; they are on the table (direct).
- Create an accent with your ictus (direct), then bring your arms wide in an open embrace of the sound (indirect).

"Out of Space"

Being "out of space" occurs when the conductor chooses to focus on other elements besides Space, such as Weight, Time, or Flow. Being "out of space" can be difficult for conductors to try, considering their sense of obligation to attend to their ensembles. However, a conductor who allows himself/herself to focus on internal space issues an invitation to the ensemble to concentrate on Weight, Time, or Flow as expressive elements, and perhaps find a more subtle and genuine interpretation.

> **Out of Space Exercise:**
> - Try shutting your eyes for a brief moment in the midst of conducting a phrase. Notice whether this aids or hampers your choir's ability to be expressive.
> - Meditate on how much energy you put out into your choir as you work. Is it balanced with their energy output, or off balance? If you find yourself acting always as the "energizer" in your work with an ensemble, challenge yourself to go "out of space" occasionally, feeling the music inside with as much vigor as you project a musical concept.
> - Focus more on the auditory and less on the visual even while keeping your eyes open. If this is difficult for you to do, look slightly above the heads of your singers for two bars, then directly back at them. It can be difficult to hear well when encountering a live ensemble's visual stimulus.

Experiencing Time: Quick and Sustained

Of Laban's four effort elements, that of Time is emphasized over any other in conventional conducting textbooks. Executing consistent tempi and knowing how to speed up and slow down is obviously a non-negotiable skill for all conductors to master. However, Laban's definition of Time is somewhat broader than what most conductors are used to. Time is related to a quality of decisiveness, and the mover decides how to move, whether in a lingering, leisurely fashion or with urgency and quickness. For this reason, musical tempo is not necessarily coupled with Time in the Laban system. A musical tempo might be quite rapid, while the conductor's gestures will be sustained (perhaps the work is notated in 4/4 but the conductor is in "2"). Or perhaps a minimalist work leads the listener to feel sustainment while the conductor is concerned with managing rapid sixteenth pulses in quick Time.

> **Quick Time Exercise:**
> - Fling a dart across the room.
> - Rush to answer the phone—it's going to be good news! Or in contrast: Turn off the cell phone at the concert—it's disturbing the players!
> - Bounce a superball. Chase it across the room when it bounces away.
> - Push the button on your car key to activate the lock.
> - Jump into a swimming pool.
> - Shout someone's name from far away.

> **Sustained Time Exercise:**
> - Linger at the library, shelf-reading.
> - Sip a cup of tea without feeling rushed.
> - Stretch out your arms above your head, and hold for ten counts.
> - It's a difficult choice: should you order the merlot or the cabernet?
> - Sing a long melodic line without taking a breath.
> - Prolong a musical cadence; let the dynamic develop fully before the cutoff.

> **Combined Time Exercise:**
> - Use a yo-yo, noticing the alternation of quick "flicking" motions and that of sustainment.
> - Rapidly fire off a typed email (quick). Stretch and yawn while still at the computer, glancing out the window (sustained).
> - Run to catch the bus! Sit quietly and read a book once you've boarded.

Efforts in Combination: States

After considering the effort elements in isolation, it is logical to begin to combine them. In any movement, at least two effort elements are present at the same time. For instance, tapping on a window can be considered quick while also being light and quick. Laban organized two effort elements into six *states:*

1. Dream
2. Awake
3. Mobile
4. Stable
5. Remote
6. Rhythm

These are listed below as polar opposites: Dream is the opposite of awake, and so on.

Dream State: Pairs Weight with Flow. (W/F)
Awake State: Pairs Space with Time. (S/T)

Remote: Pairs Space with Flow. (S/F)
Rhythm: Pairs Time with Weight. (T/W)

Mobile: Pairs Time with Flow. (T/F)
Stable: Pairs Weight with Space. (W/S)

Below are some examples of how each state "feels" either in the body or in the imagination. These descriptors are designed to help you as you explore *ideas connected to movement,* because Laban intended each state or drive to be linked to inward concepts.

Dream State

Dream state takes one's awareness away from the environment (Space) and elements of Time, and instead draws the mover inward to Weight (focused on the body) and gradations of bound vs. free Flow. The sensation is one of "a dream" in that there is little perception of time passing, and one is focused inwardly, not on one's surroundings. To feel this state, initially close your eyes. With an inward focus, you are controlling and/or freeing your feelings (Flow) with a sense of lightness or pressure in the body (Weight).

You may feel strong Weight/bound Flow (controlled conviction, "I will not budge!"), light Weight/free Flow (effervescent joy and possibility, like you are spinning around quickly and playfully), bound Flow/light Weight (union with another in an embrace), or free Flow/strong Weight (Tai Chi movements). As you move, remove any metric or defined sense of Time, either sustained or quick. As you continue to vary the pacing of the movement, you will be more likely to access variations in Flow rather than Time. If you open your eyes, keep an inward focus on your body rather than being drawn "into space."

Dream State Listening:
- Palestrina "Agnus Dei I" from *Pope Marcellus Mass*
- Anton Bruckner "Sanctus" from *Mass in E Minor*

Awake State

As the title suggests, awake state is the opposite of "the dream." It emphasizes qualities of Space (awareness of environment) and Time (quickness or sustainment). The sensation is that of gradual or sudden realization, following a hunch or experiencing an epiphany. To feel this state, open your eyes, engage with the outside world, be decisive (quick Time) or inquisitive (sustained Time).

There is a certitude and clarity experienced even if the movements are sustained. Awake state can be quick Time/direct Space (chopping vegetables with precision, cueing tympani), quick Time/indirect Space ("What is that sound? Is someone calling my name? Shh… be quiet so I can hear…."), sustained Time/direct Space ("I see a dollar bill on the pavement, I want to pick it up before someone else does, I am moving slowly and directly towards the bill…"), or sustained Time/indirect Space ("I'm walking on the street at night, gradually I'm becoming aware that someone is behind me, I'm going to turn slowly to see who it is…")

Awake State Listening:
- Josquin des Prez *El Grillo*
- Charles Stanford *Beati Quorum Via*

Mobile State

Mobile state engages the body in variations of bound Flow vs. free Flow and variations of Time. Because both Time and Flow may be fluctuating and there is a lack of orientation to Weight or the Space around you, it is a very active, instinctive, and perhaps even disoriented, way of moving.

Mobile state may be quick Time/free Flow (you have walked through a cobweb and are rapidly brushing your hair free of the cobweb with a sense of disorientation; collapsing into fits of giggles), sustained Time/free Flow (floating in water; roller skating), quick Time/bound Flow (shivering in cold weather; hammering a small nail into the wall), sustained Time/bound Flow (drawing away from someone in embarrassment; pulling into yourself).

Mobile State Listening:
- Carlo Gesualdo *Ahi, disperata vita*
- John Tavener *Song for Athene*
- Benjamin Britten *Flower Songs, Movement 1* ("Fair Daffodils")

Stable State

Stable state focuses on the opposite effort elements as found in mobile state—that of Weight and Space. Here you make your presence known with clear structure, either using power and strength (a kingly procession), or using lightness (the belle at the ball enters down the staircase). A parent disciplining a child, "Eat your vegetables!" is in stable state, exerting his/her Weight in direct dialogue with the child, while the child's reaction, that of wiggling in discomfort at the table, is in mobile state. Imagine marching in a procession (direct Space/strong Weight), turning a heavy crank (indirect Space/strong Weight), picking a piece of lint off your jacket (direct Space/light Weight), or balancing a wine glass on the palm of your hand (indirect Space/light Weight).

Stable State Listening:
- William Billings *Africa*
- J. S. Bach "Gloria" from *B Minor Mass*

Remote State

Remote state is concerned with Flow (binding or freeing) and Space (direct or indirect). Flow is about feeling, and Space is about thinking. You are either freeing or controlling your thoughts while examining a variety of options. Perhaps you are ruminating too long about a project that needs to be completed or solving a math problem with great concentration (bound Flow/direct Space), feeling distracted or paranoid (indirect Space/bound Flow). Conversely, a "positive" association of indirect/free could be thinking creatively about something (brainstorming; being in the flow of a writing project; surfing the internet). To feel direct Space/free Flow, try staring at a tree while "spacing out." You are still engaging with the environment by looking at something intently, but your mind is free to wander. Indirect Space/free Flow might be accessed when you look around your environment with no particular goal (strolling through an art museum; taking in the sights at the Space Needle, or for an extreme example, jumping out of a plane as a skydiver).

Remote State Listening:
- Arvo Pärt *Magnificat* (first minute, after which some gradations of weight begin to emerge, taking it into dream state)
- Steve Reich *Proverb*

Rhythm State

Perhaps the archetypal view of a conductor is that of a person moving in rhythm state. Here, one is working with gradations of Time and Weight. Varying Time and Weight is frequently mentioned in conducting textbooks, variations of Time for obvious goals (rubato, accelerando, decelerating), varying Weight for contrasts in dynamics or articulations. Weight is about sensing, and Time is about deciding, but because rhythm state is "out of space," the sensation is less about thinking or intellectualizing than one might feel in awake state. A quick/strong movement is smashing a can with your foot. A sustained/strong movement is pulling on a rope in tug of war. A quick/light movement is playing the snare drum. A sustained/light movement is petting a cat that is lying in the sun.

Rhythm State Listening:
- Michael McGlynn *Dulaman*
- Igor Stravinsky *Credo* (mass)

Efforts in Combination: Drives

Laban defined a *drive* to encompass three elements of movement. Rather than memorizing a drive for what three elements it contains, it may be simpler to memorize what is *not* emphasized or present in the movement.

Action Drive:	Lacks Flow (S, T, W)
Passion Drive:	Lacks Space (W, F, T)
Vision Drive:	Lacks Weight (S, T, F)
Spell Drive:	Lacks Time (S, W, F)

For a more in-depth look at the states and drives with corresponding "inner attitudes," consult Vera Maletic's workbook, *Dance Dynamics: Effort and Phrasing*.[96]

Action Drive (Space, Time, Weight)

The action drive is useful for executing specific movements requiring "clear spatial attending, an intentional use of Weight, and a good sense for Time,"[97] where gradations of Flow are not necessary or even ideal. Laban defined eight action drives in all:

1. Punch (thrust)
2. Float
3. Press
4. Flick
5. Glide
6. Slash
7. Dab
8. Wring

---

96   Vera Maletic, *Dance Dynamics: Effort and Phrasing* (Columbus: Grade A Notes, 2005).
97   Maletic, 42.

Action Drive Listening:
- Britten "This Little Babe" from *A Ceremony of Carols*
- Haydn "Kyrie" from *Lord Nelson Mass*

Passion Drive (Weight, Time, Flow)

Passion drive takes a person out of a sense of Space (thinking) and journeys into sensations of Weight, Time, and Flow (flamenco dancing; abandoning control of emotion; giving birth; daydreaming).

Passion Drive Listening:
- Durufle "Kyrie" from *Requiem*
- Faure *Cantique de Jean Racine*
- Bruckner *Christus Factus Est*

Vision Drive (Space, Flow, Time)

Vision drive removes the sensation of being in the body, with an emphasis on heightened thinking or imagining (Space) in leisurely or hasty fashion (Time), with abandonment or restraint (Flow).

Vision Drive Listening:
- Handel "All We Like Sheep" from *Messiah*
- Debussy "Dieu! Qu'il la fait bon regarder" from *Trois Chansons*

Spell Drive (Space, Weight, Flow, Lacks Time)

Spell drive abandons time while magnifying the elements of Weight, Flow, and Space. The sensation may be that of compliant or reluctant yielding, being spellbound or hypnotized.

Spell Drive Listening:
- Barber *Agnus Dei* (based on Adagio for Strings)
- Glass *Koyaanisquatsi*

Experiencing the States

In my graduate choral conducting seminar, I invited my private teacher in Laban movement, Carol Schouboe, to work with conductors on various states and drives. After training the group in separate movement elements and trying various combinations, she gave us a helpful exercise to try.

> **Group Exercise:**
> - Each student received a piece of paper with a State listed, as well as details about the quality of movement in the State (for instance, the paper might read, "Dream State, Light Weight, Bound Flow").
> - Students were placed in pairs and asked to engage in a "movement dialogue" that lacked verbal communication of any kind. Each person was not aware of the state the other partner had to portray. For example, perhaps one person was asked to show "direct Space and quick Time," while the person "replying" was tasked with being in "indirect Space and bound Flow." The fascinating task was (1) to try to identify states or elements of movement while watching others move and (2) to feel how different perspectives could change the dynamic in the room. If one person moves in strong Weight and direct Space, followed by a person in free Flow and quick Time, it will feel like a "movement dissonance."

Because much of what singers "pick up" from conductors is unconscious perception, an exercise like this can be illuminating. Trying on different states in movement is useful not only in communicating musical intent but also as a reminder that we have choices in how we approach our ensemble in rehearsal. Varying our "podium presence" helps us to connect authentically to the music. Not all rehearsal concepts need to be communicated in stable state if the music is "in the dream"!

Experiencing the States in Rehearsal

Attempt to conduct a series of warm-ups in a particular state, emphasizing that state. Think about how it feels to breathe and sing in each state, and customize the warm-ups to help the ensemble discover the differences.

What does it feel like to be in vision drive or stable state while on the podium? How does it change, enhance, or complicate the normal dynamic between yourself and the choir? Can you "give yourself permission" to be less attentive to certain details and more attentive to others in your movement? How does the sound change? Ask your singers after the experiment what it felt like for them.

In my experience, working with various states has allowed my choir to be more versatile in their expression. This exercise is especially helpful if you are willing to use a state that feels less natural to you.

Beyond the Action Drive

The "drive" most commonly written about for conducting is the *action drive,* which combines Weight, Time, and Space, and omits Flow. The various action drives are dab, flick, slash, punch, float, glide, wring, and press. They are a valuable starting point for conductors exploring Laban movement concepts because they offer distilled, potent archetypes for movement, rich in contrast. Action drives, like dance steps, can train a person to be aware of specific elements in movement, but a fuller movement palette is accessed by training with *all* the states and drives, some of which include the element of Flow. To attempt to stay in an action drive is difficult because in the world of dance, action drives are used primarily as points of transition between various states and drives.

Through private studies in Laban movement with Carol Schouboe,[98] a Certified Laban Movement Analyst, I have explored the potent capabilities of all ten states and drives for conductors. These discoveries have continued to bear fruit in my work coaching choral conducting students. Not only has Laban training helped me to determine the movement signature of each conductor I encounter, but it has offered me a specific yet subtle palette of prompts for movement that allow conductors to diversify choices of how to conduct.

The states and drives can be useful in score study as well as physical gesture. Often I ask conductors to prepare a score by considering a hierarchy of important

---

[98] Carol Schouboe has done pioneering research and teaching of Laban Space Harmony with the Integrated Movement Studies Laban/Bartenieff Movement Analysis faculty, and has developed in-depth hands-on skills in Bartenieff Fundamentals for use in rehabilitation. She also served as an assistant faculty member in University of Washington's Laban certification program from 1989–1990. I am grateful to her for providing inspiration for many of the descriptions for movement in states and drives in this chapter.

musical elements, and then select a state or drive that might best reflect that hierarchy in gesture. Conductors consider which aspects of music (Weight, Space, Time, or Flow) they most need to emphasize in their movement and track changes in the hierarchy throughout the piece based on musical elements, such as harmony, texture, rhythm, tempo, dynamics, and articulation. The identification of specific states and drives allows for nuanced choices with clear affective experiences, beyond simply deciding to "add resistance" or "create an accent with the left hand." The use of various effort elements is intended to have an affective, or emotional, purpose both in the conductor as he/she moves and in those who watch.

Other invaluable considerations beyond effort training include Laban's system of *body*, *shape*, and *space*, which will be addressed in other chapters.

Movement Signatures

Laban considers a movement signature to be an individual's natural way of organizing their physical movements in life. This signature is often present from early childhood and persists into adulthood. When working with young conductors such as my undergraduate music education majors, I can often identify aspects of their "movement signature" even before they begin to conduct. With more experienced conductors, a movement signature may also include how they were trained to conduct in the past. The goal is to make a student aware of physical predispositions in movement so they can make conscious choices when on the podium. To grossly oversimplify, a student who is commonly known to speak very fast, move quickly (quick Time) and scatter their attention across many things at once (indirect Space) may have trouble accessing sustainment or strong weight when conducting.

My work with undergraduates incorporating "effort training" (teaching Weight, Space, Time, and Flow in addition to traditional conducting skills) has been quite useful. Since incorporating Laban, I have noticed a rapid improvement in what students are able to do expressively with gesture. Young conductors quickly acquire a language to describe what each movement feels like and a means for discussing possibilities of movement correlated to expressive marks in the score.

Many conductors need to discover qualities in gesture that are currently lacking in their signatures. Barbara Adrian, in her text *Actor Training the Laban*

Way writes, "Our affinities and disaffinities are often revealed through what we are able to see or not see."[99] This quote suggests that Laban training could improve what we are capable of imagining in ourselves, and perhaps in our art. For instance, many young conductors struggle to understand how to introduce strong Weight into their gesture, while others cannot distinguish between direct and indirect Space orientation. When you begin to explore effort, notice when you unconsciously want to "recover" into a different effort (sustained Time giving way to Flow, or bound Flow giving way to direct Space). Challenge yourself to maintain the state until you consciously wish to "modulate" to something new.

Later in this chapter, we will do some guided listening together with the purpose of honing a specific movement "profile" for a musical work.

Expressivity in Conducting

Is the affective aspect of conducting really important? In other words, has it been demonstrated that an expressive conductor can improve the performance level of an ensemble? Do audiences respond to certain styles of conducting more than others? And how much has the role of "master conductor" changed over the years? Leon Botstein posits that our society's focus on visual media has led to an increased interest in a highly expressive conductor.

> In modern conducting, the burden has shifted from preparation [of the score] to the moment of performance and the capacity of the conductor to put nuance on the stage in terms of dynamics, articulation and balance, with the hands alone…Although Monteux admonished conductors not to conduct for the audience, in an age dominated by television and film, the visual impression the conductor makes has become far more influential than might seem reasonable.[100]

The definition of a conductor's roles and resultant audience expectation have changed over time, as was suggested by Botstein's remarks above. The "conductor as time keeper/ensemble leader" of the Baroque and Classical periods (i.e., Lully), evolved into "conductor as interpreter" of the Romantic era (i.e., Berlioz), which has evolved into "conductor as expressive mover" (think

---

99   Barbara Adrian, *Actor Training the Laban Way* (New York: Allworth Press, 2008), 144.
100   Leon Botstein, ""Conducting," *The New Grove Dictionary of Music,* accessed online April 17, 2011.

Dudamel, Bernstein, Tilson Thomas, and so on). In modern times, previous expectations of the conductor's role are bundled in with the added burden of being highly communicative through gesture. The development towards a society that favors the physically "virtuosic" mover is not just due to an increased exposure to television and film but also serves a practical purpose, allowing a conductor to communicate ideas efficiently to an ensemble in the age of the jet-set "guest conductor."

Some writers interpret the role of the conductor even more broadly. Witness Stephen Cottrell's assertions in the article "Music, Time and Dance in Orchestral Performance: The Conductor as Shaman." Cottrell outlines the archetypal audience's impression of conductor as a person appointed by a culture to conjure up the spirit of the composer and provide a window back in time, a heroic figure shrouded in black, standing with their backs to the audience, who with mysterious gesticulations can effect the orchestra's sound without themselves making a single utterance…[101] Cottrell goes on to assert that,

> I then consider the nature of the conductor's gestures within these events, and argue that these can be constructed as a form of dancing, and that the functional ambiguity of these gestures serves only to enhance their symbolic significance; their greater importance, in fact, is in connection with the creation of another world of time within orchestral performance.[102]

William J. Finn in his hallmark textbook on choral conducting implies that the conductor must act as hypnotist, bringing an ensemble into communal belief:

> He must exercise a certain hypnotic influence on the singers; they must recognize the mood he is trying to recreate, and be so impressed by his sincerity as to be guided altogether by his mind, as though they were in reality hypnotized.[103]

But is any of this substantiated by evidence? Does a conductor who keeps his left hand in his pocket (as was recommended by Richard Strauss) really fare any worse than a conductor who attempts to use a large variety of expressive movements on the podium?

---

101 Stephen Cottrell, "Music, Time and Dance in Orchestral Performance: The Conductor as Shaman," *Twentieth-Century Music*, 3 (1) (March 2006).
102 Ibid.
103 William J. Finn, *The Art of the Choral Conductor* (Boston: CC Birchard and Company, c. 1939), 263.

Fortunately, quantifiable research into the impact of expressivity on an audience is beginning to take place.[104] Dr. Steven Morrison of University of Washington, along with Harry Price, Carla Geiger, and Rachel Carnacchio, completed a study in which audiences watched two conductors using high and low expressivity in their gestures, set to the same recording of a university wind ensemble. The conducting changed, but the musical recording did not. Despite the identical recording, the performance of the wind ensemble under the high-expressivity conductor received a higher rating by the audience than the same recording under the low-expressivity conductor. In the article entitled "The effect of conductor expressivity on ensemble performance evaluation," published in JRME (Journal of Research in Music Education), April 2009, the researchers concluded:

> Ultimately, one's judgment of a live ensemble performance may be only partly attributable to what one **hears** (the ensemble members' singing or playing) after factoring in such variables as what one **sees** (e.g., the conductors' actions). Specifically, one may judge a performance as more or less expressive depending on the perceived expressivity of the conductor.[105]

In a subsequent study featuring a university choir, Stephen Morrison and collaborator Jeremiah Selvey observed similar results. Identical performances were evaluated differently depending on how expressive the conductor was. Further analysis revealed that, at least in the case of this particular choral performance, it was the instances of inexpressive conducting that actually depressed the evaluations. Beyond simply demonstrating the value of expressive conducting, such findings offer a compelling illustration of the consequences that may await the conductor who lacks an expressive gestural vocabulary.[106]

The stunning discovery that an audience actually *perceives a different sound* from the same recording based on the perceived expressivity of the conductor

---

104 Beyond Morrison's research, try reading Liz Garnett, *Choral Conducting and the Construction of Meaning: Gesture, Voice, Identity* (England: Ashgate Publishing Limited, 2009), Gail B. Poch, "Conducting: Movement Analogues through Effort Shape" *Choral Journal* 23/3 (1982), Michele Menard Holt "The Application to Conducting and Choral Rehearsal Pedagogy of Laban Effort/Shape and its Comparative Effect upon Style in Choral Performance" (DMA Dissertation, University of Hartford, 1992) and Therees Tkach Hibbard, "The Use of Movement as an Instructional Technique in Choral Rehearsals" (DMA Dissertation, University of Oregon, 1994).

105 Steven J. Morrison et al, "The effect of conductor expressivity on ensemble performance evaluation," *Journal of Research in Music Education* 57 (1) 2009.

106 Steven J. Morrison and Jeremiah Selvey, "The effect of conductor expressivity on choral ensemble evaluation" (Paper presented at the 19th International Symposium on Research in Music Behavior, Barcelona, Spain, February 2011).

builds a solid case for the value of Laban training in the conductors' overall education. But how new is the application of dance to conducting? Apparently not very according to anecdotal evidence, such as a *Time Magazine* article from 1940 entitled "Serge's Dream." It describes Serge Koussevitsky's decision to hire Erick Hawkins, choreographer and dancer partner to Martha Graham, to teach conductors at the renowned summer festival at Tanglewood's Berkshire Music Center. Today many leading conductors readily incorporate Laban movement in their conducting classes or touch on other important methods, such as Tai Chi, Reiki, Yoga, and Alexander Technique.

What are the correlations between dance and conducting? Here is a brief summary of similarities between the art forms.

Dance and Conducting: Correlations
1. Fleeting live creations of art
2. Music as "muse"
3. Use of learned, refined movements that reflect symbolic meaning
4. Learned through "methods" with "do's" and "don'ts"
5. Demand agility, flexibility, kinesthetic awareness, sensitivity to contrasts in gesture

---

If conductors are to some extent dancers, and if high-expressivity conductors are favored by audiences over low-expressivity conductors, then should conductors also be choreographers, deciding in advance what gestures they should use for a given passage of music? It is my assertion that the best conductors use movement that approximates "improvisatory dance" rather than "fixed choreography." Conductors may begin with a concept of how to conduct a piece, but will hone their gesture throughout the preparation and performance of the work based on the needs of the ensemble. Being able to "change gears" physically is a skill polished over many years on the podium, and attaining such flexibility is a sign of a master conductor. In the words of Neal Bartee:

> For the conductor to incorporate the use of improvisational movement in learning to conduct a score, he must use the nearest source available: the study of improvisational movement in dancing and acting. In these disciplines artists are constantly using the improvisational process in creating a dance or a character. One should expand the range of movement expression of one's body to communicate the shades of emotion required.

The conductor should expand his awareness from the incipient stages of learning technique so that his study will be fruitful creatively as well as mechanically.[107]

However, emphasizing expressive movement in the early education of a conductor is easier said than done. Conductors spend their youth honing musical technique, not moving across a dance floor. Conducting teachers are not necessarily trained movers, and conducting classes are rarely taught in rooms with mirrors, where students can actually see what they look like.

Conducting textbooks often relegate "expressive conducting" to a single chapter based on certain articulations encountered in the score (legato, tenuto, staccato, and marcato). Yet consider this message from pianist, composer, and teacher Arthur Schnabel: "The performer does not underline anything which the composer has already made obvious. He has to take care of whatever the composer has left for him to take care of."[108]

It takes something of a sea change to understand that the conductor may do best to emphasize what is *not* in the score but needs to be brought forth from the musicians to realize the work most fully. In doing so, the conductor begins to suggest higher outcomes in performance rather than simply reflect musical intent through gesture. For example, a musical score may imply but not specify the following aspects of expressivity: rubato, mezza da voce phrasing, singing "with line," vowel shape and vowel modification, breath support, inner intent, imagination, singing in tune, varying vocal color, etc. Each of these expressive aspects may require different, carefully detailed gestures.

Laban's purpose in life was to help all individuals become more well-rounded in their physicality so all potentials could be tapped. There is no point in creating a method of conducting that would actually limit a conductor to a specific way of moving. Laban was not attempting to create a strict "method" that all dancers should adhere to, and as an act of honoring the diverse way each person perceives movement possibilities, this chapter does not prescribe specific gestures. It will, however, offer suggestions for how to narrow choices of "states" or "drives" based on certain musical works.

---

107 Bartee, 174.
108 Frederick Prauznits, Score and Podium: A Complete Guide to Conducting, 263.

Listening with Laban: Creating a Kinesthetic Analysis of the Score

As dancers have shown us, moving to recorded music can provide a useful vehicle to connect the effort elements (Weight, Space, Time, and Flow) to specific musical events. In this day and age, recordings can serve as an "aural history" as well, allowing us to compare the interpretations of masterworks by many conductors over the years. However, conductors are ultimately responsible for creating their own interpretations of music separate from any recording they may encounter. Musical decisions must be made based on a thorough analysis of the score from all angles.

In my chapter, "Incorporating Laban Actions in the Rehearsal," from *Music for Conducting Study*,[109] I identify various musical elements that *may* lead to efforts in a specific set of pieces. Charles Gambetta suggests a broad approach to coupling musical events with Laban efforts for any musical work in his 2005 dissertation, "Conducting Outside the Box: Creating a Fresh Approach to Conducting Gesture through the Principles of Laban Movement Analysis."[110] However, without examining all the elements in combination, it is difficult to know what gesture makes the most sense.

Musical Elements

Melodic Shape, Motivic Length, Motivic Development (or lack thereof)
Harmony vs. Dissonance (along a continuum)
Harmonic Rhythm and Development
Rhythm and Articulation
Tempo and Pulse/Meter
Phrase Lengths and Overall Form
Dynamics
Texture and Density
Tone Color and Timbre
Textual Meaning (in the case of texted music)

---

109 James Jordan with Giselle Wyers, *Music for Conducting Study* (Chicago: GIA Publications, 2008).
110 Charles Gambetta, "Conducting Outside the Box: Creating a Fresh Approach to Conducting Gesture Through the Principles of Laban Movement Analysis" (D.M.A. diss., University of North Carolina at Greensboro, 2005).

In music, all of the elements listed above are present simultaneously. Yet a conductor's job is to make choices about what to emphasize in the music, not to reflect all parts with equal emphasis. As you look at a piece, ask yourself: What would I write home about in this piece? What is driving this work's identity? What elements assert themselves over and over, and what elements are continually changing? Remember that a state or drive in dance is a *perspective* for the mover that may change throughout the performance; the same is true in musical works.

Listening while moving can be a powerful way to hone an awareness of how we should "feel" when we conduct. When you first try moving to music, imagine you are 75 percent dancer and 25 percent conductor. Do not be concerned with pattern unless it helps you to connect to the intent of the music. Ask yourself: As I am moving, what is coming to the forefront? Am I demonstrating Time, Space, Weight, Flow, or a combination of these elements? What is the '"prime movement element" I tend to emphasize? What am I not showing? Is this intentional or due to force of habit? Refer back to the kinesthetic exercises described earlier in this chapter. Treat them as points of comparison with how you feel as you move to this piece of music.

Of course, some of the movement choices you make while simply listening and moving may change when you are in front of an ensemble because you will be attempting to offer "physical solutions" to various issues in the score, especially vocal challenges. You also may be distracted by the interpretation of the work you have chosen to move to if it does not match your vision. It is important that you choose carefully when listening to recordings and find performances that you trust to inform your own interpretation.

All of these caveats aside, you will find that many of the movement choices you make unconsciously while improvising will be retained because they reflect a sort of archetype for the sound.

Here are some questions you may ask as you are listening and moving to music:

Hearing Time (Decision Making):
Hearing time as a conductor, one is used to thinking of tempo and pulse. Try considering Laban's broader definition of "time" as a refinement of your previous view.

Is the music…
- Acting decisively with haste and urgency?
- Postponing a decision through leisurely sustainment?
- Switching between the two options above?

Hearing Space (Thinking, Imagining):
Hearing space may cause you to be drawn into your thinking either abstractly (as you sense dimension to the sound) or with specific mental images.

Is the music…
- Causing you to see specific images or "scenes" in your mind?
- Bringing a sense of landscape either with two-dimensional (flat) or three-dimensional (round) images?

Hearing Weight (Physical Intention):
Hearing weight is linked to your physical sense of the music. Weight tends to draw you more into your body and the inward sensation of the sound.

Is the music…
- Causing you to draw into your body's sensations?
- Asserting a specific intent either lightly or with force?

Hearing Flow (Progression, Feeling):
Hearing flow is linked to density, dissonance or consonance, and rhythmic consistency or instability.

Is the music…
- Suggesting progression unfolding either freely or with careful control?
- Bringing up intuitive responses to the music that are hard to quantify or describe?

Exploring Choral Works in Detail

Below I offer a personal interpretation of how to conduct a series of well-known choral works. Effort training can feel different for every individual based on personal aesthetics, preferences, and movement signatures. One person may mostly feel the element of Time (Quick or Sustained) in gesture, while another person might be more apt to translate his/her perception of time into Bound Flow or Free Flow. One person might easily know how to access Weight in gesture to intensify sound, while another will naturally move into Bound Flow or Direct Space for a similar effect.

The same can be said when considering the needs of a choir. One choir may be gifted at dealing with lightness without becoming breathy; if so, the conductor can easily access light gestures without concern of causing the ensemble's pitch to fall. Another choir may need a conductor to access Bound Flow to serve as a reminder of how to support the sound with *appoggio*, or conversely, may need the conductor to use freer flow in the gesture to keep them from tightening their throats as they exhale air. The possibilities from ensemble to ensemble, and from day-to-day in rehearsal, are limitless.

Therefore, try the suggestions below and then come to your own conclusions. Let those conclusions always be inspired first by the needs of your ensemble.

Morten Lauridsen's *Dirait-On*

When I conduct Lauridsen's *Dirait-On*, I "write home" about Time (mostly sustained, some quick depending on tempo choices and use of rubato) and changing aspects of Weight (light, stronger, light again, etc.), followed by some contrasts in Flow (mostly free, at times bound). I feel less of a "spatial" awareness, which Laban defined as "thinking." If I choose the "Top 2" elements of movement as Time and Weight, I am emphasizing the rhythm state. If I add Flow as a third element, I am conducting in the passion drive.

By doing this kinesthetic analysis, I begin to realize that when conducting this work, it will be important to emphasize sustainment in the gesture, retain a fairly light but sometimes stronger amount of Weight, and examine opportunities for the Flow to bind slightly, most likely at the ends of phrases or in response to building harmonic tension. I am reminded also to spend less time in Direct Space with the singers and adopt a more introspective, intimate approach in rehearsal, allowing them to focus inwardly as they are learning the work.

Michael McGlynn's *Dulaman*

The first thing I notice in this piece is the assertion of Quick Time. Constant fluctuations in text stress, uneven phrase lengths, and changing meters keep my focus on tracking time. Any element that is constantly fluctuating will cause one to feel its presence. If time elements (such as pulse, meter, or articulation) are in statis, time might actually seem less imperative to emphasize.

In *Dulaman*, I feel gradations of weight, mostly light but at times more strong and deliberate. The weight changes are manifest mostly in subtle shifts of dynamic but also occur in octave shifts upward and in the thickening or opening of texture. Weight combined with Time is rhythm state, the same state chosen for Lauridsen's *Dirait-on*. But notice the variation needed between these pieces, considering that *Dirait-on* is concerned with sustainment and *Dulaman* is concerned with quickness!

In *Dulaman*, the element of Flow seems unchanging, always somewhat "free." Space or the "thinking" component comes into our focus more readily, as though we are watching something very intriguing (Space) unfolding rapidly (Time) while affecting our bodies (Weight). Time/Weight/Space becomes action drive. In this case, trying various combinations between Dab, Flick, Slash and Punch could bring useful clarity to the conducting gesture.

Samuel Barber's *Agnus Dei*

From the start of this piece, I feel many dimensions to the sound. The piece begins famously with sopranos singing alone, followed by the entrance of the rest of the choir. The sensation is clearly that of Direct into Indirect Space, as though you as listener are looking at something very specific that then opens into something much wider—the lighthouse, then the ocean. Flow is also present with a quality of progression unfolding slowly but deliberately. There is a steady vacillation between bound flow and freer flow (but never fully free). Space and Flow combined become remote state, and when the subtle but still present fluctuations of Weight are factored into the equation, we have a good example of spell drive. Spell drive in music is the closest thing to hypnosis one can experience.

By doing this physical analysis of *Agnus Dei,* I am reminded as conductor to attempt to remove my ictus of a strong emphasis on meter and approach a "timeless" quality in the gesture. I am convinced of the importance of teaching my students about various textures in the sound (direct/indirect) and helping them to use careful attention to breath support and pacing to bring out the variations in bound flow, where the breath will move more cautiously, with a sense of suspending the tone, and more freely, when the breath will move faster. I am reminded to help my singers feel the changes in weight that I experience when I conduct, so the full *fortés,* which come late in the piece, can be rich, not overly effortful, and grounded in the entire body, not focused in the throat where tension may arise.

Claude Debussy's *Dieu! Qu'il la fait bon regarder*

Debussy's modal inflections along with fluctuations in triple/duple rhythms and quick/sustained articulations lend a sense of constant change to this work, but the Weight never seems to vary, remaining relatively light. Time and Flow combined become mobile state, and when Space is added (sensed mostly in the poem's description of a beautiful woman) in both direct and indirect permutations (driven by texture changes in the music) we arrive at vision drive, with a heightened sense of thinking and feeling but with less perception of the physical body (which would involve Weight). This tendency to de-emphasize the body fits with the chivalrous text, where a woman is admired and even idolized.

As I prepare to conduct this work, I will notice when the harmonic and textural shifts seem to "bind themselves inwardly" and when there is a sense of moving forward with abandon and rapture. Here, Time and Flow can work together to demonstrate these shifts, with *rubato* driven by the natural stress of the language and Debussy's harmonic progressions. I will be less concerned with varying Weight, since when I wish to intensify sound, I will only need subtle shifts in Flow to accomplish the task. Concentrating on Weight would most likely bog down an otherwise smooth and linear melodic line.

These musical examples tend to stay in the same state or drive, and therefore are useful as teaching pieces. However, be aware that many works, especially longer pieces, will involve shifts between states and drives.

In all of the above examples, I have given you a look at my personal interpretation of the works. Even if you choose to take each work in different directions, the act of experimentation with Weight, Flow, Space, and Time is already part of the learning process. Some combinations may feel like they "make sense," while others may seem preposterous. For instance, imagine trying to conduct Pierre Passereau's *Il est bel et bon* in Spell drive (where the emphasis on time in music and gesture is missing)! Perhaps you will find certain elements that you are always listening for in the music. For instance, you may tend to hear melody first, or conversely, rhythmic momentum. Challenge yourself to not let your listening predisposition overly influence your choices for gesture. Conversely, challenge your gesture to truly reflect what you feel is important, not simply what your "movement signature" might lead you to favor.

A Brief Discussion of Laban's "Shape" System

As mentioned earlier in this chapter, a full discussion of Laban must include body, shape, space, *and* effort. For a concise and well-organized look at all aspects of the Laban system, consult Lisa Billingham's text *The Complete Conductor's Guide to Laban Movement Theory*.[111] Although this chapter is focused primarily on the states and drives using the effort elements, I encourage all conductors to also familiarize themselves with Laban's "shape" system, which includes descriptions for *shape qualities* and *modes of shape change*.

Shape Qualities (Affinities)

- Rising with lightness
- Sinking with strength
- Advancing with sustainment
- Retreating with quickness
- Spreading (opening) with indirectness
- Closing (narrowing) with directness

---

[111] Lisa Billingham, *The Complete Conductor's Guide to Laban Movement Theory* (Chicago: GIA Publications, 2009).

As you experiment with gesture, carefully consider how you direct and place your ictus. The idea of "rising with lightness" is fairly intuitive for conductors, as they attempt to create a decrescendo, for instance. Yet a conductor might try to speed up a tempo by leaning forward, a gestural choice that Laban would consider a "disaffinity." Disaffined gestures are not "wrong" but can seem quite dramatic since they play on the contrast between what people expect to see and what is actually shown.

Modes of Shape Change

- Shape flow – how the body changes shape in relation to itself (shrugging shoulders; stretching; etc.)
- Directional – how the body moves outwards into the environment (can be either spoke-like and straight or arc-like and curved)
- Carving – moving outwards in a way that encourages a sense of sculpting dimension in the space between you and the environment

In conducting, experiment with concepts of directional vs. carving gestures. The opening bars of Stravinsky's *Symphony of Psalms* likely calls for a sense of directional movement (conducted with a straight-angled, spoke-like approach) but Poulenc's *O Magnum Mysterium* will demand a wider variety in shape, recruiting "carving" to represent a "sphere of sound" felt in the rich harmonies and supple vocal lines.

Conclusion

Understanding the potential of each separate effort element (Weight, Time, Space, and Flow) and their combinations in states and drives can provide a powerful vehicle for personal expression, as well as a qualitative description of the energy present in movement. Effort brings an evocative, often unconscious response to both the mover and those observing the movement (our ensembles and audiences). Considering the impact subtle changes in movement dynamics can bring to observers, a thorough training in effort and all of the states and drives is highly recommended.

PART 4

Bodying Forth:
Developing a Kinesthetic Vocabulary
and Movement Language

CHAPTER 13

The Laban Connection to Mirror Neurons: The Importance of Learning and Re-Learning Movement

The distinctive feature of brains such as the one we own is their uncanny ability to create maps. Mapping is essential for sophisticated management, mapping and life management going hand in hand. When the brain makes maps, it *informs* itself. The information contained in the maps can be used nonconsciously to guide motor behavior efficaciously, a most desirable consequence considering that survival depends on taking the right action. But when brains make maps, they are also creating images, the main currency of our minds. Ultimately consciousness allows us to experience maps as images, to manipulate those images, and to apply reasoning to them.

Maps are constructed when we interact with objects, such as a person, a machine, a place, from the outside of the brain toward its interior. I cannot emphasize the word *interaction* enough. It reminds us that making maps, which is essential for improving actions as noted above, often occurs in a setting of action to begin with. Action and maps, movements and mind, are part of an unending cycle.... (pp. 63–64)

—Antonio Damasio
in *Self Comes to Mind*

Everything should be as simple as it is, but not simpler. (p. 141)

—Albert Einstein
in John Daido Loori,
The Zen of Creativity

We forget at times that conducting gesture is composed of an intricate series and sequence of gestures, rotations, and body movements that communicates rhythmic intent and evokes musical responses from musicians. Many times, however, in our haste to get to the end product—the pattern—we ignore all of the subparts that make up our conducting technique. And to go a step further, we almost never revisit the "basics" once we begin conducting.

This chapter addresses all of those basic elements that must be practiced as individual technical events. In many writings about Zen practices, there is an overriding theme that one needs to spend time with the simple if one ever hopes to understand the complex. In fact, according to Zen philosophy, one will never experience the whole without a concentrated and focused effort on learning the simple elements.

> Zen teaching and practice tends to be expressed very directly, without excessive ornamentation. The design of the typical Zen monastery reflects this. The space is sparse, unobtrusive, and uncluttered. We see this in the simple flower arrangement on the Buddhist altar, in the architecture of the monastery's buildings, in its gardens and pathways. We also see it in the kind of food that is served and the way it is served, as well as in the practitioner's vestments. All of it reflects a simplicity that allows our attention to be drawn to that which is essential, stripping away the extra. (p. 135)
>
> —John Daido Loori
> in *The Zen of Creativity*

Conducting technique needs to be built slowly and carefully, one element at a time. While the learning and execution of conducting patterns seems to be the end goal, in reality there are many simple technical elements that give meaning to those patterns. Remember that conducting patterns are a large representation of forward movement of sound. Patterns are given meaning and evocative power when they are a composite of smaller, specific elements. It is almost as if the pattern is a template of sorts, over which we lay specific elements that imbue our patterns with meaning. It is the small, technical elements (not necessarily the larger pattern) that evokes musical responses from musicians. If a golfer wants to improve his or her golf swing, he or she would ask a golf pro to analyze the swing. The golf pro would, inevitably, suggest a "back to basics" approach that focuses on specific weak elements of the person's technique.

So, you could consider this a "back to basics" text for the development and improvement of conducting technique. For both beginners and experienced conductors, it tries to identify those simple elements of conducting technique that will later comprise the whole. Spend time with each of the individual exercises. Consider creating a chart or a log to keep track of when you have revisited a certain element of technique and to help you make sure you have covered all of the specifics of conducting technique in a simple, yet logical fashion.

I hope that what you will discover is not only an increased comfort level with your technique, but a newfound awareness about the important simple elements that comprise your gestural vocabulary.

Understanding Mirror Neurons

At an intuitive level, conductors for the most part understand that their gesture affects others, and more importantly, directly affects sound. Many conductors believe that conducting gesture is merely the transport system for rhythmic precision and textural clarity. While they believe there are other influences upon sound, those influences happen almost as accidents because they do not fully invest in the powers that awareness and consciousness carry for the art. This inconsistency in philosophy is created by a lack of understanding of the real nature of how things work—that is, how our consciousness is carried through the way we move and breathe through our gesture.

The term "mirror neurons" has been developed to describe this magical and mystical process by which we influence sound and spirit through our gesture, breathing, and being. Simply stated, what is happening in the truest psychological sense is that the sound within us, obtained from experience and score study and birthed through fantasy, is wirelessly transmitted to the musicians who sit in front of us. In essence, other persons receive the energy from the mirror neurons firing in our consciousness *and* unconsciousness, and then intuitively respond in sound and human expression. It is our task in conducting pedagogy to develop our "mirror neurons" through score study, breathing, and kinesthetic language.

The Laban Efforts in Combination provide a direct link to the development of these "mirror neurons." In the conducting world, there are mirror neurons for the kinesthetic of movement, the color of sound, the human message within and among notes that are all developed through score study, kinesthetic study, and the journey within oneself that must occur with every piece of music. As conductors, we must develop the mirror neurons that will be fired in others because the movements we choose for the scores we conduct are acquired through a rich movement awareness experience that we then begin to organize and catalog through the Laban Efforts in Combination.

The skill sets that follow can be considered small units in the path to mirror neuron development. It is very clear from Damasio's work that body maps of all kinds transfer immediately and wordlessly to those who experience them in real time. Viewed in a sharper perspective, Laban Effort/Shape (and more specifically, the Efforts in Combination) is a way for conductors not only to acquire a movement vocabulary, but also to trust in the power of that movement when bonded with music to communicate motion and phrase shape, and all the "other" musical ideas that are carried within the breath. A leading psychologist in the Body Mapping/neuron mirroring theories, Antonio Damasio states it perhaps the clearest:

> So-called mirror neurons are, in effect, the ultimate as-if body device. The network in which those neurons are embedded achieves conceptually what I hypothesized as the as-if body loop system: the simulation, in the brain's body maps, of a body state that is not actually taking place in the organism. The fact that the body state simulated by mirror neurons is not the subject's body state amplifies the power of this functional resemblance. If a complex brain can stimulate someone else's body state, one assumes that it would be able to simulate its own body states. A state that has already occurred in the organism should be easier to simulate since it has already been mapped by precisely the same somatosensing structures that are now responsible for stimulating it.[112]

---

112 Antonio Damasio, *Self Comes to Mind* (Pantheon, 2010), p. 103.

Laban, Mirror Neurons, and Breath

Given the information so eloquently summarized in the previous quote, I would like to focus our thoughts on the miracle of conducting gesture upon ensembles. To be sure, motion learned through re-living movement already experienced through the reality of life will bring immediate honesty into one's gestural vocabulary. But what Damasio suggests above is that not only are mirror neurons fired in an ensemble when they experience the conductor's gesture, but the *breath* prior to any phrase and between any phrase is probably a far larger "igniter" of responses in musicians. In *The Musician's Breath* (2010), my co-authors (Mark Moliterno and Nova Thomas) and I make a passionate case for the power of one's breath and trusting what it carries. Movement learned through the Laban Efforts in Combination is the igniter for our mirror neurons; the breath incinerates our musical ideas, and it is the breath in marriage with our movement that fires the mirror neurons in the singers and players in our ensembles. As Damasio points out, we need to fire our own mirror neurons through an examination of movement and score study. But once that is in place, our delivery system for firing the neurons of others is gesture and breath. Trust in this idea is central to the understanding of the conductor's art.

The chapters that follow will guide you stepwise to "fire" your own neurons so that what you do on the podium and rehearsal can have an immediate mirror effect on all who sing and play with you. As you begin your study of movement through the genius of Laban, consider the following:

> Explanations of the existence of mirror neurons have emphasized the role that such neurons can play in allowing us to understand the actions of others by placing ourselves in a comparable body state. As we witness an action in another, our body sensing brain adopts the body state we would assume were we ourselves moving, and it does so, in all probability, not by passive sensory patterns but by a pre-activation of mirror structures—ready for action but not allowed to act yet—and in some cases by actual motor activation.[113]

---

113 Damasio, p. 104.

SKILL SETS
Acquiring Conducting Technique

Using the Principles of Laban

SKILL SET ONE
Developing Movement Observation and Self-Perception Skills

That the body, in most of its aspects, is continuously mapped in the brain and that a variable but considerable amount of the related information does enter the conscious mind is a proven fact. In order for the brain to coordinate physiological states in the body proper, which it can do without our being consciously aware of what is going on, the brain must be informed about the various physiological parameters at different regions of the body. This information must be current and consistent, from time to time, if it is to permit optimal control. (p. 101)

—Antonio Damasio[114]
in *Self Comes to Mind*

---

114 It should be noted that this text continues to emphasize the importance of both awareness in both conductor and musician, and the importance of body maps for conductors. Antonio Damasio, a faculty member of The University of Southern California, is a leading psychologist who has not only defined Body Mapping as a necessary science but has also made significant inroads in convincing the scientific community of how body maps are crucial to our consciousness and unconsciousness. Pivotal quotes from his most recent book, *Self Comes to Mind*, are dispersed throughout this text. The work of Laban and the images and thought processes it evokes are essential for the development of one's conducting body map that is experience-based. Damasio's work concerning Body Mapping and the role of mirror neurons is essential to the development of a conductor and central to one's understanding of how gesture creates an action/reaction synergy between conductor and ensemble.

The exercises in this skill set are designed to gain a kinesthetic organization of the entire body and an awareness of how weight interacts with movement activity. When conducting, you must not only experience an entire world of movement in your upper torso, but your lower torso must be grounded *and* centered for you to perceive the Efforts in Combination in the upper torso. It is also important to note that this sense of weighted "core" or "center" is necessary when moving within the crystals in later skill sets (e.g., sphere, cube, icosahedron, etc.). For those readers who want more information regarding the spiritual and physical aspects of center, consider reading *Toward Center* (GIA, 2009).

BODY KINESTHETIC EXERCISE 1: Weight at Center

Feeling Weight at Your Center

The feeling of weight at your center is an important kinesthetic for conductors. When you are "centered," you feel a certain "weight" that grounds your gesture. Center must be a "kinesthetic" thing. You must "feel" where it is; it defies description or exact anatomical location.

When I studied at the Laban/Bartenieff Institute for Movement Studies in New York, I took a course on what are known as the Efforts in Combination: Flow, Weight, Time, and Space. We were lead through a number or exercises that would allow us to experience, as much as is possible, each of those efforts in isolation. The exercise for weight that I learned then remains the best way for me to "relocate" my center (i.e., to experience it in its proper "low," centered position within my body). The exercise that follows, called the *Towel Slap Exercise,* is one of the most important exercises for either discovering center or relocating a center that is too high.

> **Towel Slap Exercise:**
> 1. Using a large, thick towel, slap the towel against the floor to obtain the loudest possible sound.
> 2. As you slap the towel, analyze your movement patterns to determine which Efforts in Combination produces the loudest towel slap.

About This Exercise:

- You will find that if you grab the end of the towel and begin the exercise with your hands extended backward over your head, bringing the towel directly over the top of your head and following the midline of the body will produce the loudest sound.
- What you experience as the towel is slapped is a sudden use of weight.
- As the towel slaps the floor, you should feel the sudden dispersion of weight into the floor.

Important to this exercise are (1) body alignment, (2) beginning and ending location of the towel, and (3) focus of your energy as the towel hits the floor. The diagrams below show the beginning, middle, and final positions of the towel slap exercise.

Figure 24. Beginning position for towel slap exercise.

Figure 25. Middle position for towel slap exercise.

Figure 26. Ending position for towel slap exercise.

The secret to this exercise is that first you need to bring the towel through the center or midline of the body. You can achieve a loud slap with the towel only if the body is in perfect alignment. However, the most important part of this exercise is that, at the moment when the energy is released in the loud slap as the towel meets the floor, you feel the "true" location of center within your body. Once that has been experienced through this exercise, then you can recall it through a sense of "kinesthetic imagination" whenever needed.

Aside from the towel slap exercise above, the following exercises have been equally effective in helping to locate the kinesthetic location of center.

BODY KINESTHETIC EXERCISE 2:
Learning the Kinesthetic of Withholding Weight

The exercises that follow can provide you with the ability to either take weight out of your conducting gesture or withhold weight from your gesture in a way that is both free and unencumbered. Buoyancy, lightness, hovering are all possible synonyms for this valuable kinesthetic tool. Mastery of these life activities can then be associated with specific efforts and can also be applied to sudden changes of Effort.

Tiptoe Exercise:
1. Tiptoe around the room, making as little sound as possible.
2. What does your body feel like? Where do you fell your center of levity?

About This Exercise:
- In this exercise, you most likely feel your center of levity *high* in your body.
- To tiptoe quietly, you actually hold back the displacement of weight as you move, or in other words, you experience lightness, which is a *withholding* of weight.
- This exercise is important because it teaches us what center is *not*! When you withhold weight, or avoid sensing weight, your center raises.

Skipping Exercise:

1. Perform this exercise in an area that affords the use of a large floor space.
2. Begin skipping across the floor. Try to make it across the room with as few skips as possible, making your skips as high as possible.
3. As you skip, make sure your upper body remains free.
4. What image will help you to skip higher? Where do you feel your center of levity as you skip?

About This Exercise:

- Skipping is one of the most valuable of all movement activities because the entire body is carried by an energy continuum that can only be felt if the body is centered.
- The constant releasing of energy coupled with a dynamic inertia that centers itself around the core makes this an essential exercise to master.
- You will find that the more you can "hold back" your weight at the top or highest point of the skip, the higher you will be able to skip.

Tug of War Exercise:

1. Engage in a tug of war with someone else using a long, heavy bath or beach towel.
2. Both of you grasp the ends of the towel, count to three, and begin to tug. If done correctly, neither of your should win; it should be a standoff.
3. Perform the tug of war again, and experiment with the positioning of your body to achieve the lowest possible center of levity, which translates into a sensation of weight. You will find that a condition of equilibrium occurs when both of you squat in an apelike position so your center of levity, or center of weight, drops into your pelvis area.
4. When the condition of equilibrium occurs, where do you feel your center? Do you feel it low in your body?

About This Exercise:

- You should "feel" your center of levity in that "tug-of-war" place when you conduct. If you do, you will find that when you breathe, the air will be able to drop to the same place where you feel your center of levity.

BODY KINESTHETIC EXERCISE 3:
Learning the Kinesthetic of the Body Interacting with the Effort of Weight in Relative Isolation

Experiencing Dimensions of Time

For musicians, the isolated Effort Element of Time is the most difficult to grasp. Musicians tend to think or conceptualize time in evenly divided segments. For Laban, time was to be viewed in larger units that would parallel real-life experience. These exercises are designed to re-orient musicians toward Laban's conception of Time.

Blindfold Exercise:

1. Perform this exercise in pairs.
2. Blindfolded, one person should walk around the room for ten minutes.
3. The other person should function as a guide. The role of the guide is not to influence the path about the room by the blindfolded partner, but to merely look out for the partner's well-being. The guide should anticipate dangerous situations before they occur and steer the partner away from those situations.

About This Exercise:

- This activity stresses the Effort Element of Time. Without the aid of the sense of sight, the blindfolded person will experience sustained time.

Experiencing Various Interactions of Time, Weight, and Space Using the Body

Mirrored Mime Exercise:
1. This is a valuable exercise to perform in a class setting.
2. The class should mirror the instructor's movements as if they are the mirrored image.
3. The instructor should create various vignettes where Weight, Time, and Space are changed so the class can experience changes in Flow.

About This Exercise:
- This activity is recommended as a daily warm-up for conducting classes.

Walking Mime Exercise:
1. This is a valuable exercise to perform in a class setting.
2. Have each student select a partner. The exercise has more dramatic results if the partner is either of the opposite sex or physically different in height and/or weight.
3. One person is the leader, while the other person follows.
4. The followers should imitate the gait of their partner as closely as possible.

About This Exercise:
- Following this activity, have students talk about how different their bodies felt as they imitated the walk of their partner.

Play Acting Exercise:
1. This is a valuable exercise to perform in a class setting.
2. Ask the students to swing their arms. First, ask them to use only their upper bodies.
3. Then ask them to employ their entire bodies into the swing.

About This Exercise:
- Following this activity, have the students discuss the importance of both lightness and strength to their arm swing.

SKILL SET TWO
Unlocking the Conductor's Architecture

The tree of life is immensely large and complex, and we of the human species are one twig on that tree. A twig is not representative of the whole tree but is a very specialized development of it, so that, if we wished to understand the whole tree, we would avoid looking at it from the twig's specialized point of view and choose, instead, that of the roots and trunk. (p. 3)

—Thomas Hanna
in *The Body of Life*

Before we discuss the particulars of Laban architecture and the specifics of Effort/Shape in the skill sets that follow, there is a necessary readiness that must be in place as you explore your own sphere of movement.

It stands to reason that you will not move well unless you are able to move. An intimate understanding of the structure of your body is necessary for you to move.[115]

In applying the powerful Body Mapping information in my teaching, I have found that unless one specific part of the arm structure is released, it will be almost impossible for a conductor to move freely or expressively—and more importantly, breathe! All of the exercises and movement paradigms presented in this skill set require a free and engaged upper body. As conductors, none of us would argue that our arms are important tools in our communicative work. What many of us do not understand is that our arms must be "unlocked" so the full architectural and lever advantage can be used in both horizontal and vertical movement.

The Unlocking Joint: The Point of Gestural Release

Access to a full range of arm usage is almost solely dependent on a conductor's ability to *access* free movement through the "shoulder joint." A freely moving, released shoulder ball and socket unlocks the sterno-clavicular joint, which is the first joint of the arm. To access this all-important joint, the arm must be used at an angle in relationship to the body that is close to an embrace. This angle provides a space in the armpit that not only unlocks the shoulder ball and socket but also allows for a free and supple movement connection directly into the sterno-clavicular joint. Without this access "space" under the arm, it is almost impossible to enjoy free and expressive movement. Stated another way,

---

115 I would encourage all those reading this book to study the *Anatomy of Conducting* DVD that accompanies the Second Edition of *Evoking Sound* (GIA, 2009).

conductors unlock the full range of motion through the constant engagement of the *full* arm unit. Read the description above while studying the illustrations in Figures 27 and 28.

Figure 27. Point of release created by space between the arm and ribs.

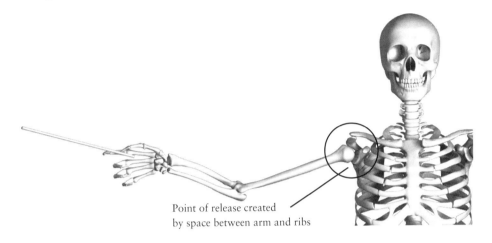

Figure 28. Space between the arm and ribcage.

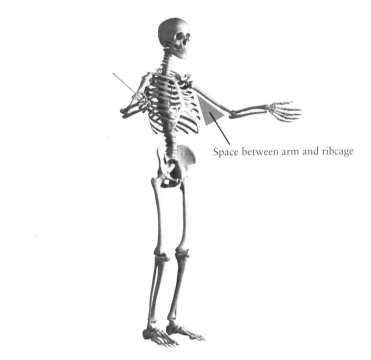

For further study of Body Mapping, view *The Anatomy of Conducting DVD* and complete *The Anatomy of Conducting Workbook* (GIA).

SKILL SET THREE
Accurately Perceiving Your Architecture

Our body is constructed in a manner which enables us to reach certain points of the kinesphere with greater ease than others. An intensive study of the relationship between the architecture of the human body and its pathways in space facilitates finding harmonious patterns. Knowing the rules of the harmonic relations in space we can then control and form the flux of our motivity....

It is natural for all living organisms to use the simplest and easiest paths in space when fighting, not only when a fight is a matter of life and death, but also in other activities, since all working is a kind of fighting and struggling with objects and materials. Everywhere economy of effort is in evidence, including all kinds of bodily locomotion. (p. 23)

—Rudolf Laban
in Irmgard Bartenieff,
Body Movement

The flow of movement is strongly influenced by the order in which the parts of the body are set in motion. We can distinguish an unhampered or "free flow" and a hampered or "bound flow." Movements originating in the trunk, the centre of the body, and then flowing gradually out towards the extremities of the arms and legs are in general more freely flowing than those in which the center of the body remains motionless when the limbs begin to move. (p. 21)

—Rudolf Laban
in *The Mastery of Movement*

Author's Note: *All of the content in this chapter is demonstrated on the DVD included with this book. The DVD icon indicates when the content is demonstrated on the DVD.*

> The control of the flow of movement is therefore intimately connected with the control of movements of the parts of the body. Body movements can be roughly divided into steps, gestures of arms and hands, and facial expressions. Steps comprehend leaps, turns. Gestures of the extremities of the upper part of the body comprise scooping, gathering and strewing, scattering movements. (p. 21)
>
> —Rudolf Laban
> in *The Mastery of Movement*

> Designing trace-forms in the air with only the extremities can lead to a kind of external form-writing. (p. 49)
>
> —Rudolf von Laban
> in Irmgard Bartenieff,
> *Body Movement*

> Human body movement is an ever-present, complex, and yet an elusive part of our lives, subject to 'tune out,' simplification, and other perceptual maneuvers. (p. 65)
>
> —Carol-Lynne Moore
> in *Beyond Words*

From my vantage point, an understanding of Laban depends on what I term "interactive perception." Conductors must have a clear conception of both the architecture of the body and what it feels like when those parts of their architecture are moving in synchronicity with sound. Earlier I described and identified the architectures of the body as a type of projective geometry for conductors. This skill set takes the geometric theory one step further. In addition to reviewing Laban's geometry of the body, this skill set will go a step further so to help you gain an understanding of the physics of moving from a Laban perspective.

The Crystals

> Laban much preferred the word "crystals" to "solids," not only because it sounded more poetic but because the image of a transparent crystal lends itself more readily to the idea of stepping inside it and moving around in its space. Ideally, each crystal should be the right size in the imagination for the person moving inside it, who should be able to reach all its extremities. (p. 27)
>
> —Jean Newlove and John Dalby
> in *Laban for All*

> The movements of our body follow rules corresponding to mineral *crystallizations* and structures of organic compounds. The shape which possibly offers the most natural and harmonious tracks for our movements is the *icosahedron*. It contains a rich series of combined inner and outer trace-lines with dimensional connections provoking "stable," i.e., easily equilibriated, movements as well as diagonal connections providing disequilibriating movements. Trace forms of movements are, however, never complete crystal patterns, but awareness of a harmonious flow resulting from crystalline tendencies increases pleasure in skill. (p. 114)
>
> The integration of body and mind through movement occurs in free performance of choreutic shapes. There is no limit to the possibilities of the study and practice of choreutics. It penetrates every human action and reaction, since all actions and reactions spring from movement within us. In the domain of the arts this fact becomes especially clear.
>
> There are visible arts such as architecture, sculpture and painting in which trace forms are fixed through the movement of drawing and the shaping of different materials. There are the audible arts, such as music and oratory (including the speaking of poetry), in which the trace-forms of bodily movements give shape to the sounds and rhythms, which characterize ideas and emotions. (p. 115)
>
> —Rodulf Laban
> in *Choreutics*

In searching for a divining logic to help explain human movement, Laban intensely studied the writings on geometry of Plato and Pythagoras. The mathematical relationships discovered by Pythagoras and Plato's delineation of the five perfect solids—*Tetrahedron, Cube, Octahedron, Dodecahedron,* and *Icosahedron*—fascinated Laban. Within those shapes, with the triangle as the basic geometric building block, Laban found sympathetic structures that allowed him to clearly view and organize human movement in all its dimensions. These crystalline shapes, whose inspiration lay in Plato and Pythagoras, became the foundation of Laban Movement Analysis and the basis of understandings in his approach to *Modern Educational Dance*.

Figure 29. The five perfect solids
(as delineated by Pythagoras and Plato).

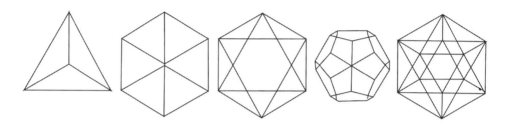

The Body: A System of Levers

The human skeleton is a miracle system of levers. Movement is achieved though a body that "levers" its way through its movement life. The systematic perception of one's body allows one to become aware of ALL the intricacies of one's movement and how those movements FEEL. It is that kinesthetic feedback and perception of how those moving levers "feel" that gives conductors their particular expressive and yes, even a stylistic vocabulary. It is the acquisition of that particular language that is the singular focus of this book. Consider the following statement by Laban:

Rationalistic explanations of the movements of the human body insist on the fact that it is subject to the laws of inanimate motion. The weight of the body follows the laws of gravitation. The skeleton of the body can be compared to a system of levers by which distances and directions in space are reached. These levers are set in motion by nerves and muscles which furnish the strength needed to overcome the weight of the parts of the body that are moved. The flow of the motion is controlled by nerve centers reacting to external and internal stimuli. Movements take a degree of time, which can be exactly measured. The driving force of movement is the energy developed by a process of combustion within the organs of the body. The fuel consumed is in the process is food. There is no doubt about the purely physical character of the production of the energy and its transformation into movement. (p. 22)

—Rudolf Laban
in *The Mastery of Movement*

Going back to James Watson's theory of the eccentric projection of feeling presented earlier, simply stated, it was Watson's belief that all movement learning was acquired through "feelings in the joints." I have never been able to locate if, indeed, Laban knew of Watson's theory. However, it is clear to me that the thought process between the two was similar. Laban went one step further to codify and describe those body "feelings" as gravity pulls that were associated with particular "weights." An understanding of these "gravity pulls" is central to the expansion of one's expressive movement vocabulary. This vocabulary, acquired in a way that guides one through a progressive and systematic study of body architecture that teaches a progression of gravity pulls, is central to gaining expressive conducting technique. The progression and study of this understanding follows:

- Accurately perceiving one's personal movement space;
- Segmentation of the body for both self-perception and study;
- Understanding and perceiving the defense scales: pure, clean dimensions with one gravity pull;
- Understanding and perceiving two-dimensional movement: moving around the defense scale (the diamond);
- Understanding and experiencing two-dimensional movement with one gravity pull: door plane, wheel plane, and table planes;
- Understanding the diagonals (movements within the cube): experiencing the interaction of two gravity pulls;
- Perceiving the world of movements and gravity pulls in the icosahedron;
- Learning to experience various expressive gesture vocabulary through the addition of the Efforts in Combination.

Additionally, it is important to ask questions about the "how" of movement:

- Which part of the body moves?
- In which direction or directions of space is the movement exerted?
- At what speed does the movement progress?
- What degree of muscular energy is spent on the movement?[116]

---

116   These questions are in Laban's own words from *The Mastery of Movement*, p. 27.

This skill set will move through a progression of geometric study of the body. These materials must be studied and understood in the sequence below. The sequence is progressive. Do not move from one concept to the next unless you fully understand and perceive each concept. The knowledge of your architecture, according to Laban, is a cumulative and progressive awareness process.

The Study of the Body Architecture and Its Hierarchy of Resultant Gravity Pulls

Geometric Divisions of the Body for Study and Self-Perception

The first step in understanding through self-perception Laban's view of the geometric organization of the body is the ability to divide the body architecture into clearly defined areas. The body should be perceived as being divided into two units: *upper unit* and *lower unit*.

- Lower unit – lower back/lower abdomen/pelvis/hip/thigh/lower leg/feet/toes – The lower unit is the center of weight and serves to transport the body and support postural changes in the upper body.
- Upper unit – head/neck/chest and upper spine/ entire arm unit beginning at scapula and moving outward toward fingertips – The upper unit is the control center for all manipulating, exploring, reaching, gathering, and gesturing activities.
- Right and left half of the body – The body is divided into two halves.

This completes Laban's segmentation of the body for perceptive purposes, all of which are represented in Figure 30.

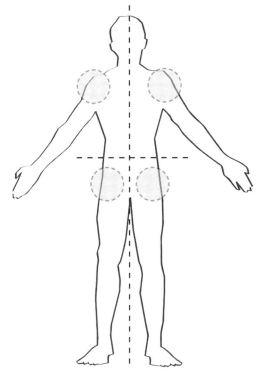

Figure 30. Basic components of the body: perceiving the body in architectural divisions.

In perceiving yourself as a mover (conductor), you should begin by doing some basic patterns, and then ask yourself the following questions:

- What part of your body initiates the movement?
- Which parts of the body are active or held?
- Is the movement leading away from the center of the body or toward it?
- Are those body parts used symmetrically or sequentially?
- Is your center of weight shifting or anchored?
- How are you grounding your body?

Perceiving Your Kinesphere and Interactive Gravity Pulls

One of the most valuable implications that the work of Laban has for conductors lies within the concept of the interaction of gravity upon the skeletal structure. Many conductors get into conducting and expressive dilemmas because their body "always feels the same." If conductors would be aware of how their body feels as it moves not only through space but also through the sound conducted, they would move their conducting to a new perceptual and expressive level. Laban wanted the body to be perceived as a three-dimensional structure with three axes: (1) a depth axis, (2) a length axis, and (3) a width axis. When standing upright, these three axes in codependence create a three-dimensional space around the body that can and should be readily perceived at all times.

Each of the motions below causes not only a different spatial experience, but also a different feeling regarding gravity pulls.

- Standing still, gravity exerts a downward pull and at the same time an upward pull along the vertical axis, or the *core* of the body.
- Being aware of the vertical axis, you can move forward or backward in the depth dimension.
- You can also move your arms to the sides of your body along what is known as a *sagittal axis*.

Laban called one's personal space their *kinesphere* (see Figure 31). It is your personal space for expressive and communicative movement.

Figure 31. The kinesphere.

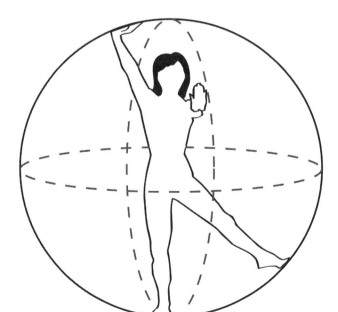

SKILL SET THREE

Spatial Distinctions and Zones for Movement

As conductors, we move our arms as a communicative and connective device. From Laban's perspective, this is done by either (1) gathering toward the body or (2) scattering away from the body. Both movements, when perceived properly by the conductor as aware acts, have decidedly different effects upon the sound. Theoretically, the gestures can be done on three different levels in Laban's world. As conductors, however, our expressive gesture is somewhat confined to the medium and high planes. These planes are most useful for left-hand technique because of the effect they can have on both color and articulation. The horizontal directions are most easily accessible for conductors.

Using the three levels in space shown in Figure 32, experience the following movement in planes:

- Move your arms around the middle plane.
- Practice exploring the corners of the upper plane with your left hand.
- Practice keeping your basic pattern anchored on or near the middle plane.
- Use both hands along the middle plane.

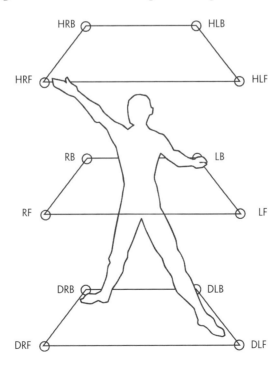

Figure 32. Three levels in space: oblique directions.

213

Sequential Exploration of the Organization of the Body with Corresponding Gravity Pulls

The Defense Scale:
The Foundation of Kinesthetic Experience for Conductors

There is no concept more important to understanding and experiencing the feelings of one's body moving through the Defense Scales. Defense scales (or derivations of them) can be found in all of the Eastern martial arts and the Eastern meditative arts. This defense scale is uniquely one-dimensional. The basic defense scale is built around the three basic axes of the body: (1) vertical axis, (2) horizontal axis, and (3) center axis that passes through the center of the body and intersects with the other two. Movement along each axis, specifically with the hand, produces what Laban termed a "pure, clean gesture" in that the mover (conductor) is experiencing only one gravity pull. Being able to experience these pure, clean dimensions gives conductors valuable expressive tools when conducting passages that need simplicity, directness, or a certain type of clarity or sound transparency. The key to the experience of the pure, clean dimensions is that you must stay connected or pass through your center to keep the purity of the single gravity pull or gravity interaction on the body. You must have the core of your body well aligned to perceive the kinesthetic of these movements accurately: movements toward center increase stability; movements outward decrease stability.

- Move your hands up and down your vertical axis and experience the "feel" of one gravity pull.
- Move each hand along a perfect horizontal plane.
- Bring your hand from behind your back, around your body, and directly though the center intersected axis, as if you are defending yourself against attack. This movement is powerful and direct when done correctly because it uses only one gravity pull. *This Defense Scale is one of the most important physical exercises for conductors to organize their own movement and clearly feel and be aware of the interaction of gravity upon their own body.*

Figure 33. The defense scale.

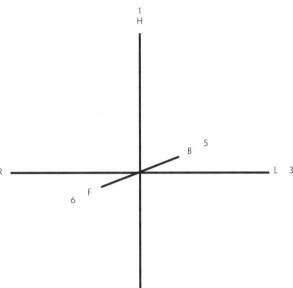

The conductor, at all times, should perceive the above defense scale in operation at all times represented in Figure 34.

Figure 34. The defense scale in operation.

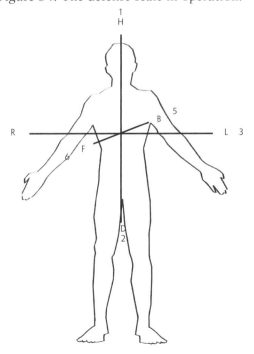

Experiencing Two-Dimensional Movement Around the Axis: Movement in the Octahedron

For Laban, it was next most important to experience movement around the cross of axis. The experience of moving from point to point around the periphery without going through center elicits yet another body feeling for conductors and yet another area for movement possibilities. These sequences afford conductors a methodical, step-by-step way to explore and experience the vast movement possibilities. Remember that movement around the periphery of the octahedron still only uses one gravity pull! An octahedron is shown in Figure 35.

- Take each hand separately and move in pure, clean dimensions along the periphery of the octahedron, from the middle of your body upward.
- Focus especially around the periphery in the middle of the octahedron.

Figure 35. Octahedron.

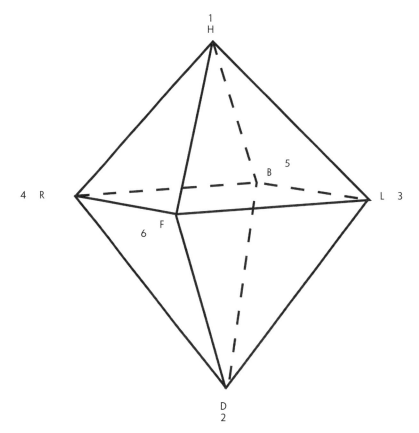

The Door, Wheel, and Table Planes: Two-Dimensional Movement

Earlier in this chapter, I emphasized the importance of the Defense Scale, with its single gravity pulls and pure, clean dimensions. Equally as important to conductors is an understanding, both intellectually and kinesthetically, of the door, wheel, and table planes. These are the planes available to conductors when reaching from one of three different axes, as shown in Figure 36.

Because of the architecture of the body, the planes form a rectangular surface. Note that for each of the planes, one of the gravity pulls is dominant over the other—that is, vertical movement is dominant over horizontal movement (with its corresponding gravity pull) in the door plane, horizontal movement dominates over sagittal movement on the table plane, and sagittal movement dominates over vertical gravity forces in the wheel plane.

Figure 36. The door, wheel, and table planes.

For conductors, a vivid perception of these three planes is fundamental to the development of conducting technique that positively affects ensemble sound no matter the nature of the ensemble. Let me be more specific.

Door Plane…The Plane of Human Connection:
This plane, when conceptualized correctly in a conductor's movement world, does not exist at the intersection of all three planes as Laban states, but is slightly altered. This plane and its independent axis, when perceived concurrently with the other planes, is forward from the core alignment of the conductor, an embrace-length away.

Once located in your perception, the door plane should come to represent the actual sound of the ensemble, almost like a sound membrane that has elastic qualities. This plane can be touched, pressed into, stroked through contact with either fingertips or baton. The contact with this membranous plane is the plane that establishes honest and meaningful connection not only with the sound in the room, but also with the human beings producing the sound. You could picture the following:

Figure 37. Visualizing the door plane.

- Practice touching the *elastic* membrane of the door plane. Remember that as a conductor, motion in your arms is generated from the fingertips backward.
- Explore with both hands the entire surface of the door plane, from the level of the horizontal table plane upward.

- If other singers or instrumentalists are available, practice singing or playing unison sounds or tone clusters each time there is contact with the door plane.

Wheel Plane...The Plane of Forward Motion:
This plane is vital for a conductor's understanding of how sound is moved forward—how sound is set in motion. If you imagine turning a water wheel, it rolls forward and back in a quasi-ellipse. This elliptical dynamic, no matter whether it is moving the entire body through space or just the arms, generates a forward-moving propulsion. This motion can be seen in the physical architecture of patterns, both on vertical beats and horizontal beats. This motion is never static. It tends to accelerate as you reach an ictus point in the pattern, and then decelerate as you come out of or leave the ictus point. This movement has a decidedly different kinesthetic sensation than the movement experience from axis outward in the door plane.

- If you are able, run forward and then backward in a large space. Run in a slight elliptical shape. The faster you run, the more you will feel a shift of weight *at* the point where you suddenly change direction.
- If you simply do vertical gestures with your arms, you will notice that you can control the acceleration and deceleration by varying the depth of the ellipse you are conducting. You will also feel an acceleration toward the bottom of the beat and a deceleration away from the beat.

**Table Plane...The Plane of Opening
and the Architectural Foundation of Conducting Technique:**
The table plane, located at the point where your forearm can be held parallel to the floor, forms the basis of the visual architecture of patterns and provides you with another gestural tool to not only move sound forward but also affect the dynamic of the sound. The table plane affords you of the chance to optimize the use of a spreading gesture that hopefully stays connected to your central core. The horizontal motion with its gravity pull is the strongest kinesthetic feeling when operating in this plane.

- To experience the gravity of the table plane, move both arms along the horizontal surface of the table plane.
- Make certain you reach for the outermost perimeters so the possible space of the table plane is mapped in your mind and that you properly use your arms to access these areas.

After experiencing each of the three planes alone, conduct standard patterns while trying to perceive all three planes simultaneously. To help clarify your perception of these three intersecting planes, imagine the following representation:

Figure 40. The three intersecting planes.

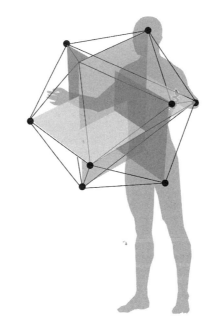

Movement within the Cube:
The Experience of Three Interactive Gravity Pulls

> The easy performance of certain efforts into definite directions or along stretches of free shapes or regular patterns makes the movement harmonious. The body is brought by grotesque movements into contorted positions when reaching to an awkwardly situated aim with an unsuitable effort. (p. 39)

—Rudolf von Laban
in *Modern Educational Dance*

In his book, *Modern Educational Dance* (1948), Laban clearly puts forward the principle that for any movement to be kinesthetically valid as a movement experience connected, body movements should cross or rather involve diagonal movement that crosses at least two planes. This is a pedagogical game changer for conductors because Laban clearly alludes that shifts in weight can only be "experienced" when one moves in diagonals within one's representational cube. Laban further writes:

> The themes of space orientation can be performed in small medium and large extension. The moving person can stop at any point on the way from the center to the most distant point he can reach. There exist, for example many points *bf*, distributed along the line *c* to *bf*. The distinction of a narrow *bf* (level with shoulders), a medium distance *bf* (level with forehead), and a wide bf (reaching as far as possible), will suffice for training purposes. The rhythm of the movements along orientation patterns can be chosen as one wishes, but it is advisable to start with regular time intervals, each stretch in space have the same time duration. (p. 37)

If you perceive yourself being placed within a cube, the space that surrounds you is organized in a clearly geometric arrangement.

Figure 41. Space within the cube:

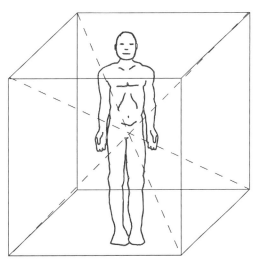

Using this geometric model, if you conceive of the possibilities of diagonal movement, the following vivid representation of the paths of *possible* movement become clear.[117]

Figure 42. The paths of possible movement.

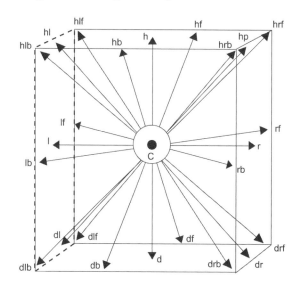

If one lists all the possibilities for movement within the cube, the following list is the result:

Key to Abbreviations in Laban Diagonal Movement Path Cube

h = high   *d* = down   *l* = left   *r* = right
b = backward   *f* = forward   *c* = center

hr	=	high right
db	=	down backward
lf	=	left forward
dr	=	down right
hb	=	high backward
rf	=	right forward
dl	=	down left
hf	=	high forward
rb	=	right backward

---

117 This illustration appeared in *Modern Educational Dance* (1948), p. 36.

SKILL SET THREE

hl	=	high left
df	=	down forward
lb	=	left backward
hrf	=	high right forward
dlb	=	down left backward
hlf	=	high left forward
drb	=	down right backward
hlb	=	high left backward
drf	=	down right forward
hrb	=	high right backward
dlf	=	down left forward

So what is the value of taking yourself repeatedly through these diagonals? I have found that variations in phrase shape, phrase direction, tempo changes, and dynamic changes can only be affected by conducting gestures that utilize the same "shifts" in kinesthesia that can be experienced first by simple movement through these diagonals. Diagonal movements allow conductors to stay connected to center while they have a change in direction, intensity, dynamic, or tempo. *As a by-product, it is the movement among and between those diagonals that provides the building block experiences of shifts of weight as one passes through center!* For the development of conducting technique, one should move through these diagonals (if possible daily, or at least weekly) as a warm-up for any rehearsal. Instead of moving through the entire cube, modify the cube to a rectangle, with the bottom being the table plane, so you focus your movement using your arms and upper torso. Remember that because of the structure of the body, it is almost impossible to perform diagonals geometrically equal. You can, however, come close to creating that illusion. It could also be argued that on some of the diagonals, depending on tempo, three gravity pulls may be experienced.

Practice the following diagonal scales:

- High/right/forward to deep/left/back
- Deep/left/ back to high/left/forward
- High/left/forward to deep/right/back
- Deep/right/back to high/left/back
- High/left/back to deep/right/forward
- Deep/right/forward to high/right/back
- High/right/back to deep/left/forward

The next, and arguably the most important step, in the development of conducting technique using Laban's principles is to move *from* the whole body movement experience within the cube and feel the gravity pulls that result, which forces you to experience the effect of gravity as you move through and between these diagonals using your upper body only as the expressive apparatus.

Again, it is the movement of the whole body within the cube that is central to establishing a strong sense of consistent tempo and, consequently, meter discrimination. It is the moving between the diagonals that connects one's center to the organic foundations of rhythm.[118] The importance of this work cannot be overemphasized as it relates to the development of an expressive conducting technique as well as a rhythmic sense that is grounded within a conductor's core. A conductor's training should first consist of moving the entire body through all of the diagonals and then refining body movement and coordination using the upper torso.

Author's Note: *At this point, the reader should view, study, and participate in real-time exercises using the segment of the component DVD that accompanies this book, as masterfully taught by Dr. Meade Andrews.*

Moving from Full Body Movement to Focusing
the Movement World on the Upper Body

The essential step in this "Labanization" process is to take the experiences of moving within the larger cube and transfer that total body kinesthetic to the upper body expressivity while maintaining the total body awareness you had in the large cube. That is, you conceptualize yourself as illustrated in Figure 42 and once again move through all of the diagonals, but on the smaller movement scale of your upper body.

---

118 This compelling pedagogical information was proved in this author's doctoral dissertation. In that study, the overall organization of the students' movement was movement within a cube via many different scenarios and the ability to feel the dimensional cross of axis. It is this author's interpretation that significant experimental results were obtained solely on the basis of this Laban principle. Consequently, this author feels strongly, as suggested by the experimental data, that the experience of the dimensional cross of axis (i.e., moving within the cube) is central to the development of a movement vocabulary.

Figure 43. Movement through all of the diagonals.

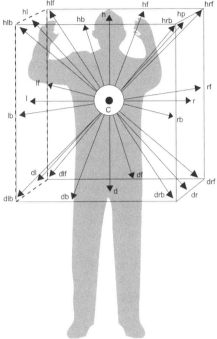

The space of the cube that surrounds your whole body is now visualized as a crystalline shape around your upper body. It is important to imagine yourself at the center of this cube. he perception of the space behind you is as important as the conception of the space in front of you! If you do not stay in awareness of the space that is behind you, then tensions develop in your basic technique. The key is to maintain an awareness and the conceptualization of the geometry of your movement. It has been my experience that conductors experience tremendous growth in expressivity and technique as long as they perceive their movement world existing in this crystalline shape of the cube.

Using the diagram shown in Figure 43 as your perceptual starting point, perform the following sequence using only your upper torso and take yourself through all the diagonals.

High/right/forward	to	deep/left/back
Deep/left/ back	to	high/left/forward
High/left/forward	to	deep/right/back
Deep/right/back	to	high/left/back
High/left/back	to	deep/right/forward
Deep/right/forward	to	high/right/back
High/right/back	to	deep/left/forward

Modified Diagonals and the Dynamic of Movement Among and Between Diagonals Create the Icosahedron

Figure 44. Icosahedron developed from planes.

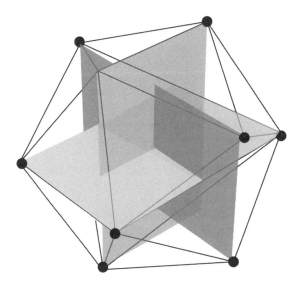

If you combine all the previous geometric/crystalline-like structures with all their intersecting planes, Laban called this visualization of one's total movement world the *icosahedron*.

The icosahedron is constructed around one kinesphere. Conductors exist primarily in the top portion of the icosahedron. This perception of the structure and geometry of one's personal space is important for the development and expansion of technique. Also note that all of these shapes exist not only in larger body movements but also in small movements. When the perception of space is right, you can move in response to your audiation of the score and react to the sounds you hear.

Conducting gestures learned and organized according to Laban's projective geometry provides the conceptual tools you need as a conductor to reflect musical idea and human message in the music you conduct.

Figure 45. The perception of the icosahedron for conductors: space for expressive movment.

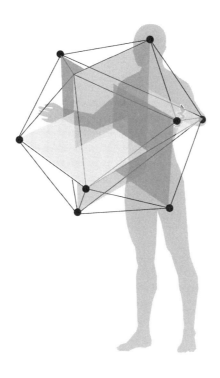

SKILL SET FOUR

Developing a Kinesthetic Vocabulary of Effort Combinations through Awakening Movement Imagination

The components making up the different effort qualities from an inner attitude (conscious or unconscious) towards the motion factors of Weight, Space, Time and Flow. (p. 13)

—Rudolf Laban
in *The Mastery of Movement*

Actions in which one or two of the elements of Time, Space, or Weight are almost entirely absent, or slightly stressed, are incomplete elemental actions. In casual movements that are neither sustained nor quick the time element has no physical import. Such movements seem to consist of Weight and Space components only. That means that there exists no definite attitude of the moving person towards the time factor. These are incomplete elemental actions which can frequently be observed as transitions between basic actions. (p. 77)

—Rudolf Laban
in *The Mastery of Movement*

Certain movements can be considered derivatives of basic actions:

Basic Action	Derivative
Punch	shove, kick, poke
Slash	beat, throw, whip
Dab	Pat, tap, shake
Flick	Flip, flap, jerk
Press	crush, cut, squeeze
Wring	pull, pluck, stretch
Glide	smooth, smear, smudge
Float	strew, stir, stroke (p. 77)

—Rudolf von Laban
in *The Mastery of Movement*

It is a mechanical fact that the *weight* of the body, or any of its parts, can be lifted and carried into a certain direction of *space,* and that this process takes a certain amount of time, depending upon the ratio of speed. The same mechanical conditions can also be observed in any counter-pull which regulates the *flow* of movement. The use of movement for a definite purpose, either as a means for external work or for the mirroring of certain states and attitudes of mind, derives from a power of a hitherto unexplained nature. One cannot say that this power is unknown, because we are able to observe it in various degrees of perfection, wherever life exists.

What we can clearly see is that this power enables us to choose between a resisting, constricting, withholding, fighting attitude, or one of yielding, accepting, indulging in relation to the 'motion factors' of Weight, Space and Time to which, being natural accidents, inanimate objects are subjected. This freedom of choice is not always consciously or voluntarily exercised; it is often applied automatically without any contribution of conscious willing. (p. 23)

—Rudolf Laban
in *The Mastery of Movement*

The variety of human character derives from the multitude of possible attitudes towards motion factors, and certain tendencies herein can become habitual with the individual. It is of the greatest importance for the actor-dancer to recognize that such habitual inner attitudes are the basic indications of what we call character and temperament. (p. 24)

—Rudolf Laban
in *The Mastery of Movement*

Laban passionately believed that to become adept with movement, a person should develop a daily routine of exploring the Efforts in Combination. In the initial stages of movement exploration, the "labeling" and understanding of the Effort Element content in everyday life activities provides the foundation of movement understanding because it grows out of one's personal experience. Laban believed that we all experience a complete spectrum of movement possibilities as children, but we have forgotten those movement experiences because the routine of our daily lives has minimized our daily movement experience. For each of the Efforts in Combination, there are suggestions below for life activities that would reawaken that particular Effort Combination within conductors. Mime each of the suggestions for each category and discover how a change in one or more of the individual Effort Elements changes the movement. Add your personal experiences to each list.

Experiencing the Efforts in Combination

It is easiest to gain an understanding of the Effort Elements through their various combinations as suggested by Laban. It is difficult to experience Flow, Weight, Time, or Space separately. By adjusting the relative intensities of Flow, Weight, Time, and Space within an activity, one can relate an infinite variety of movement possibilities. Laban assigned an action verb to each combination of three Effort Elements. Central to his theory is the simultaneous concentration on the three elements of Weight, Space, and Time taking over, or predominating, changes in Flow. Laban's action verbs, which describe combinations of Effort Elements, along with movement examples for each verb, are shown on the pages that follow. The abbreviations denote S = Space, W = Weight, and T = Time.

For each of the Efforts in Combination, the elements of Time, Space, and Weight interact to produce the illusion of Flow. In other words, the perception of one's rhythmic and gestural flow is a by-product of the interaction of Time, Space, and Weight. Flow cannot exist alone. It is the result of infinite combinations of Time, Weight, and Space, which produces an infinite variety of movement. The genius of Laban was his ability to observe how the combinations of Time, Space, and Weight could be varied to produce what is perceived as Flow. These principles are important for conductors to make them aware of the infinite potential of their own movement and to reawaken movement within themselves that may not have been used since childhood, or to reawaken movement that may not be part of their current life experience.

LABAN ACTION VERB	QUALITIES (ELEMENTS)	MOVEMENT EXAMPLES
FLOAT	indirect (S) light (W) sustained (T)	• treading water at various depths

> Floating movements can be directed into various zones of space, the most important being high, forwards, outwards, but there are endless possibilities–with each arm separately, or both together, floating downwards, upwards, across, sideways, forwards and backwards, extending into space in all directions. (p. 62)
>
> —Rudolf Laban
> in *Modern Educational Dance*

LABAN ACTION VERB	QUALITIES (ELEMENTS)	MOVEMENT EXAMPLES
WRING	indirect (S) strong (W) sustained (T)	• wringing a beach towel

> Wringing can vary from a pulling to a twisting movement, and is felt more easily in the shoulders, arms and hands than in the hips and the legs. The feeling of strength must not be lost, as the slow muscular resistance felt in pressing is also present in this effort, but wring produces a different sensation as the joints move more flexibly. (p. 63)
>
> "Indulging with" space and time, and fighting against weight, which is the essence of wringing, develops a valuable control and gives an entirely different movement experience from that gained by doing simple twisting exercises. (p. 65)
>
> —Rudolf Laban
> in *Modern Educational Dance*

SKILL SET FOUR

LABAN ACTION VERB	QUALITIES (ELEMENTS)	MOVEMENT EXAMPLES
GLIDE	direct (S) light (W) sustained (T)	• smoothing wrinkles in a cloth, • ice skating
PRESS	direct (S) strong (W) sustained (T)	• pushing a car
FLICK	indirect (S) light (W) quick (T)	• dusting off lint from clothing
SLASH	indirect (S) strong (W) quick (T)	• fencing • serving a tennis ball
DAB	direct (S) light (W) quick (T)	• typing • tapping on a window

This action is felt most easily in the hands in a light movement, such as a painter dabbing on spots of colour, or in the fingers as in typewriting. (p. 65)

In dabbing at an object, resistance is felt. "Fighting against" Space and Times connected with "indulging with" Weight (shown in a certain relaxation and lightness), which is the essence of dabbing, develops a valuable control and gives an entirely different movement experience from that gained by doing simple straight line exercises. (p. 67)

—Rudolf Laban
in *Modern Educational Dance*

LABAN ACTION VERB	QUALITIES (ELEMENTS)	MOVEMENT EXAMPLES
PUNCH	direct (S) strong (W) quick (T)	• boxing

The lists on the pages that follow appear earlier in the text as an illustrative example. These lists are expanded, with more examples given for each effort combination.

SKILL SET FOUR

FLOAT

indirect (Space)
light (Weight)
sustained (Time)

Activities Drawn from Life Experiences:

- tracing a picture with a pencil
- floating in a pool on your back
- vaulting over a high bar by means of a pole
- using a bubble wand
- spraying a room with air freshener
- lying on a waterbed
- falling into the first moments of sleep
- reaching for an unfamiliar cat
- staggering
- swinging on a rope swing
- blowing bubbles
- the moment you are dropped off a ski lift before your feet hit the ground
- walking up the stairs and thinking there's one more, but realizing there isn't
- riding an elevator
- using a butterfly net
- free fall in skydiving
- spreading a light picnic blanket on the ground
- a feather falling to the floor
- a ball falling into a pile of cushy velvet
- Tai-Chi
- holding each of the five basic positions of the arms in ballet
- slowly waving a flag
- free falling with a parachute
- a feather falling
- spraying/wafting cologne

235

WRING

indirect (Space)
strong (Weight)
sustained (Time)

Activities Drawn from Life Experiences:

- twisting a washcloth or a sweater dry
- twisting your hair in the morning
- drying out a sponge
- twisting off a bottle cap
- opening a cardboard can of prepackaged cookie dough
- washing socks
- playing with a hula hoop
- drying your hands under a blower
- loosening or tightening a jar cap
- turning over dirt with a trowel
- squeezing juice from an orange
- twisting a twist tie on a trash bag
- using a screwdriver
- pulling out the stem of an apple
- spinning a dreidel
- opening a can of sardines
- using a melon baller
- opening a stuck faucet handle
- massaging a muscle
- applying lotion to your hands
- balling up toilet paper
- turning a key in the ignition
- pouring out a liquid
- braiding hair or a rope
- peeling a banana
- opening an old car window
- scooping ice cream
- scraping the batter from a mixing bowl
- using a manual can opener
- opening a hard doorknob
- pretending to choke someone

PRESS
direct (Space)
strong (Weight)
sustained (Time)

Activities Drawn from Life Experiences:

- kissing a child gently
- pushing a shopping cart loaded with groceries
- ironing a shirt
- pressing a button on a vending machine
- pushing a child on a swing
- squeezing a tennis ball
- pressing on the floor when doing a handstand
- closing an overloaded suitcase
- pushing a lawnmower in high grass
- pushing a lawnmower uphill
- using a paper cutter
- using a hole punch
- pushing in a laundromat coin cartridge
- moving a piano
- pedaling a mountain bike uphill
- applying the brakes in a car
- kneading dough for bread
- removing a childproof cap
- walking with an umbrella against the wind
- washing a window with a squeegee
- stapling papers
- ringing a doorbell
- pushing in a thumb tack
- packing trash in a filled trash bag
- going through a revolving door
- buckling a seatbelt
- covering your ears from loud music
- climbing an elliptical machine or stair stepper
- doing push-ups
- pushing a mop
- pushing a cookie cutter into dough
- stamping a piece of paper
- pushing a book onto a crowded bookshelf
- treading water
- pushing the touch screen of a GPS or ATM
- fingerprinting
- poking a friend
- closing a three-ring binder

GLIDE

direct (Space)
light (Weight)
sustained (Time)

Activities Drawn from Life Experiences:

- reaching to shake hands
- wiping up a spill with a paper towel
- pushing off from the side of a pool
- ice skating
- erasing a blackboard or dry erase board
- dusting or wiping off a table
- drawing a violin bow across one string
- spreading butter or jelly on toast
- gently scratching your arm
- sliding down a banister
- coasting downhill on a bicycle
- roller-blading or roller-skating
- throwing a paper airplane
- sliding in socks on a newly polished floor
- painting a wall with a roller
- opening a sliding glass door
- smoothing sheets when making a bed
- putting a ring on your finger
- closing a zip-lock sandwich bag
- turning a page in a book
- smoothing cement with a trowel
- icing a cake
- water- or snow-skiing
- drawing a circle with a compass
- playing a glissando on a piano
- shaving
- slipping on sandals
- ironing a delicate fabric
- drawing in the sand
- spackling a hole
- moving your finger across the mouse pad of a laptop computer
- putting on sunscreen
- finger-painting
- icing a cake
- using a Swiffer duster

DAB

direct (Space)
light (Weight)
quick (Time)

Activities Drawn from Life Experiences:

- putting the final touches on the frosting of a cake
- tip-toeing
- playing darts (moment the dart is released from the hand)
- using a paintbrush to make dots
- poking someone's arm with your finger
- dipping a cloth in a pail of water
- breaking a balloon with a pin
- dotting an "i"
- applying antiseptic on a small cut
- tap dancing
- pushing a button on a remote control
- typing
- finger-painting
- testing hot water with your finger
- cleaning cobwebs from the ceiling
- using white glue
- cleaning a child's sticky mouth
- placing a cherry on a sundae
- covering a blemish with concealer
- painting your fingernails
- pointing to an item on a menu
- playing a single, soft note on a piano
- dabbing a sweaty brow
- touch-ups
- cell phone texting
- applying something with cotton
- tossing a pinch of salt on a food item
- clicking on something on the Internet
- painting polka dots
- lighting a candle with another candle

FLICK

indirect (Space)
light (Weight)
quick (Time)

Activities Drawn from Life Experiences:

- removing an insect off a table
- turning a light switch on or off
- leafing through the pages of a book
- lightly keeping a balloon in the air
- brushing debris off a desk or table
- shooing a fly
- wiping sweat from your brow
- shooting marbles
- touching a hot stove
- throwing a Frisbee
- snapping your fingers
- opening "flip-top" toothpaste
- brushing snow from a windshield
- taking a foul shot in basketball
- striking a match
- folding egg whites
- throwing rice
- popping soap bubbles
- moving hair from your face
- shaking mud off your shoe
- tossing a can into the recycling bin
- sprinkling salt in a recipe
- removing crumbs from your shirt
- dipping your toes in a pool to check the temperature
- turning on a desk lamp
- snapping
- flicking someone's ear
- playing badminton
- shaking off excess water from a sponge
- writing "correct" marks on the paper
- playing Wii tennis
- flicking water from your hands
- turning a car signal on
- flicking a paper football
- splattering paint

SLASH

indirect (Space)
strong (Weight)
quick (Time)

Activities Drawn from Life Experiences:

- swinging a baseball bat
- fencing
- casting a fishing line
- golfing
- opening a cardboard box with a utility knife
- wielding a knife like a butcher
- tearing a piece of paper
- using an axe to chop wood
- slamming a door
- shaking catsup from a new bottle
- employing self-defense maneuvers
- sweeping a sandy floor with a push broom
- beating a hanging rug clean
- cutting vegetables
- kicking a soccer ball
- swinging a golf club wildly
- waving excitedly to a friend
- slamming a car door
- swinging a hammer while demolishing cabinets
- sweeping
- chopping onions with a knife
- holding your hand out the window of a moving car like an airplane wing
- counting money or dealing playing cards
- ripping out a page from a magazine
- slamming something
- throwing something far away
- tennis forehand or drop shot
- bushwhacking
- using an industrial paper cutter

PUNCH

direct (Space)
strong (Weight)
quick (Time)

Activities Drawn from Life Experiences:

- plumping a pillow
- boxing
- using a punching bag
- applauding loudly
- hammering a nail
- pounding your fist on a table
- digging a hole
- serving a volleyball
- fist pumping
- throwing a drink in someone's face
- hitting a TV to make it work
- hitting a buzzer
- knocking your shoes against each other to get dirt off
- banging on a bed and watching all of the dust that comes out of it
- throwing wet laundry into the dryer
- throwing a book violently to the floor
- typing on a computer
- kneading dough for homemade bread
- push-ups
- hammering tongue-and-groove joints together
- plopping down onto a bed
- stuffing a turkey
- karate
- boxing
- playing with a punching bag
- Tae Bo exercises
- giving a friend a "pound" in greeting

SKILL SET FIVE
The Movement Imagery Exercises

Dance as a sequence of movement can be compared with spoken language. As words are built up of letters, so are movements built up of elements. As sentences are built up of words, so are dance phrases built up of movements. (p. 26)

—Rudolf von Laban
in *Modern Educational Dance*

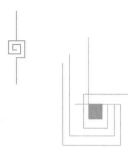

Punch / Press

Punch / Slash

Punch / Dab

Slash / Wring

Slash / Flick

Wring / Float

Wring / Press

Float / Flick

Float / Glide

Glide / Dab

Glide / Press

Dab / Flick

Without pause, quickly perform each pair of movements shown above. If the exercises are performed correctly, you will feel a sudden shift of energy between the two movement experiences of each pair. Perform each exercise first with external body movement and then with no external body movement so you can internalize the various combinations of movements and, more importantly, the changes in energy between the two movements in each combination. The quality of the Time element of each of the movements should be varied, as should the direction of each movement.

Laban did not specifically assign names to each of the eight combinations. The names of flick, dab, etc., have grown from the wide body of Laban practitioners who have found these labels useful and in keeping with the integrity of Laban's philosophical beliefs. Laban did believe that language could be more exacting about the action than it could be for the more subtle shades of experience. Transitions occur when one moves between Effort actions by changing one of the Effort Elements. For example, one may progress from punching (direct/heavy/quick) to pressing (direct/heavy/sustained). Transitions often involve the changing of a single component; it is possible, however, to change two or three components simultaneously.

The combinations of Elements attended to simultaneously are difficult to name. Laban referred to combinations of two factors (Elements), however, as an *incomplete Effort*. Those combinations are also referred to as *inner attitudes* because the combination of only two Elements suggests that the movement is not yet externalized but, instead, expresses a state of feeling Laban writes of in *The Mastery of Movement:* "It is difficult to attach names to these variations of incomplete Effort as they are concerned with pure movement experience and expression."[119]

The verbal descriptions are not precise, and they are always subject to movement validation. For each combination of two factors, you can combine the Effort Elements in four different ways. These combinations are known as *states*, or *drives*. All possible combinations of the six groups are illustrated in Figure 45. The italicized labels beneath the Effort Elements are the commonly used labels for the states, or drives. Remember that the descriptive terms in italics attempt to generally mirror internal feelings, not movements. Refer back to Chapter 12 by Giselle Wyers for in-depth discussion of these states and drives, and their importance for conducting study.

---

119   Rudolf Laban, *The Mastery of Movement*, p. 92.

Figure 46. Combinations of the Effort Elements into states or drives.

Laban Action	Time	Gestural Conducting Translation	Weight	Descriptive Syllable	Musical Sound Analogies
Float	Sustained	Indirect	Light	f	Whole tone No weight Repetitive passages.
Wring	Sustained	Indirect	Heavy	zh	Diminished chords Chopin Prel., Op. 28, No.20
Glide	Sustained	Direct	Light	s	Line Phrase
Press	Sustained	Direct	Heavy	v	Bagpipes Feminine Cadence
Flick	Quick	Indirect	Light	~ pft	Grace notes Textures requiring lightness
Slash	Quick	Indirect	Heavy	z	sfz Accents
Dab	Quick	Direct	Light	t fast tempo p slow	Staccato
Punch (side-arm)	Quick	Direct	Heavy	CH phy	with some degree of sustainment that is not tenuto
Dab/Press*	Sustained briefly	Direct	Light-Heavy	m	Tenuto
Punch/Press*	Sharp attack, sustained	Direct	Heavy	hwh *a la* Lamaze breathing	Marcato

* Hybrid combination of Laban efforts to simulate movements needed to play tenuto and marcato.

SKILL SET SIX
The Sixteen Movement Themes

The basic actions are also present in any mental or intellectual form of expression, and the outward projection of an effort can be indicative of a state of mind. Some people may have never experienced either bodily or mentally some of the efforts described here, and it will be beneficial for them to enlarge their understanding and the appreciation of a wider range of movements and the feel and comprehension of human action which such movements stimulate. (p. 52)

—Rudolf Laban
in *The Mastery of Movement*

In conclusion, it can be said that movement can be described as a composite of its shapes and rhythms, both making part of the superimposed flow of movement in which the control exerted by the moving person upon the movement becomes visible. (p. 93)

—Rudolf von Laban
in *Modern Educational Dance*

At the center of Laban's pedgagogical world are the Sixteen Movement Themes. These themes represent a progression of awarenesses of how one moves. These themes and their understandings and experiences are central to gaining an expressive conducting vocabulary. They are exactly as Laban described them and should be processed and experienced in the order suggested.

These themes, in a sense, form a type of "Zen of Conducting" curriculum for any conducting study or sequential conducting curriculum. The sixteen themes represent a stepwise and sequential method for acquiring movement vocabulary and the accompanying body kinesthesia for that vocabulary. They should not simply be studied once; they should be revisited time and time again.

These movement themes provide the foundation, combined with a clear understanding of both the spatial organization and the mechanics of the body (Body Mapping), of a sequential study of gesture.

Basic Themes

1. Themes concerned with the awareness of the body
2. Themes concerned with the awareness of weight and time
3. Themes concerned with the awareness of space
4. Themes concerned with the awareness of the Flow of the Weight of the body in Space and Time
5. Themes concerned with the Adaptations to partners
6. Themes concerned with the instrumental use of the limbs of the body
7. Themes concerned with the awareness of isolated actions
8. Themes concerned with occupational rhythms

Advanced Themes

1. Themes concerned with the shapes of movement
2. Themes concerned with the combinations of the eight basic actions

Figure 47. Themes concerned with the combinations of the eight basic actions.

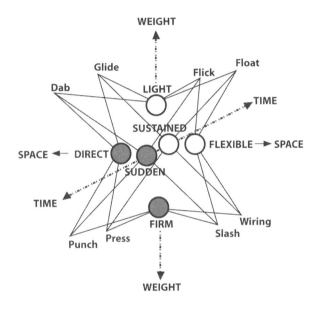

Key:
filled-in circle = fighting against Weight, Space, or Time
open circle = Indulging Weight, Space, or Time

3. Themes concerned with space orientation
4. Themes concerned with the performance of shapes and efforts by different parts of the body
5. Themes concerned with elevation from the ground
6. Themes concerned with the awakening of group feeling
7. Themes concerned with group formations
8. Themes concerned with the expressive qualities or moods of movements

Laban Movement Experience DVD: Experiencing the Movement Themes

The primary objective of the Laban Movement Experience DVD is to guide you through experiencing these movement themes. The DVD is designed to provide movement experiences to orient you to what the authors of the DVD feel are the most important themes to experience as a conductor/musician. The pedagogical integrity of the framework above cannot be underestimated. Movement experiences that cover these categories provide a balanced and aware movement experience that serves as the foundation for the use of space, but how one moves through that space. Repeated interactions with the DVD is central to your movement skill and movement perception development that will lead to a heightened level of body and movement awareness and a keen sense of body kinesthesia in many different manifestations.

SKILL SET SEVEN

Predicting and Imaging Movement to Evoke the Music: Laban Movement ∫core Analysis (LM∫A)

Music is silent screaming; motionless dance.

—Elaine Brown
Alumni Lecture
Westminster Choir College, 1989

An impulse is an activating, energizing force. A sound or group of sounds resulting in an increase in energy yields impulse. In a succession of tones of equal rhythmic value, impulse tends to result from ascending motion. Ascending motion by leap tends to result in greater impulse than ascending motion by step.

A resolution is a retracting, de-energizing force. A sound or group of sounds resulting in a decrease of energy yields resolution. If the energy gathered by the tightening of a spring is impulse, the dissipation of the energy effected by the release of the spring is resolution. Because resolution is a decrease or playing out of energy, there can be no resolution if there has been no energy gathered. (p. 13)

Imagine a motion that describes a circle (such as the motion of a person riding on a Ferris wheel). Beginning at the lowest point, the first part of the motion is an ascent. The motion continues upward along the arc on the left side until the highest point. At the highest point it has nowhere else to go but down; it returns downward along the arc on the right side, until it connects with the original point. When it connects, the circle is an indivisible unity. The whole unit is formed only when the arc of the descent matches the arc of the ascent. The boundaries are formed by the matching of the descent with the ascent. (p. 14)

—Markand Thakar
in *Counterpoint: Fundamentals of Music Making*

In a previous letter we have remarked that when a melody rises it marks in general an intensification of energy, when it falls it signifies a relaxation. Therefore, we must look for melodic fragments which bear an upward thrust, and balance them sensitively and minutely with those fragments which signify respite. (p. 70)

Convey the inner and hidden dialogue, the ying and yang, the up and down, the question and answer, male and female, boy-girl, tension and relaxation.

Be considerate of the text. It might just coincide with melodic or harmonic accentuation—and this moment is the Pentecost of song.Cultivate the forward look. Melody is a vagabond, incorrigibly searching the world for a place "really" to settle down. Even punctuation is not a period of retrospect, but of marshaling strength and scanning the horizon. The last note we sing is the one to which all others lead. (p. 71)

—Robert Shaw
in *The Robert Shaw Reader*

One of the areas of score analysis that is often overlooked has to do with the forward movement of a piece. Many of us take for granted our kinesthetic gifts—that is, understanding how a piece of music feels in our body. What we fail to either recognize or appreciate is that our singers do not always come equipped with fantasies of how music moves and feels in our bodies as we bind those sensations to the musical sounds we produce. For many of us, this is a natural, almost intuitive, process.

For vocalists, I have found that these decisions are of paramount importance. Inappropriate weight applied to musical line can directly inhibit vocal production. Vocal technique and the movement of musical line are intimately bound in the music-making process. Not to mention the "fantasy" of musical line confounds the music-making process. Moreover, if this analysis is approached with forethought, the "kinesthetic" study will transfer directly to appropriate conducting gesture—a by-product of the score study process.

While our musical intent is good, too often our gesture sends conflicting information to the choir. Our conducting gestures should match the Laban

Movement Score Analysis (LMSA). That is, we should be very clear in our minds just how the music moves forward. LMSA (or some type of study and analysis of the motion and shape of musical line) should take place before gesture is employed in either rehearsal or performance. Such analysis and the understandings it provides are central to the score preparation and musicing process.

Presented below are general rules for LMSA, followed by an explanation of each rule:

1. Make arsis/thesis decisions about the overall shape of the musical line.
2. Add weight to slow musical line; take away weight to add velocity and speed to the forward movement of the musical line.
3. Use direct gestures and efforts to propel musical line. Indirect gestures tend to slow the forward velocity.
4. Always complete movement analysis of a score before applying gestures to the movement. Then imagine yourself conducting the piece while audiating it, but do not move (imaging).
5. Mark the score with several possible analyses (LMSA) that are reflective of your desired musical intent.
6. Give the LMSA to your singers and have them mark the Efforts in Combination in red in their scores.
7. Remember that LMSA should reflect the rate of harmonic movement within any piece.
8. Have your singers speak the voiced and unvoiced LMSA syllables.

Rule #1 – Make arsis/thesis decisions about the overall shape of the musical line.

Use the Day-Tay system of Weston Noble or the Note Grouping principles of James Thurmond as a guide. In Baroque music, knowledge of the underlying dance steps contributing to the rhythmic structure is essential.

Deciding where musical lines move to—their "towardness"—is at the heart of LMSA. Use brackets labeled with "A" for arsis and "T" for thesis to mark the phrasal direction of every musical line in a score. In contrapuntal music, careful analysis is crucial to rehearsal planning and subsequent teaching. However, as conductors we tend to be too rigid in our thinking as we analyze because we believe the anacrustic part of the phrase is simply assigned to a rhythmic value, such as a pickup note. However, upon closer inspection, we often discover that the "rise" in the musical phrase occupies one or more beats and, in some situations, several measures. Text stresses combined with melodic shape and harmonic movement often provide definitive answers of a composer's intent.

To consider how phrases move in advance of the rehearsal/teaching process should become central to the rehearsal preparation process. Note, however, that many of the decisions made concerning forward movement of sound in a score are products of experience and an individual's innate musical instincts. Thus, an awareness of what is happening within your own body is central to this decision-making process.

Rule #2 – Add weight to slow musical line; take away weight to add velocity and speed to the forward movement of the musical line.

The Laban Efforts in Combination show that in many (if not all) situations, the addition of weight changes (or rather "transforms") the combinatory effort. The addition or subtraction of weight is one of the strongest determinants of Flow. Stated in Laban terms, the addition of weight into any movement changes the quality of Flow of the forward motion.

With score analysis in mind, it is important to revisit the Laban Efforts in Combination (see Figure 48).

The Laban principle is quite direct. Changing the amount of "weight" in Punch, for example, changes the "type" or "quality" of Punch. Subtle changes in weight have profound effects on musical phrasing. Allowing an ensemble to subjectively apply weight to a musical phrase diminishes the musical effectiveness of the ensemble. Instead, use your musical experience and musical instincts to provide the raw material for these important phrasing decisions.

Figure 48. Review chart for Laban Efforts in Combination to describe movement.

Laban Action Verb	Qualities (Elements)	Movement Examples
FLOAT	indirect (S) light (W) sustained (T)	• treading water at various depths
WRING	indirect (S) strong (W) sustained (T)	• wringing a beach towel
GLIDE	direct (S) light (W) sustained (T)	• smoothing wrinkles in a cloth • ice skating
PRESS	direct (S) strong (W) sustained (T)	• pushing a car
FLICK	indirect (S) light (W) quick (T)	• dusting off lint from clothing
SLASH	indirect (S) strong (W) quick (T)	• fencing • serving a tennis ball
DAB	direct (S) light (W) quick (T)	• typing • tapping on a window
PUNCH	direct (S) strong (W) quick (T)	• boxing

Rule #3 – Use direct gestures and efforts to propel musical line. Indirect gestures tend to slow the forward velocity.

Once you have made decisions that coincide with the forward movement of the musical line, the next stage of LMSA is to explore the qualities of gesture that will directly reflect the musical decisions your analysis has yielded. Conducting gesture that is more direct (i.e., angular) will always propel musical line forward, provided the gesture is physically released after the ictus. Indirect gesture, by its very nature, implies that less weight is involved. The withholding of weight inherent in indirect movement tends to allow the musical line to decelerate. After LMSA of any score has been completed, carefully consider the efforts that should be superimposed over your chosen conducting patterns.

Rule #4 – Always complete movement analysis of a score before applying gestures to the movement.

Gesture should always grow out of careful movement analysis of the musical materials at hand. While it is possible to omit the particulars of LMSA, you will find that without LMSA, you may become handicapped in the rehearsal process because of an inability to objectively describe to your singers the subtleties of the forward motion of the musical line. Without such guided instruction, singers apply their own movement instincts to the musical materials at hand: some will supply little, and others will contribute powerful movement ideas. However, the lack of a clear movement "profile" for a piece will undoubtedly lead to a mediocre rhythmic performance as a result of conflicting musical ideas within the ensemble.

Rule #5 – Mark the score with several possible analyses (LMSA) that are reflective of your desired musical intent.

Mark directly on your score the specific Laban Efforts in Combination (e.g., Float, Glide, Press, Dab, etc.) that reflect your kinesthetic feeling of how the phrase moves forward based upon your musical instincts and experience.

Rule #6 – Give the LMSA to your singers and have them mark the Efforts in Combination in red in their scores.

After you have made decisions concerning the "broad stroke" Efforts in Combination, mark the Efforts in Combination directly on the score (as shown in Figure 51 and Figure 52 at the end of this chapter).

At first glance, it might appear as though LMSA is a choreographic method, or a system that choreographs each movement of the conductor. It is not. The Laban Effort Elements represent a movement system that allows conductors to communicate their "feelings" or kinesthesia of movement through carefully chosen vocabulary. The Efforts in Combination are words that represent the energy within each movement in an attempt to verbalize the inner dynamics of movement. Hence, LMSA is a symbolic system designed to approximately represent all of the factors involved with the kinesthesia of a musical phrase.

Rule #7 – Remember that LMSA should reflect the rate of harmonic movement within any piece.

The rate of harmonic change often provides valuable insight into phrasal ideas of the composer. Yet many conductors fail to pay close attention to the rate or speed of harmonic chord changes. Harmonic motion is integral to most, if not all, phrasing decisions. Moreover, the individual "style" of a composer is highly dependent upon the composer's harmonic language, or harmonic syntax.

Remember that music has no grammar, but each composer possesses individual harmonic syntax. And while harmonic syntax has no strict rules, you can see common patterns that, in turn, define a composer's individual style.

Rule #8 – Have your singers speak the voiced and unvoiced LMSA syllables.

After you have selected the Efforts in Combination, you must be able to "translate" inherent motion into sounds. Sometimes musicians find it challenging to relate movement to sound, but this can become a valuable rehearsal technique.

Theoretical understanding of movement is one thing, but kinesthetic connection of movement to sound will enhance both rehearsal and musical performance. A modified chart of the Laban efforts is shown in Figure 49. This chart combines descriptions of each action from Philip Burton's Expressive Movement course taught in conjunction with Dalcroze training, to which Marilyn Shenenberger has added voiced and unvoiced sounds that mirror the general qualities of Float, Flick, Press, Dab, etc. I have found that the use of these syllables immediately binds kinesthetic movement ideas to musical sounds in the most effective ways. In the right-hand column of the chart, Shenenberger suggests musical structures that most often can be associated with the musical sounds (e.g., diminished chords, staccato, marcato, etc.).

Figure 49. Laban Efforts in Combination to describe movement and resulting sound.

Laban Action	Time	Gestural Conducting Translation	Weight	Descriptive Syllable	Musical Sound Analogies
Float	Sustained	Indirect	Light	f	Whole tone No weight Repetitive
Wring	Sustained	Indirect	Heavy	zh, [ʒ]	Diminished Chords Chopin Prel., Op. 28, No. 20
Glide	Sustained	Direct	Light	s	Line Phrase
Press	Sustained	Direct	Heavy	v	Bagpipes Feminine
Flick	Quick	Indirect	Light	pft	Grace notes Textures requiring lightness
Slash	Quick	Indirect	Heavy	z	sfz
Dab	Quick	Direct	Light	t fast tempo	Staccato
Punch	Quick	Direct	Heavy	CH, [tʃ]	Accents (with some degree of sustainment) that are not tenuto
Dab/Press*	Sustained	Direct	Light-Heavy	m	Tenuto
Punch/Press*	Sharp attack, sustained	Direct	Heavy	hwh a la Lamaze breathing	Marcato

* Hybrid combination of Laban efforts to simulate movements needed to play tenuto and marcato.

Choosing Appropriate Efforts in Combination

While all of the musical factors presented in this chapter contribute to the decisions regarding which Efforts in Combination to use to propel musical line, the amount of weight selected may be affected by the vocal/technical requirements of a piece. When conducting, I have often found it necessary to add more weight than originally envisioned to maintain a supported, on-the-breath sound from the singers. Fuller dynamics (resonances) sometimes also require more gestural weight than originally conceived. The deciding factor rests with the sound of the ensemble. As conductors we must constantly react to the sound and vary Laban efforts to achieve the desired musical result.

Where is weight applied to the conducting gesture? The most common misconception is that weight is added muscularly to the conducting gesture. However, weight added through increased muscular tension actually creates an undesirable response in the sound. The result is a sound that is out of tune, rigid, and hard. Instead, from an Alexander Body Mapping perspective, consider adding weight in the wrist, which is actually located in the palm of the hand. Imagine that your hand is holding a heavier object. The muscles in your arms should remain released at all times, as should the free motion in your scapulae or "shoulder blades." The weight, then, should be added and subtracted from your gesture through the addition or subtraction of weight in the palm of your hand.

Figure 50. Key to LMSA phrase markings.

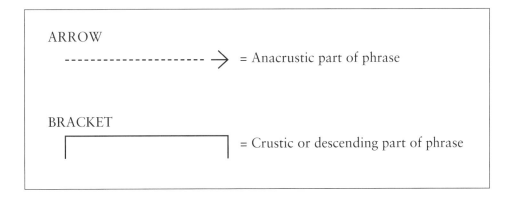

Figure 50. (Continued)

Effort Combination Label	Effort	Symbol for Score Marking
FLOAT	indirect (S) light (W) sustained (T)	**F**
WRING	indirect (S) strong (W) sustained (T)	**W**
GLIDE	direct (S) light (W) sustained (T)	**G**
PRESS	direct (S) strong (W) sustained (T)	**P**
FLICK	indirect (S) light (W) quick (T)	**FL**
SLASH	indirect (S) strong (W) quick (T)	**S**
DAB	direct (S) light (W) quick (T)	**D**
PUNCH	direct (S) strong (W) quick (T)	**PN**

SKILL SET SEVEN

Figure 51. Example of Efforts in Combination marked
in excerpt of Innisfree by Gerald Custer (GIA).

Note that this is only one LMSA approach to the musical elements in this piece; there may be many more. Also, remember that the size of the symbol is directly related to the amount of weight to be added to the conducting gesture.

*Winner of the 75th Anniversary Alumni Composition Competition,
Westminster Choir College of Rider University.*

INNISFREE
For SATB Voices and Piano

"The Lake Isle of Innisfree"
William Butler Yeats, 1865–1939

Gerald Custer

Figure 52. (Continued)

Figure 52. Example of Efforts in Combination marked in excerpt of When Spring Is Born at Last by Jackson Hill (GIA).

Note that this is only one LMSA approach to the musical elements in this piece; there may be many more. Also, remember that the *size* of the symbol is directly related to the amount of weight to be added to the conducting gesture.

SKILL SET EIGHT
Music Exercises for Practice

From where does the impulse of motion come? The impulse given to our nerves and muscles, which move the joints of our limbs, originates in inner efforts. (p. 26)

—Rudolf von Laban
  in *Modern Educational Dance*

From my vantage point, an understanding of Laban depends on what I call *interactive perception*. As a conductor you must have a clear conception of both the architecture of your body and what it feels like when those parts of your architecture are moving in conjunction with sound.

An important purpose of this book is to re-direct conductors to base conducting decisions on the harmonic motion of the works they are conducting. While melodic shapes may determine part of a phrase's trajectory, it is the harmonic structure that gives conductors information on how the "sounds" of the melody are set in motion.

In the exercises that follow, you will be asked to apply Efforts in Combination according to not only the melodic rhythm of the exercise but also, more importantly, the harmonic progression. These exercises were constructed to provide you with material to make conducting decisions.

These exercises have been recorded for your use and are available for free download at www.giamusic.com/conductorsgesture.

SKILL SET EIGHT

Dab and Glide

The conductor should make the sounds indicated while conducting.

Marilyn Shenenberger

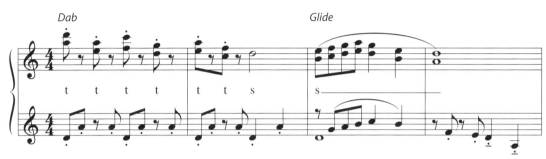
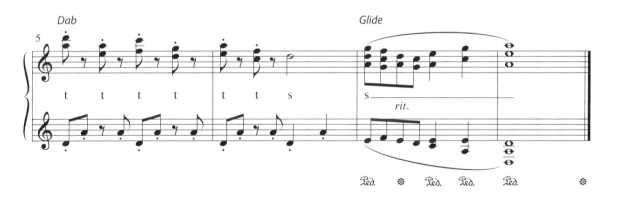

THE CONDUCTOR'S GESTURE · JAMES JORDAN

Glide, Press, Float, Dab, and Punch

The conductor should make the sounds indicated while conducting.

Marilyn Shenenberger

Track 3: ♩ = 72
Track 4: ♩ = 88

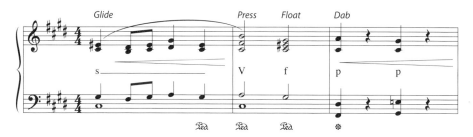
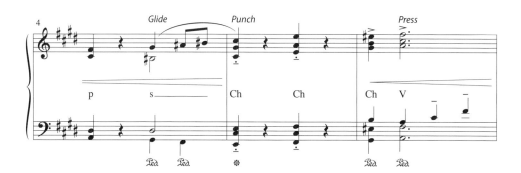
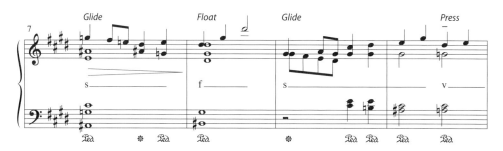

SKILL SET EIGHT

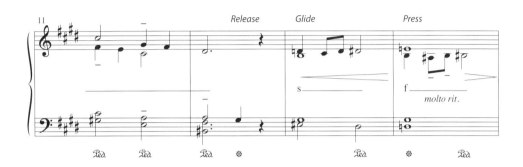

THE CONDUCTOR'S GESTURE · JAMES JORDAN

Float, Dab, Wring, Glide, and Press

The conductor should make the sounds indicated while conducting.

Marilyn Shenenberger

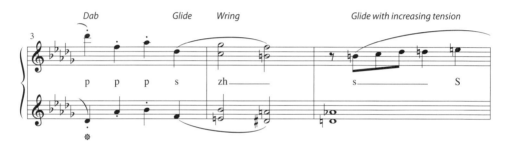

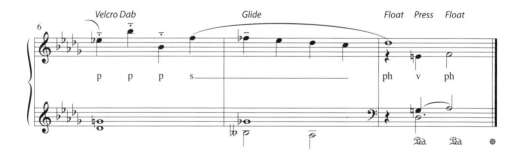

Press and Wring

The conductor should make the sounds indicated while conducting.

Marilyn Shenenberger

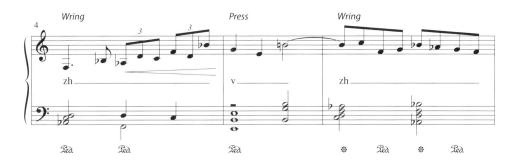

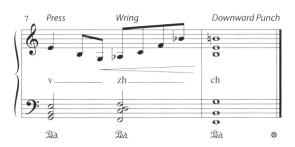

THE CONDUCTOR'S GESTURE · JAMES JORDAN

Dab and Glide over Float and Glide

This is a conducting duet. Participants should make the sound most fitting to the effort of the part they conduct.

Marilyn Shenenberger

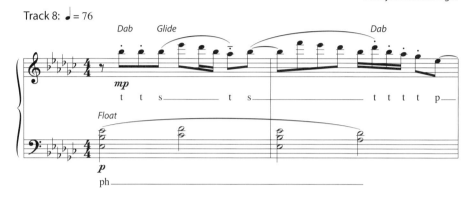

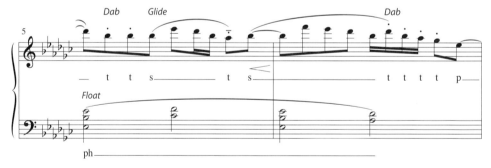

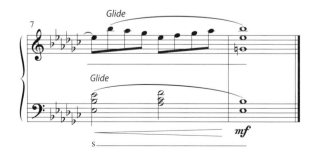

SKILL SET EIGHT

The Zoo

The conductor should make the sounds indicated while conducting.

Marilyn Shenenberger

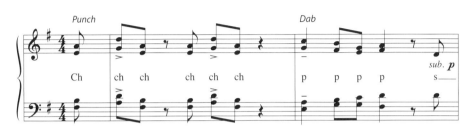

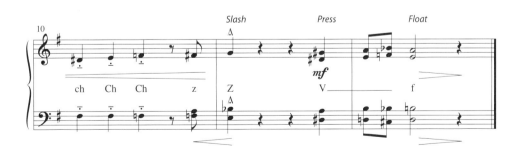

THE CONDUCTOR'S GESTURE • JAMES JORDAN

Mixolydian Conducting Round
Sing, play, and conduct as indicated.

Marilyn Shenenberger

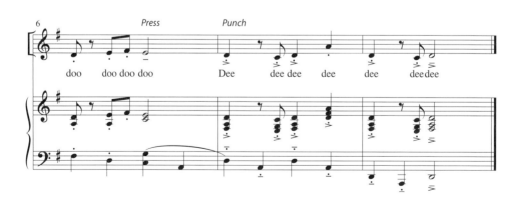

SKILL SET NINE
The Movement Experience DVD*

MEADE ANDREWS
JAMES JORDAN

* *The Conductor's Gesture DVD is found in the back inside cover of this book.*

Conductors embody the skills of an illusionist because in Frank Zappa's words: "They create designs in the nowhere that are interpreted as signals…" that impact and influence invisible sound. They are also able to convert thoughts and feelings into movement that is presented in the space that surrounds them. Through a process of "space-forming" or "space-sculpting," ideas and emotions that are encoded in the score and imbedded in the musicians are converted into shaped vibrations that transmit messages through the air to others. Even though the music cannot be seen, the consequential sensations can be felt. Therefore, conducting remains a tactile and mystical act that triggers human interaction and reaction. (p. xv)

According to Laban, Space, Weight, and Time are our allies in this pursuit. Energy, Direction, Distance, Resistance, and Speed also play a principal role. The interactions of these efforts combine to yield an inexhaustible thesaurus of gestures that can contain subtle and significant meaning. (p.xvii)

Conducting technique should demonstrate a balance of craft: the objective work of dispensing information and artistry, the subjective exploration of inspirational possibilities. Artists are responsible for developing their own imagined-ideal or aural model of a composition. Jordan cautions us that copying or mimicking someone else completely negates or defeats the creative process. When conducting technique is real, truthful, and in the moment, it generates from the inside out. To accomplish this, you need to broaden the movement potential within your body and eliminate whatever interferes with the musical goals. (pp. xviii-xix)

—Eugene Migliaro Corporon
from the *Foreword*

The chapters on this DVD are an important if not essentially vital supplement to this text. In my experience, when learning "Laban" it was my movement experiences that formed the basis of my understanding and my new conducting vocabulary. The DVD contains movement classes in which you can participate in the privacy of your own space and master classes in both choral and instrumental genres that allow you to see drill, practice, and applications to music examples. The DVD has two and a half hours of instructional material!

It is the area of application to actual conducting that has been so elusive and, in many ways, so confusing to those who have read this material in my past writings on the subject, especially in both editions of *Evoking Sound*. Students who have seen demonstrations of the material by myself, Meade Andrews, or Giselle Wyers have immediately grasped the profound implications for the development of their expressive conducting technique and their understanding of why they move and how to marry movement to the composer's musical and human intents. In the movement sections of the DVD, the authors attempt to provide similar content and experiences to what they experienced at the Laban Institute for Movement Studies in an effort to allow you to acquire movement experiences that are central to understanding Laban's theories.

Simply put, one cannot perceive one's movement space and its architecture unless one has moved in it and self-perceived it. Similarly, one cannot apply *any* of the Laban gestural language unless one has defined that language through one's personal movement experience. In many respects, while the written content of this text is important to a theoretical understanding of the frameworks of Laban's thought, it is the visual material on the DVD that will refine and define your understanding of this remarkable material. It is only after actually moving through this material that you can begin to apply this new "language" to your conducting to cause reactions to your gesture in the sound of your ensemble. The experiences of Dr. Andrew's movement classes are core to the experiences of this book and will form the foundation of your kinesthetic understanding of the genius of Laban.

The Discipline of Etudes for the Development of Conducting Technique

At the risk of being repetitive, I must re-emphasize that what is demonstrated on the DVD is a very detailed approach to the practicing and acquiring of movement experiences that form the foundation of a gestural vocabulary to be called on later in time and to be used to evoke the composer's intent from the ensemble. The material you will see in the classes in addition to your lists of *your* Efforts in Combination and the Movement Imagery Exercise suggested by Laban form a conductor's book of daily etudes for both the development and deepening of organic and natural gestural understandings.

One viewing of Dr. Andrew's classes will not engrain these concepts in your mind, but repeated study, reading, and thought will. Based on my own experience and the material that Giselle Wyers offers, I can assure you that these experiences will profoundly broaden your conducting technique and your ability to communicate through gesture in ways you never would have imagined.

Finally, there is a wealth of material contained in not only the choral master classes, but also in the work that was done with wind conductors and the Wind Symphony of The University of North Texas. In some cases, the changes are small, but they yield tremendous changes in the sound of the ensemble. As you view and study this portion of the DVD, be careful to not only *observe* the subtle changes that the Efforts in Combination bring about in the gesture of each conductor, but also *listen* for the changes that occur within the sound of the ensemble. By observing the subtle changes in gesture and hearing the immediate and often dramatic changes in the sound of the ensemble, you will begin to understand the potential impact of this material upon our art.

F. M. Alexander and Rudolf Laban: A Symbiotic Relationship

Meade Andrews

Continents apart, F. M. Alexander (1869–1955) and Rudolf Laban (1879–1958) have both become known as unique contributors to the exploration of the field of the mind-body connection: engaging the power of thought to influence and direct movement, and vice-versa. In Australia, Alexander developed his work out of the need to address his pattern of chronic laryngitis. He wrote: "The so-called 'mental' and 'physical' are not separate entities….all training…must be based on the indivisible unity of the human organism." In Germany, and later in England, Laban also made this discovery: "Movement is first and fundamental in what comes forth from a human being as an expression of his intentions and experiences. It is one of man's languages and as such must be consciously mastered."

Both men realized that we live because we have a need to move, to express the complexity of our unique selves, creating our identity in the world. In fact, they each discovered that we are designed for movement and that we are uniquely "wired" for the creative interaction between thought and movement, both in our daily activities and in the complex skills of artistic and athletic performance.

Alexander built the foundation for the exploration and integration of the three-dimensional organization of the body via his process of *directional thinking*: "I wish my neck to be free, to allow my head to poise forward and up, so that I may have a lengthening and widening back." He was concerned with the psychophysical unity of the whole person—the self, as he identified the individual in all of his/her myriad possibilities in life. Laban also concerned himself with the journey of the whole person in time and through space; he explored the relationship of the three-dimensional architecture of the body in relation to the three-dimensional architecture of space. And subsequently, he went further to explore the dynamic and varied energy of individual expression through the four effort elements—the elements of Time, Space, Weight, and Flow—which guide the mover's inner attitudes toward movement and relationship with the environment and other human beings. The crystallization of these efforts, as they combine and re-combine with each other, create the full effort actions known as Float, Glide, Press, Punch, Flick, Dab, Wring, and Slash.

SKILL SET NINE

Together, Alexander and Laban, with their unique and often similar concerns for the unity of the whole person in a whole body in relation to the environment, have richly influenced the depth and breadth of what it means to be fully human and expressive in these contemporary times. These interrelated, almost symbiotic ideas carry much import for the study of conducting. Conductors must, *in the same moment,* monitor their bodies and dynamically perceive how they are moving in space to affect the sounding of music. "I am not interested in a wide spreading of my personal methods of mastering movement. I am interested in the possibility that a very great number of individuals should share my outlook on life, which is a dynamic outlook towards harmony between men." (Laban)

How to Use the DVD for Practice and Study

It is recommended that you first study the DVD following the outline below and then view the DVD again multiple times, moving and participating in the class with Dr. Andrews. What follows is an outline of the content in the order that it appears on the DVD.

NOTE TO VIEWER: *Whenever possible, actively participate with Dr. Andrews in the movement exploration sequences. These activities are the foundation of all understanding of Laban and its application to conducting.*

SELF-STUDY OUTLINE
THE CONDUCTOR'S GESTURE DVD[120]

Introduction
James Jordan

1. Problem with conducting pedagogy is that we are faced with three problems.

   - The perception of the self moving
   - The perception of others moving
   - The understanding of one's architecture so movement can be expressive

2. Why study movement?

   - Issue of mirror neurons (as discussed in the text)

---

[120] Participants in the Meade Andrews movement classes and in the choral conducting master class were drawn from volunteer members of graduate and undergraduate conducting classes at Westminster Choir College who are studying with James Jordan, Joe Miller, and Amanda Quist. Their names can be found on separate menus within the DVD.

Chapter 2: The Laban Masterclasses
Meade Andrews

> **MENU TITLE**
> Understanding Our Architecture and Space for Movement

General Introduction: Dr. Meade Andrews
The Architecture of the Body
The Architecture of Space
Effort and Efforts in Combination

The Architectural Design of the Body:
The Interaction and Mutual Dependence of Laban and Alexander Technique

- The body is designed for movement: the architecture of the joints. It is through the joints that we perceive both our own motion and the motion of others. In her introduction, Dr. Andrews provides basic introductory material concerning the use of the Alexander Technique that readies the body for movement, while focusing on the architectural aspects of organization of the body that Laban espoused.

Defining and Delineating Your Personal Space:
Exploring the Dimensions of Movement

This section takes students through basic movement that Laban defines as the "pure-clean" dimensions of movement—that is, pure clean dimensions, when experienced alone, have only *one gravity pull* interacting with that movement.

- Defining the parameters of the body – balancing the body from the feet through the top of the head, becoming aware of front and back space
- Laban's belief that movement is sequential and one has the ability to move through space
- Defining the dynamic directions of the body – defining the width and space of the body that are all interconnected in one's self-perception of movement

- The interrelationship of vertical and horizontal spaces (i.e., moving in a three-dimensional space)
- Vertical space-opposites whose energy moves both upward and downward
- The parameters of one's width that moves around the vertical space
- The importance of back space and one's perception of that back space
- The awareness of one's front space—the dynamic directions
- The exploration of space
- The perception of one's three-dimensional space
- Reactions of students on how they "feel" after they have been taken through these various awarenesses

Exploring the Planes of Movement:
The Door Plane, Wheel Plane, and Table Plane

As a conductor you must learn the large planes of movement so those planes can be transferred to your upper body movement when conducting. The important aspect of this "kinesthetic learning" is that you must first perceive the geometric space you occupy before you can move within it expressively.

- **Door plane** – defining the door plane dimensions and movement: the cartwheel dynamic, the axis of movement or center – There is a central axis in the door plane…the sagittal axis! The sagittal axis is extremely important to conductors, condensing around center and re-expanding again around an axis.

- **Wheel Plane** – exploring the forward roll; exploring the dimensions of forward/down, back and upward; defining the axis in the wheel plane by moving around that axis; moving forward and down and backward and up

- **Table Plane** – defining the axis of the table plane – Movement is side to side and forward to back. Use "swinging" to open the back and front of your body.

- **Importance of the three planes to define the possibilities and space of movement** – Perceiving space, even though you do not use all of it all the time, is crucial to conducting.

- **The Kinesphere** – defining your total personal space; moving within your kinesphere; your self-perception of the space that you have the potential to move within

- **Fingertip exploration in many spaces** – As a conductor you must perceive this space even though you don't access it for conducting.

- **Taking your personal kinesphere for a walk** – perceiving your personal space while moving; keeping your back and sides in your awareness and perception – Being aware of your back actually opens the front space to both your perception and the perception of the ensemble.

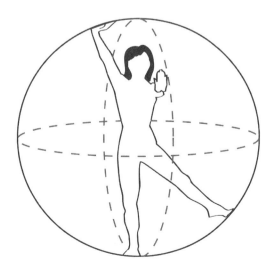

Experiencing the Diagonals of the Cube
(26:35)

NOTE TO VIEWER: *The movement within the cube explored in this section is central to the acquisition of an expressive vocabulary for conductors. Movement between the diagonals is central to the development of expressive conducting technique that is rooted in Center.*

- Diagonals are important to conductors because they define one's center and core that directly influences sound.

NOTE TO VIEWER: *It is important to view moving through the diagonals many times to make sure you can access these diagonals in an expressive way, all on an expressive Center.*

- It is important to view all movement in this section through movement in the cube.

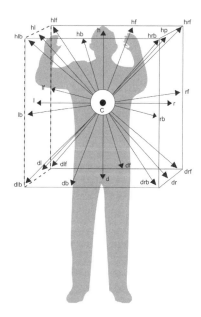

SKILL SET NINE

MENU TITLE
Experiencing the Efforts and Efforts in Combination

How to Connect the Fundamental Core of Connection of Your Body
Opening into Three Dimensions
Opening out into Space
How to Bring Energy into Aspects of Dynamic/Artistic Expression

The Defense Scale:
Definition and Application Using Time, Weight, and Space

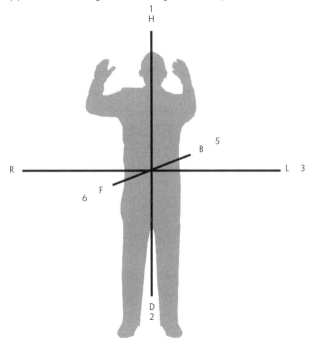

1. Moving through the Defense Scale with Effort qualities:

    Rising with *lightness*   —   Sinking with *strength*
    Narrowing with *directness*   —   Widening with *indirectness*
    Retreating with *quickness*   —   Advancing with *sustainment*

Exploring the Isolated Efforts Through Movement:
The Building Blocks of Expressive Conducting Gesture

It is important for conductors to have clearly defined extremes of *each* Effort as defined by what it feels to move within the envelope of the effort.

285

Experiencing the Efforts in Isolation Through Life Movement Situations

While it is not possible to experience each effort solely isolated, it is possible to experience each effort as the predominant effort, as demonstrated on the DVD.

2. **Exploration of Time** – indulging in Time through life situations; defining the extremes of Time (sustained Time and quick Time)

3. **Exploration of Space** – defining direct Space and indirect Space through movement experiences

4. **Exploration of Weight** – defining light Weight and strong Weight experienced through movement

5. **Exploration of Flow** – experiencing free Flow and bound Flow

Experiencing the Efforts in Combination Through Movement Experiences

Acquiring a Movement Vocabulary Through Effort in Combination Experiences

Experiencing Efforts and Efforts Juxtaposed

NOTE TO VIEWER: *It is important to experience the exercises along with the participants on the DVD.*

1. Float
2. Wring
3. Punch
4. Press
5. Float
6. Dab
7. Flick
8. Glide

SKILL SET NINE

Chapter 3:
Applying the Efforts in Combination to Patterns:
Drill and Practice Examples
James Jordan

MENU TITLE
Experiencing the Efforts in Combination

In this section, Dr. Jordan demonstrates how to practice applying the Laban Efforts in Combination to standard patterns. It should be noted that the students are employing patterns as detailed in *Evoking Sound* (Second Edition) and demonstrated on the *Anatomy of Conducting* DVD.

Chapter 4:
Choral Conducting Masterclass – Practical Application
James Jordan and Meade Andrews

MENU TITLE
Masterclass with Choral Conductors: Application of Efforts in Combination

Music:
O Vos Omnes by Blake Henson (GIA G-6483)

Choral ensemble:
Students from undergraduate and graduate choral conducting classes at Westminster Choir College

In this section of the DVD, students are asked to conduct, employing and experimenting with different efforts to discover how the sound of the ensemble is affected. Meade Andrews also coaches students to stay in awareness of their bodies through various teaching procedures of the Alexander Technique to keep them aware of their bodies so the Laban Efforts in Combination can clearly transmit their musical intention.

Chapter 5: Instrumental Conducting Masterclass – Practical Application
James Jordan

> MENU TITLE
> Masterclass with Instrumental Conductors

Instrumental ensemble:
University of North Texas Wind Symphony

In this lengthy segment, Dr. Jordan works in great detail with conductors to experiment, adapt, and change their gesture to evoke different sounds from this gifted wind ensemble. You are encouraged to take meticulous notes regarding how the efforts are applied and how the sound changes in the ensemble. Part of learning the Efforts is hearing the sometimes subtle and other times dramatic changes that occur in the musicing when gesture causes other colors, articulations, and music intent from the ensemble on this DVD.

This segment demonstrates how Laban Efforts can influence color, articulation, and the expressiveness of the ensemble. The interaction of the Efforts and how those Efforts in Combination impact the forward movement of sound through the Note Grouping principles of Marcel Tabuteau are also demonstrated, especially in the segment with Carlos Jung.

North Texas Conductor's Collegium
University of North Texas
Winspear Performance Hall

North Texas Wind Symphony

Clinicians:
James Jordan
Eugene Migliaro Corporon

Collegium Conductors:
Courtney Barnes
Carlos Jung
Seth Wallum

All conductors were given instruction on the Laban Efforts in Combination prior to these rehearsals. All were asked to have various Laban solutions to employ to change ensemble sound.

Courtney Barnes

Suite from Mass
Arr. Michael Sweeney
Amberson Holdings LLC and Stephen Schwartz
Boosey & Hawkes, sole selling agent

Carlos Jung

Farewell to Gray
Donald Grantham
Piquant Press
P.O. Box 29449
Austin, TX
(512) 343-6098

Seth Wallom
New World Dances
Martin Ellerby
Studio Music Company

SKILL SET TEN

Preparatory Audiation and Laban Efforts CD/MP3 Download for Conducting Technique Development (with Jonathan Palmer Lakeland, piano)

A conductor's interpretation shares the same origin. These two elements must emerge as a unified entity through the gesture. Music has movement analogues — music originates from movement: the flow of a line, the weight of maestoso, the quickness of staccato, the relaxation of a cadence, the irregularity of recitative, or the ease of jazz. What a conductor must accomplish through his gesture is the recovery of these movement analogues in order to represent the expressive origins of the music. This quality of the gesture must convey the inherent movement in the music.

—Gail B. Poch
in "Conducting: Movement Analogues through Effort Shape"
The Choral Journal, 1982

CD/MP3 download available for free at www.giamusic.com/conductorsgesture

The Acquisition of Conducting Analogues

The final step in this pedagogical journey is to kinesthetically acquire the Laban Efforts and associate them to sounds acquired through audiation of specifically designed exercises. This process is designed to provide your first experience with the Efforts in Combination and prepare you for the actual rehearsal experience. Understand that this CD is meant for familiarization, experience, and technical practice only to apply and gain facility of the Efforts in Combination. While you may believe that you are acquiring the "movements," in actuality you are acquiring the kinesthesia, or the body feeling, of what the Efforts in Combination actually feel like.

You must follow the steps as suggested for the Laban Efforts to be acquired, not as choreography, but rather as movement that grows out of music that is audiated first. When music is audiated through score study, the value of the Laban Efforts is that you can then explore your newly found gestural vocabulary (Analogues) and begin to experiment with what gesture *may* evoke sounds within the ensemble that you hear in audiation.

For those who may be familiar with the term, *audiation* is the term coined by Edwin Gordon to describe the ability of musicians to hear sound without it being physically present. This skill is a necessary one for all of us who conduct. Without sound to inform our gesture, conducting gesture carries no communicative meaning or ability to be intimately connected to sound.

Using Movement Imagery for Conducting Study

The idea behind this CD is to practice *audiating* the exercises designed by my colleague, Marilyn Shenenberger, without the sound being physically present. After you can hear the exercises without the actual sound of the CD, then you can begin to conduct while audiating those exercises to prepare yourself for a live interaction with sound. Hearing sound moving and responding to sound is a highly specific skill set in conductors. Only by hearing the exercises live and using the Laban Efforts in Combination can you begin to truly acquire the expressive vocabulary that is the pedagogical focus of this book. Hopefully, you will find that the sound responds in a very immediate and personal way to changes in Effort, and is quite sensitive to changes in Effort.

Pedagogical Concept Behind the CD/MP3: Movement Imaging

Through neurological studies done at The Ohio State University, it was discovered that conductors can "image" or imagine their movement without moving, similar to the imaging done by figure skaters and other athletes. That is, it was found that the MRIs of conductors who conducted while they audiated music and conductors who audiated music and imagined their movement *after* moving to sound was identical. This skill set is designed to provide conductors with this kind of movement imaging skill to assist in their preparation for both rehearsal and performance. To do this in a pedagogically correct way, the following procedure is suggested:

1. Study and listen to the musical exercises one at a time. Repeat listening until you can hear the example without playing the example.
2. When the example is committed to audiation, choose the Efforts indicated in the examples from your life experiences that you designed in Skill Set Four.
3. Audiate the music and conduct the music in silence, applying the Efforts.
4. With each repetition, choose other Efforts in Combination, varying the Weight, Time, and Space to achieve possible other Efforts to use when you work with live sound.
5. Now hear the exercise and imagine yourself conducting. Repeat this step many times so the Laban Efforts become part of your "movement imagery vocabulary."
6. If possible, conduct a live ensemble singing these exercises.

The drill and practice of the exercises as described above will provide you with an initial framework and conducting movement "vocabulary." These exercises are just that: exercises. But they offer a "way in" to an expansion of expressive gesture based upon the movement theories of Laban. These exercises should continually be revisited and the DVD should be continually re-viewed. The experiences on the DVD that explore the Efforts in Combination and the use and perception of Space are the tools of technique acquisition for conductors.

SUMMARY

A Retrospective on a Conducting Method Based Upon the Theories of Rudolf von Laban

> One may be said to "own" or "possess" one's body—at least its limbs and movable parts—by virtue of a constant flow of incoming information, arising ceaselessly, throughout life, from the muscles, joints, and tendons. One has oneself, one is oneself, because the body knows itself, confirms itself, at all times, by this sixth sense. (p. 47)
>
> —Oliver Sachs
>   in Carol Lynne Moore,
>   *Beyond Words*

Now that you have been through this book, I think it is helpful to take a step back and look at Laban applied to conducting with an overall perspective. This book has attempted to define the important understandings of Laban through a conductor's viewpoint. The chart below represents a visual overview of our journey and how the pieces of the pedagogical puzzle fit together.

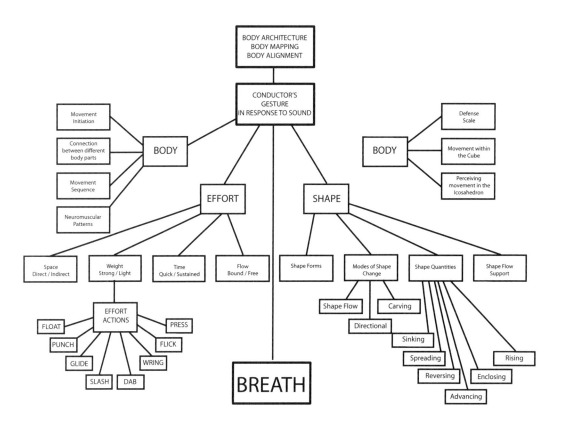

A Compendium of Thoughts for Re-Study

The work and thought of Laban provides insight into a mind that seemed to explore every possible aspect of the movement experience. There is certainly no shortage of words by Laban himself to try to provide insight into his movement thought. Whether one reads *Modern Educational Dance* or *The Mastery of Movement,* or even the articles he wrote for the *Art of Movement Guild Magazine,* one can always find clarity in Laban's words.

SUMMARY

In my study of Laban, my mentor in my doctoral research[121] always cautioned me about consulting original resources. While there are many "interpreters" of Laban (whose ranks I now join), one should never move far afield from the original sources. Because those sources are becoming harder and harder to find, I hope that quotes in this text not only keep Laban's words alive but also allow us to stay true to his original teachings.

———

In all my study and revisiting of these materials over the years, it is the quotes and the original sources that keep me aligned with Laban's original thought and intentions. In my application of his work to both rhythm and conducting, I have tried to parallel his thoughts as applied to music rather than re-interpret his ideas. In much interpretation of Laban that I read applied to music, the original language Laban used to describe the Efforts in Combination, States and Drives, and the Crystals has been altered. You can be assured of one thing in this volume: While the interpretations and applications of his work are products of my own thought and teaching experience, the language describing movement is Laban's. The genius of Laban, at least for musicians, is the language he developed to describe something that defies description…movement. The genius of his work lies in the words of the English language he has chosen that causes one to understand an entire movement world. This language is particularly effective for those of us who are not movers, or come to movement as an afterthought…as conductors.

———

If you digest the skill sets in this book, not only will you acquire more movement "words" with which to speak as a conductor, but you will also gain a language to communicate both in the classroom and in rehearsal. After all, as Marcel Tabuteau and his student, John DeLancie, said music is "motion." Tabuteau was fascinated with the sound in motion. As conductors, to understand the organic nature of movement, to have a clear paradigm through which we can experience and learn about movement, is invaluable. To then have movement

---

121 The title of this research: James Jordan, *The Effects of Movement Instruction Based upon the Principles of Rudolf von Laban and Its Effects on the Rhythm Achievement of High School Students*, Doctor of Philosophy Dissertation, Temple University, 1985.

as the "evoker" of the sound in our ensembles is perhaps the tool many of us have searched for all these years. The work of Laban truly opens up a new communicative life for all who take the time to master it.

———

While there are quotes distributed throughout this text, I have found it helpful to group the quotes in one place and use them as both a review of the concepts in this book and as a source to clarify one's thought about Laban's work. If you stay with his words, you protect yourself from getting too far afield and possibly risking misinterpretation of these crystalline ideas. The quotes are here to revisit, master and, at times, ponder the genius of this man and his ideas.

> The essential thing is that we should neither have preference for nor avoid certain movements because of physical or psychical restrictions. We should be able to do every imaginable movement and then select those which seem to be most suitable and desirable for our own nature. These can be found only by each individual himself. For this reason, practice of the free use of kinetic and dynamic possibilities is of the greatest advantage. We should be acquainted both with the general movement capacities of a healthy body and mind with the specific restrictions and capacities resulting from the individual structure of our own bodies and minds. (p. 112)
>
> —Rudolf Laban
> in *Choreutics*

> Dance as a sequence of movement can be compared with spoken language. As words are built up of letters, so are movements built up of elements; as sentences are built up of words, so are dance phrases built up of movements. This language of movement, according to its content, stimulates activity of the mind in a similar but more complex manner than the spoken word. (p. 26)
>
> —Rudolf Laban
> in *Modern Educational Dance*

SUMMARY

Man moves in order to satisfy a need. He aims by his movement at something of value to him. It is easy to perceive of the aim of a person's movement if it is directed to some tangible object. Yet there also exist intangible values that inspire movement. (p. 1)

—Rudolf Laban
in *The Mastery of Movement*

Looking at the whole range of innate and acquired impulses of man, one is tempted to search for a common denominator...this denominator...is movement with all its spiritual implications. (p. 17)

—Rudolf Laban
in Hodgson and Dunlop,
Rudolf Laban

Movement can be studied like any other reality of existence. One can see its mechanical implications, coming from the instrumental character of our body. The parts of our skeleton are levered by our muscles in a way not dissimilar from the function of a mobile crane with which we lift and transport merchandise. But in the crane sits a mastermind, the crane driver, who organizes the motions of the crane, enabling this contraption to serve a definite job. We can all know about every single screw and pulley of the crane without being able to drive it by our thinking only. For the driving we need movement.

The body is the crane and crane-driver in one assembled unit, and this unit follows—knowingly or unknowingly—the invariable rules of the bodily and mental motion. (p. 5)

—Rudolf von Laban
in *The Laban Art of Movement
Guild Magazine, No. 19* (November 1957)

I have seen all too many dancers who throw themselves into the air without any sign of inner participation. On the contrary, such large movements are frequently very externalized, comparable to hollow shells in which not the slightest indication of real life or an integration of body and mind could be discovered. (p. 7)

—Rudolf von Laban
in an unfinished article entitled
"The Educational and Therapeutic Value of Dance"
*The Laban Art of Movement
Guild Magazine*, No. 22 (May 1959)

But what are symbolic actions? They are certainly not just imitations or representations of the ordinary actions of everyday life. To perform movements, as if chopping wood or as if embracing or threatening someone, has little to do with the real symbolism of movement. Such imitations of everyday acts may be significant, but they are not symbolic. Man in those silent movements, pregnant with emotion, may perform strange movements which appear meaningless, or at any rate inexplicable. Yet, and this is the curious thing, he moves with the same actions he uses in chopping, carrying, mending, assembling or doing any everyday operation; but these actions appear in specific sequences having shapes and rhythms of their own. Words expressing feelings, emotions, sentiments or certain mental and spiritual states will but touch the fringe of the inner responses which the shapes and rhythms of bodily actions are capable of evoking. Movement can say more, for all its shortness, than pages of verbal description.

—Rudolf Laban
in *The Mastery of Movement*

What one experiences through movement can never be expressed in words; in a simple step there may be a reverence of which we are scarcely aware. Yet through it something higher than just tenderness and devotion may flow into us and from us.

…It is impossible, of course, to describe the essence of the movements. But sometimes one can experience the same sort of impulse to move, for example, in a fight, in danger, in ecstasy and in passion, in short, in times of excessive emotion.

…Movement is first and fundamental in what comes forth from a human being as an expression of his intentions and experiences. One must remember that all sound productions, such as speaking, singing, shouting, spring from physical actions, or in other words, from movements. Whether I bang a table or make it resound, or vibrate the air with shouts, it is always the same thing—movement made audible.

…Is it possible to express all this through movement, through dance? Only if the participants know and believe that dance has ethical life and only when they have become able to let this experience infiltrate their demeanour and movement drive.

…But the main aim of the movement choir must always be the shared experience of the joy of moving. Actually, the expression "joy of moving" does not fully describe the fundamental idea. It is to a great extent an inner experience and, above all a strengthening of the desire for communion.

—Rudolf Laban
in *A life for Dance*

SUMMARY

Looking at the whole range of innate and acquired impulses of man, one is tempted to search for a common denominator. In my opinion this denominator is not mere motion, but movement with all its spiritual implication.... What has to be done today—and our time seems to stand on the threshold of a new awareness of movement—is to acknowledge movement as the great integrator. This involves, of course, the conviction that movement is the vehicle which concerns the whole man with all his physical and spiritual facilities. To be able to see this great unity is not the privilege of the artist alone. Everybody, every single human individual, has this unity at the basis of his natural tendencies and impulses, which can be lifted out of the treasure of forgotten truth and cultivated in all the various ramifications of life.

> —Rudolf Laban
> in "Movement Concerns the Whole Man"
> *The Laban Art of Movement Guild*
> Magazine, No. 21 (November 1958), pp. 12–13.

In order to discern the mechanics of motion within living movement in which purposeful control of the physical happening is at work, it is useful to give a name to the inner function originating such movement. The word used here for this purpose is *effort*. Every human movement is indissolubly linked with an effort, which is, indeed, its origin and inner aspect. Effort and its resulting action may be both unconscious and involuntary, but they are always present in any bodily movement; otherwise they could not be perceived by others, or become effectual in the external surroundings of the moving person. Effort is visible in the action movement of a worker, or a dancer, and it is audible in song or speech. If one hears a laugh or cry of despair, one can visualize in imagination the movement accompanying the audible effort. The fact that the effort and its various shadings can not only be seen and heard, but also imagined, is of great importance for their representation, both visible and audible, by the actor-dancer. He derives a certain inspiration from descriptions of movements that awaken his imagination.

> —Rudolf Laban
> in *The Mastery of Movement*

In conclusion, it may be repeated that effort, with all its manifold shadings of which the human being is capable, is mirrored in the actions of the body. But bodily actions performed with imaginative awareness stimulate and enrich inner life. Therefore, mastery of movement is not only of value to the stage artist, but to everyone since we are all concerned, whether consciously or subconsciously, with perception and expression. The person who has learnt to relate himself to Space, and has physical mastery of this, has Attention. The person who has mastery of his relation to the Weight factor of effort has Intention, and he has Decision when he is adjusted to Time. Attention, intention and decision are stages of the inner preparation of an outer bodily action. This comes about when through the flow of movement effort finds concrete expression in the body.

—Rudolf Laban
in *The Mastery of Movement*

The significance of the time-rhythms of movement can be observed in individual dancers who have clearly discernible preferences for special rhythms. While one dancer will be more tempted to interpret music in which the sharp metricality of regular beats prevails, another might be repelled by the exact metricality and prefer the free, irregular unfolding of time-rhythm. The precision of the metrical dancer is in strong contrast to the expressiveness of the dance-mime-actor preferring free rhythm. There exist many shades between the two extreme contrasts of regular and irregular rhythm. To a certain degree it is true that the dancer's legs and feet prefer metrical function; but feet, arms, and hands should equally be able to express the qualities of a free time-rhythm. In fact, the whole body should be able to express the regular and irregular vibrations and waves of movement. Although an understanding and appreciation of music, which is an abstract expression of movement, can help the actor in his grasp of rhythm, it is not in itself sufficient. Even the dancer, who interprets music, has to translate it into the effort sequences from which his or her expressive steps and gestures arise. In dance, the rhythm of movement is mainly expressed by the steps, and this is particularly true of traditional ballet which uses a number of basic steps and characteristic combinations of these.

—Rudolf Laban
in *The Mastery of Movement*

SUMMARY

We should be able to do every imaginable movement possible and then select those which seem to be most suitable and desirable for our own nature. These can be found only by each individual himself. For this reason, practice of free use of kinetic and dynamic possibilities is of the greatest advantage. We should be acquainted both with the general movement capacities of a healthy body and mind and with the specific restrictions and capacities resulting from the individual structure of our own bodies and minds. (p. 17)

—Rudolf Laban
in Irmgard Bartenieff,
Body Movement

The Effort elements are the attitudes of the moving person towards the motion factors of Weight, Space, Time and Flow. (p. 8)

—Rudolf Laban
in *Modern Educational Dance*

Dynamic space, with its terrific dance of tensions and discharges is the fertile ground in which movement flourishes. Movement is the life of space. Dead space does not exist, for there is neither space without movement nor movement without space. All movement is an eternal change between binding and loosening, between the creation of knots with the concentrating and uniting power of binding, and the creation of twisted lines in the process on unifying and untwisting. Stability and mobility alternate endlessly. (p. 101)

—Rudolf von Laban
in Irmgard Bartenieff,
Body Movement

It can be said that a movement can be described as a composite of its shapes and rhythms, both making part of the superimposed flow of movement in which the control exerted by the moving person upon the movement becomes visible. (p. 93)

A refreshing swim in the sea is a wonderful and healthy thing, but no human being could live constantly in the water. It is a very similar case with the occasional swim in the flow of movement which we call dance. Such swimming, refreshing in many aspects for the body, the mind and for that dreamy part of our being which has been called the soul, is an exceptional pleasure and stimulation. As water is a widespread means to sustain life, so is movement. (p. 95)

When we realize that movement is the essence of life, and that expression, whether it be speaking, writing, singing, painting or dancing, uses movement as a vehicle, we cannot help seeing the importance of understanding this outward expression of the living energy within, and this we can do through effort study. (p. 99)

Music or any rhythms of sounds are produced by movements of the musician which show also variations in their shape and space evolution. In musical rhythm, the Time element is used in a highly differentiated manner. (p. 92)

Rhythm, however, is only a part of music, a kind of skeleton around which the main content of the musical composition—the melodies and harmonies of tones—are built up. In dance, the melody and harmony of tones recede and the importance of rhythm increases. (p. 92)

—Rudolf Laban
in *Modern Educational Dance*

The movements of our body follow rules corresponding to mineral *crystallizations* and structures of organic compounds. The shape which possibly offers the most natural and harmonious tracks for our movements is the *icosahedron*. It contains a rich series of combined inner and outer trace-lines with dimensional connections provoking "stable," i.e., easily equilibriated, movements as well as diagonal connections providing disequilibriating movements. Trace forms of movements are, however, never complete crystal patterns, but awareness of a harmonious flow resulting from crystalline tendencies increases pleasure in skill. (p. 114)

The integration of body and mind through movement occurs in free performance of choreutic shapes. There is no limit to the possibilities of the study and practice of choreutics. It penetrates every human action and reaction, since all actions and reactions spring from movement within us. In the domain of the arts this fact becomes especially clear.

There are visible arts such as architecture, sculpture and painting in which trace forms are fixed through the movement of drawing and the shaping of different materials. There are the audible arts, such as music and oratory (including the speaking of poetry), in which the trace-forms of bodily movements give shape to the sounds and rhythms, which characterize ideas and emotions. (p. 115)

—Rodulf Laban
in *Choreutics*

Awareness of bodily perspective will assist in the discrimination between spatial feeling and understanding the spontaneous activity of our limbs. Following trace-forms in their pure kinespheric form can be the first step towards meaningful use of the limbs. Later the faculty of discrimination between the quality and inner impulse and the outer form which is present in all movements will grow. The definite and joyful execution of an integrated movement will be the final result. (p. 114)

—Rudolf Laban
in *Choreutics*

Sequences of movements can be performed so that each movement is directed to a certain point in the space round the body and change from one point to the next is harmonious and flowing, forming definite patterns. This means with a definite space orientation. These patterns may extend chiefly in the air around the body, when they are known as peripheral, or they may pass close to the body, and are more central in character. Patterns most frequently combine with central and peripheral movements. (p. 35)

Dance as a sequence of movement can be compared with spoken language. As words are built up of letters, so are movements built up of elements; as sentences are built up of words, so are dance phrases built up of movements. This language of movement, according to its content, stimulates activity of the mind in a similar but more complex manner than the spoken word. (p. 26)

—Rudolf Laban
in *Modern Educational Dance*

BIBLIOGRAPHY

Allport, F. H. *Theories of Perception and the Concept of Structure*. New York: Wiley, 1955.

Anatasi, Anne. "Heredity, Environment, and the Question: 'How?'" *The Psychological Review,* 1958, 65 (4), pp. 197–208.

Apel, Willi. *The Notation of Polyphonic Music: 900–1600*. Cambridge, MA: Medieval Academy of Music, 1953.

Aristotle. "Tabula Rasa Mind." In W. S. Sahakian (ed.), *History of Psychology.* Itasca, IL: Peacock Publishers, 1980, p. 14.

Bartenieff, Irmgard. *Body Movement: Coping with the Environment*. New York: Gordon and Breach, 1980.

Billingham, Lisa. *The Complete Conductor's Guide to Laban Movement Theory.* Chicago: GIA Publications, Inc., 2008.

Birdwhistell, R. L. *Introduction to Kinetics*. Louisville, KY: University of Louisville Press, 1952.

Boring, E. G. *Sensation and Perception in the History of Experimental Psychology.* New York: Appleton-Century Crofts, Inc., 1942.

Bradley, Karen K. *Rudolf Laban*. Abingdon, Oxon: Routledge, 2009.

Braly, K. W. "The Influence of Past Experience in Visual Perception." *Journal of Experimental Psychology,* 1933, 16, pp. 613–633.

Briggs, Megan M. *Movement Education*. London: MacDonald and Evans, Ltd., 1974.

Brunswick, E. "The Conceptual Focus of Systems." In M. Marx (ed.), *Psychological Theory*. New York: MacMillan and Company, 1951, pp. 131–143.

Carr, H. A. *An Introduction to Space Perception*. New York: Longman's Green, 1935.

Chapman, Sara A. *Movement Education in the United States: Historical Developments and Theoretical Bases*. Philadelphia, PA: Movement Education Publications, 1974.

Chosky, Lois. *The Kodaly Context*. Englewood Cliffs, NJ: Prentice-Hall, 1981.

———. *The Kodaly Method*. Englewood Cliffs, NJ: Prentice-Hall, 1981.

Collins, Claudette. *Practical Modern Educational Dance*. London: MacDonald and Evans, 1969.

de Condillac, Etienne Bonnot. "French Sensationalism." In W. S. Sahakian (ed.), *History of Psychology*. Itasca, IL: Peacock Publishers, 1980, pp. 44–48.

de Moura Silva, Maristela. "An Examination of Rudolf Laban's Theory of Modern Educational Dance to Derive Implications for Program Development in the Elementary School." Ed. D. dissertation. Philadelphia, PA: Temple University, May, 1983.

Cutting, James E. "Coding Theory Adapted to Gait Perception." *Journal of Experimental Psychology: Human Perception and Performance,* 1981, 7, pp. 71–87.

Damasio, Antonio. *Self Comes to Mind: Constructing the Conscious Brain*. New York: Pantheon Press, 2010.

Davies, Eden. *Beyond Dance: Laban's Legacy of Movement Analysis*. New York: Routledge, 2006.

Dell, Cecily. *A Primer for Movement Description*. New York: Dance Notation Bureau, 1977.

Eosze, Laszlo. *Zoltan Kodaly: His Life and Work*. Trans. Istavan Farkas and Gyula Gulyas. Boston, MA: Crescendo Publishing Company, 1962.

Escalona, Sibylle, and B. Heider. *Prediction and Outcome*. New York: Basic Books Inc., 1959.

Feller, Y., and E. McNear. "An Essay on Perception from Infants to Adults." *Archeological Psychologist*, 1954 (Geneva), 36, pp. 253–327.

Findlay, Elsa. *Rhythm and Movement: Applications of Dalcroze Eurhythmics*. Evanston, IL: Summy-Birchard Company, 1971.

Freud, Anna. "Problems of Infantile Neurosis." *Psychoanalytic Study of the Child*, Vol. IX. New York: International Universities Press, Inc., 1954, pp. 69–71.

Garner, W. R., H. W. Hake, and C. W. Eriksen. "Operationism and the Concept of Perception." In J. M. Vanderplas, *Controversial Issues in Psychology*. Boston, MA: Houghton-Mifflin Company, 1966, pp. 321–335.

Gesell, A. "Maturation and Infant Behavior Patterns." *Psychological Review*, 1929, pp. 307–319.

———. "Reciprocal Interweaving in Neuromotor Development." *Journal of Comparative Neurology*, 1939, 70, pp. 161–180.

Gesell, A., F. I. Ilg, and G. E. Bulls. *Vision: Its Development in Infant and Child*. New York: Paul Hoeber, 1949.

Gibson, E. J. *Principles of Perceptual Learning and Development*. New York: Appleton-Century Crofts, 1969.

Gibson, J. J. "The Concept of Stimulus in Psychology." *The American Psychologist*, 1960, 15, pp. 694–703.

———. "What Gives Rise to the Perception of Motion?" *The Psychological Review*, 1967, 15, pp. 335–346.

Gibson, J. J., and E. J. Gibson. "Perceptual Learning: Differentiation or Enrichment?" *The Psychological Review*, 1955, 62, pp. 32–41.

Gibson, J. J., P. Olum, and F. Rosenblatt. "Parallax and Perspective During Aircraft Landing." *American Journal of Psychology*, 1955, 68, pp. 372–385.

Goodenough, F. *Developmental Psychology: An Introduction to the Study of Human Behavior*. New York: Appleton-Century Crofts, 1934.

Gordon, E. E. *Learning Sequences in Music*. Chicago: GIA Publications, Inc., 1980.

———. *Learning Sequences in Music.* Chicago: GIA Publications, Inc., 1984.

———. *Musical Aptitude Profile.* Boston: Houghton-Mifflin, 1965.

Hartley, David. "Association of Ideas." In W. S. Sahakian (ed.), *History of Psychology.* Itasca, IL: Peacock Publishers, 1980, pp. 49–52.

Heidbredder, E. *Seven Psychologies.* New York: Appleton-Century Crofts, Inc., 1953.

Helmholtz, H. von. *Handbook of Psychological Optics,* Vol. III. Trans. J. P. C. Southall. New York: Optical Society of America, 1925.

Hobbes, Thomas. *Human Nature.* London, 1651.

Hochberg, Julian E. *Perception.* Englewood Cliffs, NJ: Prentice-Hall, 1964.

———. "Perception: Space and Movement." In Kling and Riggs (ed.), *Sensation and Perception.* New York: Holt. Rinehart and Winston, 1972.

———. "Perception: Toward the Recovery of a Definition." *Psychological Review,* 1956, 63, pp. 400–405.

Hodgson, John. *Mastering Movement: The Life and Work of Rudolf Laban.* New York:Routledge, 2001.

Hodgson, John, and Valerie Preston-Dunlop. *Rudolf Laban: An Introduction to His Work and Influence.* Plymouth, Great Britain: Northcote House, 1990.

James, William. *Principles of Psychology.* Chicago: Encyclopaedia Britannica, 1952. (Originally published 1891.)

Jansson, G., and E. Borjesson. "Perceived Direction in Rotary Motion." *Perception and Psychophysics,* 1969, pp. 19–26.

Jaques-Dalcroze, Emile. *Rhythm, Music and Education.* Trans. Harold F. Rubenstein. London: The Riverside Press, 1967.

Johansson, G. "Rigidity, stability and motion in perceptual space." *Acta Psychologica,* 1958, 14, pp. 359–370.

———. "Visual perception of biological motion and a model for its analysis." *Perception and Psychophysics,* 1973, 14, pp. 201–211.

Johansson, Gunnar. "Projective Transformations as Determining Visual Space Perception in Perception." In Robert B. MacLeod and Herbert L. Pick (ed.), *Essays in Honor of James J. Gibson.* Ithaca, NY: Cornell University Press, 1974, pp. 117–138.

Jordan, Diana. *Childhood and Movement.* Oxford: Blackwell and Mott, Ltd., 1966.

Jordan, James. *Evoking Sound,* Second Edition. Chicago: GIA Publications, Inc., 2009.

Jordan, James, and Eugene Migliaro Corporon. *The Anatomy of Conducting.* (DVD) Chicago: GIA Publications, Inc., 2007.

Kant, Immanuel. "The A Priori Intuition of Space." In W. S. Sahakian (ed.), *History of Psychology.* Itasca, IL: Peacock Publishers, 1980, pp. 69–70.

———. "The A Priori Intuition of Time." In W. S. Sahakian (ed.), *History of Psychology.* Itasca, IL: Peacock Publishers, 1980, pp. 70–72.

Kestenberg, Judith. *Children and Parents: Psychoanalytic Studies in Development.* New York: Aronson, 1975.

———. *The Role of Movement Patterns in Development,* Vols. I and II. New York: Dance Notation Bureau, 1971.

Koffka, Kurt. *The Growth of the Mind.* New York: Harcourt, 1931.

Kraus, R., and S. Chapman. *History of the Dance in Art and Education.* Englewood Cliffs, NJ: Prentice-Hall, Inc., 1981.

Laban, Rudolf. *A Life for Dance.* London: MacDonald and Evans Ltd., 1975.

———. *Choreutics.* Lisa Ullman, ed. London: MacDonald and Evans, 1966.

———. *Modern Educational Dance.* Lisa Ullman, ed. Boston, MA: Plays, Inc., 1980.

———. "Movement Concerns the Whole Man." *The Laban Art of Movement Guild Magazine,* November 1958, 21, pp. 12–13.

———. *The Mastery of Movement.* Lisa Ullman, ed. Boston, MA: Plays, Inc., 1975.

———. *The Mastery of Movement.* Lisa Ullman, ed. London: MacDonald and Evans Ltd., 1980.

———. *Rudolf Laban Speaks about Movement and Dance.* Lectures and articles selected and edited by Lisa Ullman. Addlestone, Surrey: Laban Art of Movement Centre, 1971.

———. "The Rhythm of Effort and Recovery." *The Laban Art of Movement Guild Magazine*, 1960, 24, pp. 12–19.

———. "The World of Rhythm and Harmony." *The Laban Art of Movement Guild Magazine*, 1958, 20, pp. 5–9.

Laban, Rudolf, and F. C. Lawrence. *Effort.* London: MacDonald and Evans, 1947.

Lamb, Warren. *Posture and Gesture.* London: Gerald Duckworth and Company, 1965.

Locke, J. *Essay Concerning Human Understanding, 1690.* Philadelphia, PA: Troutman and Hays, 1853.

Loori, John Daido. *The Zen of Creativity: Cultivating Your Artistic Life.* New York: Ballantine Books, 2005.

MacLeod, R. B. "Phenomenology: A Challenge to Experimental Psychology." In W. T. Wann (ed.), *Behaviorism and Phenomenology.* Chicago: University of Chicago Press, 1964, pp. 47–74.

Maletic, Vera. *Body-Space Expression: The Development of Rudolf Laban's Movement and Dance Concepts.* Berlin/New York/Amsterdam: Mouton de Gruyer, 1987.

McCaw, Dick (Ed.), *The Laban Sourcebook.* London: Routledge, 2011

McDougall, William. "Social Psychology and Instincts." In W. S. Sahakian (ed.), *History of Psychology.* Itasca, IL: Peacock Publishers, 1980, pp. 166–168.

McGill, David. *Sound in Motion: A Performer's Guide to Greater Musical Expression.* Bloomington, IN: Indiana University Press, 2007.

McGraw, M. B. "From Reflex to Muscular Control in the Assumption of a Correct Posture and Ambulation in the Human Infant." *Child Development*, 1932, 3, pp. 291–297.

Merleau-Ponty, Maurice. *The Primacy of Perception.* Chicago: Northwestern University Press, 1964.

Mill, James. "Association of Ideas." In W. S. Sahakian (ed.), *History of Psychology*. Itasca, IL: Peacock Publishers, 1980, pp. 57–60.

Mittelman, Bela. "Motility in the Therapy of Children and Adults." *Psychoanalytic Study of the Child*, Vol. XII. New York: International Universities Press, Inc., 1957, pp. 284–319.

Nash, Grace C. *Creative Approaches to Child Development with Music, Language and Movement*. Sherman Oaks, CA: Alfred Publishing Company, Inc., 1974.

Newhall, Mary Anne Santos. *Mary Wigman*. New York and London: Routledge, 2009.

Newlove, Jean. *Laban for Actors and Dancers*. New York: Routledge, 1993.

Newlove, Jean, and John Dalby. *Laban for All*. New York: Routledge, 2004.

North, Marion. *Body Movement for Children: An Introduction to Movement Study and Teaching*. Boston, MA: Plays, Inc., 1972.

———. *Composing Movement Sequences*. London: Marion North, 1961.

———. *Personality Assessment Through Movement*. Boston, MA: Plays, Inc., 1975.

Partsch-Bergsohn, Isa, and Harold Bergsohn. *The Makers of Modern Dance in Germany: Rudolf Laban, Mary Wigman, Kurt Joos*. Hightstown, NJ: Princeton Books, 1973.

Piaget, J. *The Child's Conception of Movement and Speed*. New York: Basic Books, 1970.

———. *The Mechanisms of Perception*. Trans. G. N. Seagrim. New York: Basic Books, Inc., 1969.

———. *The Origins of Intelligence in Children*. New York: International Universities Press, 1952.

Piaget, J., and B. Inhelder. *The Child's Conception of Space*. New York: W. W. Norton, 1967.

Postman, L. *Psychology in the Making*. New York: Alfred A. Knopf, 1962.

Preston, Valerie. *Handbook for Modern Educational Dance*. London: MacDonald and Evans Ltd., 1973.

Redfern, Betty. *Introducing Laban Art of Movement.* London: MacDonald and Evans, Ltd., 1965.

Seashore, Carl Emil. *The Psychology of Musical Talent.* New York: Silver Burdett and Co., 1919.

Skinner, B. F. *About Behaviorism.* New York: Alfred A. Knopf, 1974.

Spitz, Rene A. *No and Yes.* New York: International Universities Press, Inc., 1957.

Thelen, Esther. "Kicking, Rocking and Waving: Contextual Analysis of Rhythmical Stereotypes in Normal Human Infants." *Animal Behavior,* 1981, 29, pp. 3–11.

———. "Rhythmical Behavior in Infancy: An Ethological Perspective." *Developmental Psychology,* 1981, 17, pp. 237–257.

Thelen, Esther, and Donna M. Fisher. "From Spontaneous to Instrumental Behavior: Kinematic Analysis of Movement Changes During Early Learning." *Child Development,* 1983, 54, pp. 129–140.

———. "Newborn Stepping: An Explanation for a Disappearing Reflex." *Developmental Psychology,* 1982, 18, pp. 760–775.

Thelen, Esther, G. Bradshaw, and J. A. Ward. "Spontaneous kicking in month-old infants; manifestation of human central locomotor program." *Behavioral and Neural Biology,* 1981, 32, pp. 45–53.

Thorton, Samuel. *Laban's Theory of Movement: A New Perspective.* Boston, MA: Plays, Inc., 1971.

Thurmond, James Morgan. *Note Grouping.* Camp Hill, PA: JMT Publications, 1982.

Titchener, E. B. *A Textbook of Psychology.* New York: MacMillan and Company, 1910.

———. "The Postulates of a Structural Psychology." *Philosophical Review,* 1898, 7, pp. 449–465.

Todd, James T. "Perception of Gait." *Journal of Experimental Psychology: Human Perception and Performance,* 1983, 9 (1), pp. 31–42.

Ullman, Lisa. *Rudolf Laban Speaks about Movement and Dance.* Woburn Hill, Addelstone, Surrey: Laban Art of Movement Centre, 1971.

Watson, J. B. *Behaviorism.* New York: W. W. Norton and Company, 1925.

Werner, H. *Comparative Psychology of Mental Development.* New York: Science Editions, 1961.

Wigman, Mary. *The Language of Dance.* Connecticut: Wesleyan University Press, 1966.

> *Note: Mary Wigman (1886–1973) was a choreographer and student of Laban's. She is considered one of the founders of modern dance in Germany. She also studied Dalcroze pedagogy, but abandoned those teachings early in her career.*

Wigman, Mary, and Walter Sorell. *The Mary Wigman Book: Her Writings.* Connecticut: Wesleyan University Press, 1973.

Zelazo, P. R. "From Reflexive to Instrumental Behavior." In L. P. Lipsett (ed.), *Developmental Psychobiology: The Significance of Infancy.* Hillsdale, NJ: Erlbaum, 1976.

RHYTHM BIBLIOGRAPHY

Azzara, Christopher D., Richard F. Grunow, and Edwin E. Gordon. *Creativity in Improvisation*. Chicago: GIA Publications, Inc., 1997.

Barenboim, Daniel. *Music Quickens Time*. London: Verso Books, 2008.

Bartenieff, Irmgard. *Body Movement: Coping with the Environment*. New York: Gordon and Breach, 1980.

Bentov, Itzhak, *Stalking the Wild Pendulum*. Rochester, VT: Inner Traditions, 1988.

Bernstein, Leonard. *Findings*. New York: Doubleday, 1982.

———. *The Conductor's Art*. McGraw-Hill, 1965.

———. *The Joy of Music*. New York: Simon and Schuster, 1959.

Bertalot, John. *Five Wheels of Successful Sightsinging*. Minneapolis, MN: Augsburg, 1993.

Blum, David. *Casals and the Art of Interpretation*. Los Angeles: University of California Press, 1977.

Bouhuys, Arend. *The Physiology of Breathing*. London: Grune and Stratton, 1977.

Boulez, Pierre. *Orientations*. London: Faber and Faber, 1986.

Broad, William, "Complex Whistles Found to Play Key Role in Inca and Maya Life," New York Times, Tuesday, March 29, 1988.

Brubach, Holly. "A Pianist for Whom Never was Never an Option." *The New York Times*, June 10, 2007: 25–7.

Campbell, Don G. *Master Teacher: Nadia Boulanger.* Washington, DC: The Pastoral Press, 1984.

Chapman, Sara A. *Movement Education in the United States: Historical Developments and Theoretical Bases.* Philadelphia, PA: Movement Education Publications, 1974.

Clifton, Thomas. *Music as Heard.* New Haven, CT: Yale University Press, 1983.

Cooper, Grosvenor, and Leonard B. Meyer. *The Rhythmic Structure of Music.* Chicago: University of Chicago Press, 1960.

Copland, Aaron. *Music and Imagination.* New York: New American Library, 1952.

Dart, Thurston. *The Interpretation of Music.* New York: Harper and Row, 1963.

Davis, Martha. *Towards Understanding the Intrinsic in Body Motion.* New York: Arno Press, 1972.

———. *Understanding Movement: An Annotated Bibliography.* New York: Arno Press, 1972.

Decker, Harold A., and Julius Herford. *Choral Conducting Symposium.* 2nd ed. Englewood Cliffs, NJ: Prentice-Hall, 1988.

Dell, Cecily. *A Primer for Movement Description.* New York: Dance Notation Bureau, 1977.

Duckworth, William. *Talking Music: Conversations with Five Generations of American Composers.* New York: G. Schirmer, 1995.

Ehmann, Wilhelm. *Choral Directing.* Minneapolis, MN: Augsburg Publishing House, 1968.

Ericson, Eric. *Choral Conducting.* New York: Walton Music Corporation, 1976.

Finn, William J. *The Art of the Choral Conductor.* Vols. 1–2. Evanston, IL: Summy-Birchard Company, 1960.

———. *The Conductor Raises His Baton.* New York: Harper and Brothers, 1944.

Fonatana, Alberto E., and Julia A. Loschi. "Combined Use of Music with Sound of Heart Beats and Respiration Rhythms in Psychotherapy." *Acta Psiquiatrica y Psicologic de America Latina,* March 1979.

Fowler, Charles, ed. *Conscience of a Profession: Howard Swan.* Chapel Hill, NC: Hinshaw Music, Inc., 1987.

Froseth, James O., and Phyllis Weikart. *Movement to Music in Confined Spaces.* Chicago: GIA Publications, 1981.

Gajard, Dom Joseph. *The Solesmes Method.* Collegeville, MN: Liturgical Press, 1960.

Gallwey, W. Timothy. *The Inner Game of Tennis* New York: Bantam Books, 1989.

Gardner, Howard. *Frames of Mind.* New York: Basic Books, 1983.

Garlinghouse, Burton. "Rhythm and Relaxation in Breathing." *NATS Bulletin* 7 (1951): 2.

Gordon, Edwin E. *Harmonic Improvisation and Readiness Record and Rhythm Improvisation Readiness Record.* Chicago: GIA Publications, Inc., 1998.

_____. *Improvisation in the Music Classroom.* Chicago: GIA Publications, Inc., 2003.

———. *Learning Sequences in Music: Skill, Content, and Patterns.* 1993 ed. Chicago: GIA Publications, Inc.

———. *Learning Sequences in Music: Skill, Content, and Patterns.* 2006 ed. Chicago: GIA Publications, Inc.

———. *Manual for the Advanced Measures of Music Audiation.* Chicago: GIA Publications, Inc., 1989.

———. *Manual for the Primary Measures of Music Audiation and the Intermediate Measures of Music Audiation.* Chicago: GIA Publications, Inc., 1986.

———. *Primary Measures of Music Audiation.* Chicago: GIA Publications, Inc., 1979.

———. *Taking a Reasonable and Honest Look at Tonal Solfege and Rhythm Solfege.* Chicago: GIA Publications, Inc., 2009.

———. *The Manifestation of Developmental Music Aptitude in the Audiation of "Same" and "Different" as Sound in Music.* Chicago: GIA Publications, Inc., 1981.

———. *The Nature, Description, Measurement, and Evaluation of Music Aptitudes.* Chicago: GIA Publications, Inc., 1987.

Green, Barry. *The Inner Game of Music.* New York: Doubleday, 1986.

Green, Barry, Donna Hallen Loewy, et al. *The Inner Game of Music Solo Workbook for Voice.* Chicago: GIA Publications, Inc., 1995.

Godwin, Joscelyn. *Harmonies of Heaven and Earth.* Rochester, VT: Inner Traditions International, 1987.

Haberlen, John. "Microrhythms: The Key to Vitalizing Renaissance Music," *The Choral Journal* 13 (November 1972): 11–4.

Hackney, Peggy. *Making Connections: Total Body Integration through Bartenieff Fundamentals.* New York: Routledge, 2002.

Hanna, Thomas. *The Body of Life: Creating New Pathways for Sensory Awareness and Fluid Movement.* Rochester, VT: Healing Arts Press, 1993.

Harnoncourt, Nikolaus. *Baroque Music Today: Music as Speech. Ways to a New Understanding of Music.* Portland, OR: Amadeus Press, 1988.

Hartley, Linda. *Somatic Psychology: Body Mind and Meaning.* Philadelphia, PA: Whurr Publishers, 2004.

Henke, Herbert H. "The Application of Emile Jaques-Dalcroze's Solfege-Rhythmique to the Choral Rehearsal." *The Choral Journal* 25 (December 1984): 11–7.

Herford, Julius. "The Conductor's Search." *The Choral Journal* 32, (December 1991): 23–6.

Hindemith, Paul. *Elementary Training for Musicians.* New York: Schott Music Corporation, 1974.

———. *The Craft of Musical Composition.* Book I: Theory. Mainz: Scott, 1942.

Hobart, Janet E. and F. "Effects of Music on Physiological Response." *Journal of Research in Music Education*, Vol. 22, 1974.

Houle, George. "Meter and Performance in the Seventeenth and Eighteenth Centuries," *The Journal of Early Music America* 2 (Spring 1989).

———. *Meter in Music, 1600–1800*. Bloomington: IN University Press, 1987.

Jaques-Dalcroze, Emile. *Eurhythmics Art and Education*. New York: Benjamin Blom, Inc., 1972.

Jones, A. J. "A Study of the Breathing Processes As They Relate to the Art of Singing" (Ph.D. diss., University of Missouri, Kansas City, 1970) *Dissertation Abstracts International*, 1971, 31/10A, 5447. University Microfilms no. 71–3693.

Jordan, James. "Audiation and Sequencing: An Approach to Score Preparation." *The Choral Journal* 21 (April 1981): 11–3.

———. *Evoking Sound: Fundamentals of Choral Conducting*, Second Edition. Chicago: GIA Publications, Inc., 2009.

———. "Laban Movement Theory and How It Can Be Used with Music Learning Theory." In *Readings in Music Learning Theory*. Edited by Darrel Walters and Cynthia Crump Taggart, 316–33, Chicago: GIA Publications, Inc., 1989.

———. "Music Learning Theory Applied to Choral Performance Groups." In *Readings in Music Learning Theory*. Edited by Darrel Walters and Cynthia Crump Taggart, 168–83, Chicago: GIA Publications, Inc., 1989.

———. "Rhythm Learning Sequence." In *Readings in Music Learning Theory*. Edited by Darrel Walters and Cynthia Crump Taggart, 26–37, Chicago: GIA Publications, Inc., 1989.

———. *The Choral Rehearsal*, Vol. I. Chicago: GIA Publications, Inc., 2007.

———. *The Choral Rehearsal*, Vol. II (Inward Bound). Chicago: GIA Publications, Inc., 2008.

———. "Toward a Flexible Sound Ideal through Conducting: Some Reactions to Study with Wilhelm Ehmann." *The Choral Journal* 25 (November 1984): 5–6.

Jordan, James, and Michele Holt. *The School Choral Program*. Chicago: GIA Publications, Inc., 2008.

Kemp, Helen. *Of Primary Importance*. Garland, TX: Choristers Guild, 1989.

Kern, Jan, ed. *Jubilate Deo: Easy Latin Gregorian Chants for the Faithful*. Chicago: GIA Publications, Inc., 1974.

Kohut, D. L. *Musical Performance: Learning Theory and Pedagogy*. Englewood Cliffs, NJ: Prentice-Hall, Inc., 1985.

Laban, Rudolf von. *A Life for Dance*. London: MacDonald and Evans Ltd., 1975.

———. *Choreutics*. Edited by Lisa Ullman. London: MacDonald and Evans Ltd., 1966.

———. *Modern Educational Dance*. Edited by Lisa Ullman. Boston: Plays Inc., 1980.

———. *Modern Educational Dance*. London: MacDonald and Evans, Ltd., 1948.

———. "Movement Concerns the Whole Man." *The Laban Art of Movement Guild Magazine* 21 (November 1958): 12–3.

———. *The Mastery of Movement*. Edited by Lisa Ullman. London: MacDonald and Evans Ltd., 1980.

Laban, Rudolf von, and F. C. Lawrence. *Effort*. London: MacDonald and Evans, 1947.

Lamb, Warren. *Posture and Gesture*. London: Gerald Duckworth and Company, 1965.

Le Hurray, Peter. *Authenticity in Performance: Eighteenth-Century Case Studies*. Cambridge: Cambridge University Press, 1990.

Leinsdorf, Erich. *The Composer's Advocate*. New Haven, CT: Yale University Press, 1981.

Leonard, C. *The Silent Pulse*. New York: E. P. Dutton, 1978).

Leonard, George, *The Silent Pulse*. New York: E. P. Dutton, 1978.

Lieberman, Philip. *Intonation, Perception and Language*. Cambridge: M.I.T. Press, 1967.

Little, Meredith, and Natalie Jenne. *Dance and the Music of J. S. Bach*. Bloomington, IN: Indiana University Press, 1991.

Long, Dorothy. *The Original Art of Music.* Lanham, MD: The Aspen Institute and University Press of America, Inc., 1989.

Maisel, E., ed. *The Resurrection of the Body—The Essential Writings of F. M. Alexander.* Boston, MA: Shambhala Inc., 1986.

Mark, C. "Simplicity in Early Britten." *Tempo* 147 (December 1983): 8–14.

Marshall, Madeleine. *The Singer's Manual of English Diction.* New York: G. Schirmer, Inc., 1953.

McElheran, Brock. *Conducting Technique for Beginners and Professionals.* New York: Oxford University Press, 1966.

Meyer, Leonard B. *Emotion and Meaning in Music.* Chicago: University of Chicago Press, 1956.

———. *Explaining Music: Essays and Explorations.* Los Angeles: University of California Press, 1973.

———. *Music, the Arts, and Ideas.* Chicago: University of Chicago Press, 1967.

Meyer, Leonard, and Grosvenor Cooper. *The Rhythmic Structure of Music.* Chicago: University of Chicago Press, 1960.

Moore, Carol-Lynne, and Kaoru Yamamoto. *Beyond Words: Movement Observation and Analysis.* New York: Gordon and Breach, 1988.

Monsaingeon, Bruno. *Mademoiselle.* Manchester, England: Carcanet Press Limited, 1985.

Noble, Weston. *Creating A Special World.* Chicago: GIA, 2004.

Persichetti, Vincent. *Twentieth-Century Harmony.* New York: W. W. Norton and Co., Inc., 1961.

Picasso, Pablo. *In His Words.* San Francisco: Collins Publishers, 1993.

Piston, Walter. *Harmony.* (Third Edition) New York: W.W. Norton and Company, 1962.

Preston, Valerie. *A Handbook for Modern Educational Dance.* London: MacDonald and Evans, 1963.

Robinson, Ray. "Wilhelm Ehmann: His Contributions to the Choral Art." *The Choral Journal* 25 (November 1984): 7–12.

Rorem, Ned. *Setting the Tone*. New York: Limelight Editions, 1983.

Rudolph, Max. *The Grammar of Conducting*. New York: G. Schirmer, 1950.

Sachs, Curt. *Rhythm and Tempo: A Study in Music History*. New York: W. W. Norton, 1953.

———. *World History of the Dance*. New York: W. W. Norton, 1937.

Sacks, Oliver. *An Anthropologist on Mars: Seven Paradoxical Tales*. New York: Alfred A. Knopf, 1995.

Saito, Hideo. *The Saito Conducting Method*. Tokyo: Min-On/Ongaku, 1988.

Schopenhauer, Arthur. *The World as Will and Representation*. 2 vols. New York: Dover, 1966.

Schuller, Gunther. *The Compleat Conductor*. New York: Oxford University Press, 1997.

Sessions, Roger. *The Musical Experience of Composer, Performer and Listener*. New Jersey: Princeton University Press, 1950.

———. *The Musical Experience of Composer, Performer, Listener*. New York: Atheneum, 1965.

Shaw, Robert. Blocker, Robert, Ed. *The Robert Shaw Reader*. New Haven: Yale University Press, 2004.

———. "Letters to a Symphony Chorus." *The Choral Journal*. 26 (April 1986): 5–8.

———. *Preparing a Masterpiece: The Brahms Requiem*. Carnegie Hall. Videocassette.

Shrock, Dennis. "An Interview with Margaret Hillis on Score Study." *The Choral Journal* 31 (February 1991): 7–12.

———. "An Interview with Paul Salamunovich on Aspects of Communication." *The Choral Journal* 31 (October 1990): 9–18.

———. "An Interview with Weston Noble." *The Choral Journal* 32 (December 1991): 7–11.

Shuter-Dyson, Rosamund, and Gabriel Clive. *The Psychology of Musical Ability*. London: Methuen, 1981.

Spector, Irwin. *Rhythm and Life: The Work of Emile Jaques-Dalcroze.* Dance and Music Series, no. 3. Stuyvesant, New York: Pendragon Press, 1990.

Storr, Anthony. *Music and the Mind.* New York: Ballantine Books, 1992.

Stravinsky, Igor. *An Autobiography.* New York: M. and J. Steuer, 1958.

———. *Poetics of Music.* Cambridge: Harvard University Press, 1974.

Swan, Howard. *Conscience of a Profession.* Chapel Hill, NC: Hinshaw Music, Inc.

———. "The Development of the Choral Instrument." In *Choral Conducting: A Symposium.* Edited by H. Decker and J. Herford. Englewood Cliffs: NJ: Prentice-Hall, Inc., 1973.

Szell, George, and Paul Henry Lang. "A Mixture of Instinct and Intellect." *High Fidelity* 15 (January 1965): 42–5, 110–12.

Tacka, Philip, and Michael Houlahan. *Sound Thinking: Developing Musical Literacy.* New York: Boosey and Hawkes, 1995.

Tagg, Barbara, and Dennis Shrock. "An Interview with Helen Kemp." *The Choral Journal* 30 (November 1989): 5–13.

Thakar, Markand. *Counterpoint: Fundamentals of Music-Making.* New Haven, CT: Yale University Press, 1990.

Thomas, Kurt. *The Choral Conductor.* English adaptation by Alfred Mann and William H. Reese. [Published as a special issue of the *American Choral Review* 13, nos. 1 and 2.] New York: Associated Music Publishers, 1971.

Thornton, Samuel. *Laban's Theory of Movement: A New Perspective.* Boston: Plays, Inc., 1971.

Thurmond, James Morgan. *Note Grouping.* Ft. Lauderdale, FL: Meredith Publications, 1980.

Toch, Ernst. *The Shaping Forces in Music.* New York: Criterion Music Corporation, 1948.

Tovey, Sir Donald Francis. *Essays in Musical Analysis.* London: Oxford University Press, 1941.

Treitler, Leo. "Structural and Critical Analysis." In *Musicology in the 1980's.* Edited by Holman and Palisca. 67–77. New York: Da Capo Press, 1982.

Vinquist, Mary, and Neal Zaslaw, eds. *Performance Practice: A Bibliography.* New York: W. W. Norton and Co., Inc., 1971.

Walter, Bruno. *Theme and Variations.* New York: Alfred A. Knopf, 1947.

Webb, Guy B, ed. *Up Front.* Boston: ECS Publishing, 1993.

Wehr, David A. "John Finley Williamson (1887–1964): His Life and Contribution to Choral Music." Ph.D. diss., University of Miami, 1971. University Microfilms 72–12,878.

Weikart, Phyllis. *Teaching Movement and Dance: A Sequential Approach to Rhythmic Movement.* Ypsilanti, MI: High Scope Press, 1989.

Zuckerkandl, Victor. *Man the Musician.* Translated by Norbert Guterman. Princeton: Princeton University Press, 1973.

———. *Sound and Symbol.* Translated by Willard R. Trask. New York: Pantheon, 1956.

———. *The Sense of Music.* Princeton: Princeton University Press, 1959.

ABOUT THE AUTHORS

JAMES JORDAN

James Jordan is recognized and praised from many quarters in the music world as one of the nation's preeminent conductors, writers, and innovators in choral music. He has been called a "visionary" by *The Choral Journal. Gramophone,* in reviewing his CD *Angels in the Architecture,* called him a conductor of "forceful and intimate choral artistry." His career and publications have been devoted to innovative educational changes in the choral art that have been embraced around the world. A master teacher, Jordan is one of the country's most prolific writers on the subjects of the philosophy of music making and choral teaching. He has authored thirty major textbooks and DVDs, and is editor for several choral series. His choral conducting book, *Evoking Sound,* was named as a "must read" on a list of six books by *The Choral Journal.*

Dr. Jordan is Professor and Senior Conductor at Westminster Choir College in Princeton, New Jersey, the leading center for the study and performance of choral music in the world. At Westminster, he teaches graduate and undergraduate choral conducting; he also conducts the Westminster Schola Cantorum and is the founding conductor of the Westminster Williamson Voices. With over forty publications to his credit, his writings have influenced not only choral conducting but also orchestral and wind conducting and pedagogy. Dr. Jordan's multi-faceted career, which has straddled both music performance and research, has provided him opportunities for unique insights and connections between the disciplines of psychology of music and performance.

Early in his career, Dr. Jordan researched rhythm pedagogy, which led to connections to conducting pedagogy through study, interpretation, and application of the work of Laban to those areas. For over thirty years, Dr. Jordan has continued his research and thinking on this subject. His experimental research concerning the use of Laban Efforts and rhythm performance have had a profound and permanent effect on how rhythm and movement is taught to both children and adults. His dissertation "The Effects of Movement Instruction Based upon the Principles of Rudolf von Laban and Its Effects on the Rhythm Achievement of High School Students" (Doctor of Philosophy, Temple University), was the first major experimental study to validate the effectiveness of Laban's movement principles upon rhythm teaching and learning. His theories of how we learn rhythm using the work of Laban have likewise transformed rhythm pedagogy. Dr. Jordan was the first researcher in music to apply the movement theories of Laban (1985) to facets of music teaching and learning. His first exposure to Laban and its implications for conducting was through his conducting study with Gail B. Poch of Temple University.

Dr. Jordan was the recipient of a Temple University Fellowship, which funded his research and study at The Laban Institute of Movement Studies in New York. Dr. Jordan pursued additional studies in psychology at Bucknell University under David Milne. At Temple, he also studied Laban Modern Educational Dance with Sarah Alberti Chapman. His study with Edwin Gordon, also at Temple University, pertaining to Music Learning Theory was pivotal in the development of his theories. His first published connection between Laban and choral pedagogy appeared in *Readings in Music Learning Theory* (1989). His theories of rhythm pedagogy are extensively detailed in *The Choral Rehearsal, Vol. 1* (2007).

Dr. Jordan continued his observational and pedagogical study of the application of Laban's work to rhythm pedagogy and movement when he served on the faculty of The School of the Hartford Ballet, the only Laban-based ballet school in the world. The initial application of Laban movement theory to rhythm pedagogy was shared at the Sugarloaf Conferences in Music Learning Theory. The first edition of *Evoking Sound*: *Fundamentals of Choral Conducting* (1996) was the first time that the work of Laban was placed within a methodological framework for conductors. The second edition of *Evoking Sound* (2009) refined that pedagogy. This book represents a culmination and expansion of those applications and provides a comprehensive resource and defined methodology for conductors to understand and assimilate the genius of Rudolf von Laban and its implications for conducting.

GISELLE WYERS

Giselle Wyers is Assistant Professor of Choral Studies and Voice at the University of Washington, where she conducts the University Chorale and teaches courses in choral conducting and voice. University Chorale's 2008 performance of the *Genesis Suite* with Seattle Symphony was termed "brilliant" by the *Seattle Times*. Under her direction, the University Chorale has enjoyed high-profile performances for the President of Latvia as well as the Crown Princess Victoria of Sweden. The chorus tours regularly; recent trips have taken them to San Francisco as well as Estonia, Finland, and Latvia.

As a guest conductor, Wyers has led high school honor choirs in New York (Alice Tully Hall, Lincoln Center), Idaho, Connecticut, Alaska, and Vancouver, Canada. In 2011, she will guest conduct semi-professional ensembles in Seattle, Boston, Montana, and Germany, including an upcoming performance with the Chamber Choir of Europe.

Wyers is a leading national figure in the application of Laban movement theory for conductors. She has team-taught summer choral conducting courses with James Jordan at Westminster Choir College, and her chapter entitled "Incorporating Laban Actions in the Rehearsal" is available as part of *Music for Conducting Study* (GIA, 2009).

As a composer, Wyers' works are published by Santa Barbara Music Publishing Company as part of the *Giselle Wyers Choral Series*, and have been premiered in the United States and abroad. Her choral series features works by Wyers and champions the works of other emerging composers. Her work "The Waking" was recorded by Choral Arts Ensemble on the Gothic Records label.

Wyers' dedication to exposing audiences to the music of contemporary American composers has led to publications in various national journals. She is especially interested in exploring how modern composers use music as a form of peace-making and social justice. "Waging Peace through Intercultural Art in Kyr's Ah Nagasaki," which appears as the cover article of the May 2008 *Choral Journal*, discusses how the act of creating and premiering a musical work can serve as a gesture of reconciliation between cultures.

Wyers holds a D.M.A. in Conducting from the University of Arizona, where she studied with Maurice Skones and minored in Historical Musicology with John Brobeck. She earned her master's degree from Westminster Choir College, where she founded the Greater Princeton Youth Chamber Orchestra, and her bachelor's degree from UC Santa Cruz, where she founded the San Lorenzo Valley Community Chorus and Orchestra.

MEADE ANDREWS

Dr. Meade Andrews is an internationally recognized certified senior teacher of the Alexander Technique. She currently teaches as guest artist-in-theatre at Rider University in Lawrenceville, New Jersey, where she also maintains a private practice in Alexander work. In the Princeton area, she offers classes and workshops at Westminster Choir College. Former director of the Dance Program at American University, Meade continues to teach workshops at the Studio Theatre in Washington, DC, her professional base for twenty years. She has also served as a movement coach for over thirty theatrical productions. In addition, she has completed a ten-year apprenticeship with Carol Boggs (CMA) in the work of Rudolf Laban and Irmgard Bartenieff. Meade travels extensively throughout the U.S. and abroad, introducing the Alexander Technique to a wide range of students, teachers, and professionals in the performing arts.

EUGENE MIGLIARO CORPORON

Eugene Migliaro Corporon is Conductor of the Wind Symphony and Regents Professor of Music at The University of North Texas. As Director of Wind Studies, he guides all aspects of the program, including the master and doctoral degrees in wind conducting. He has held positions at the University of Cincinnati College–Conservatory of Music, Michigan State University, University of Northern Colorado, University of Wisconsin, and California State University–Fullerton. He is a distinguished alumnus of California State University–Long Beach, and Claremont Graduate University.

Corporon's ensembles have performed at the Midwest International Band and Orchestra Clinic, the Southwestern Music Educators National Conference, the Texas Music Educators Convention, the International Trumpet Guild Conference, the International Clarinet Society Convention, the North American Saxophone Alliance Conference, the National Wind Ensemble Conference, the College Band Directors National Association Conference, the Japan Band Clinic, and the Conference for the World Association of Symphonic Bands and Ensembles. His groups have released more than fifty recordings, two of which have appeared on the Grammy nomination ballot. Corporon is past president of the College Band Directors National Association.

GERALD CUSTER

Gerald Custer is a multifaceted choral musician, active as conductor, composer, editor, teacher and author. A native of Baltimore, he earned his B.Mus. in Choral Music Education at Westminster Choir College, where he studied conducting with Robert Simpson, Dennis Shrock, and Robert Carwithen; choral literature with Elaine Brown; and composition with Harold Zabrack and Malcolm Williamson. He also served as Assistant Conductor of Westminster's Collegium Musicum, directed student choral and operatic ensembles, and participated in conducting masterclasses with Wilhelm Ehmann and Robert Shaw.

Custer earned his M.Mus. in Orchestral Conducting with additional work in Historical Musicology at George Washington University, where he founded and conducted the University Chamber Singers and served as Assistant Conductor of the Alexandria (Virginia) Symphony Orchestra. While a graduate student at GWU, he was appointed adjunct instructor in the university's Department of Music, teaching voice and music theory in the Columbian College of Arts and Sciences. He is presently pursuing his Doctor of Musical Arts in Choral Conducting at Michigan State University.

GEOFFREY BOERS

Geoffrey Boers is Director of Choral Activities at the University of Washington–Seattle, where he is the Mary K. Shepman Endowed Professor of Music.